THE MORAL RULES

THE MORAL RULES

A NEW RATIONAL FOUNDATION FOR MORALITY

by *Bernard Gert*

The utility of moral and civil philosophy
is to be estimated, not so much by the
commodities we have by knowing these
sciences, as by the calamities we receive
from not knowing them.

—THOMAS HOBBES

HARPER TORCHBOOKS
Harper & Row, Publishers
New York, Hagerstown, San Francisco, London

To my mother and father in gratitude for having provided me with the understanding of morality that this book makes explicit

CONTENTS

PREFACE

This book is meant to make a difference, not only in one's understanding of morality, but also in the way one acts. I do not expect all those who understand this book to become morally good men; it takes more than understanding to make one morally good. But I hope to prevent those immoral actions that are a result of misunderstanding the nature of morality. There are far more of these than one realizes. I want to provide such a clear and convincing account of morality that no one who reads this book will be able to act immorally without knowing that he is doing so. Though such knowledge will not prevent all immoral action, I do think it will prevent some. A clear understanding of morality should also significantly affect one's political attitudes. I hope to make it much harder to defend immoral political policies and much easier to support morally good ones. In short, I wish to increase as much as possible the influence of moral considerations, not only in the life of each reader, but also in the life of our entire society.

This book defends traditional morality, at least as much of it as can be defended. It is not a traditional defense. In fact, some may not regard it as a defense at all, but rather as an attack. It is an attack on many traditional ways of thinking about morality, but it seems to me that the only way to defend traditional morality is to attack the traditional ways of thinking about morality. The current attacks on traditional morality are, I am convinced, due to a misunderstanding of morality. But it is a very widespread and deep-rooted misunderstanding. The proper task of moral philosophy is to clarify our thinking about morality. The goal of this book is to provide a clear understanding of the nature of morality.

One will not find in this book stirring appeals to one's emotions. The only appeal this book makes is to one's understanding. However, unlike many people, I think one's understanding can affect one's action. I hope that after I have provided a clear understanding of morality, others with greater persuasive powers than mine will be encouraged to use them to support morality. Both moral reasons and reasons of self-interest lead me to hope that this book will have a universal appeal. I hope this book is read not only in schools but also in churches and legislatures, for religion and politics affect one's attitude toward morality more than education. It is also important that it be read in the home; for the proper attitude toward morality should be taught from the very earliest age.

The key concept, the one which makes my account of morality possible, is the concept of reason. The realization that the familiar dichotomy between rational and irrational concealed an important distinction led to the introduction of the concept "allowed by reason." The recognition that hypocrisy is allowed by reason permitted the distinction between what reason requires and what reason publicly requires. And this latter distinction is necessary in order to distinguish between providing a justification of morality and giving an answer to the question "Why should one be moral?" Though there are similarities between what I say about reason and what others have said, there are also crucial differences. Insofar as the reader does not agree that everything I call irrational is irrational, he will not agree with the conclusions that I reach. It is not necessary that he agree that everything I call rational is rational. Disagreement on this point need not result in any further disagreement. It is agreement on what is irrational that is crucial.

The account of reason presented in this book has application far beyond the field of moral philosophy. Reason and the related concept of justification play a central role in almost all traditional philosophical problems. In this book, the concepts have not been developed sufficiently to make their application to other philosophical problems sufficiently clear; however, a useful beginning has been made. The application of my account of reason to the traditional philosophical problems results in a view I call "empirical rationalism." The concept of reason is also important, in varying degrees, in all of the social sciences. In psychology, especially in psychiatry, a proper account of reason would be extremely valuable. Again, only a beginning has been made in this book, but it is a beginning with possibilities.

To the professional philosopher, the most important chapters in the book will be the first four, together with the chapter on moral judgments. These chapters are primarily concerned with analyzing concepts. In Chapters 1 and 4, I am concerned with the concept of morality, in Chapter 2 with the concept of reason, and in Chapter 3 with the concepts of good and evil. I believe this book provides the first correct analyses of these concepts. Though I realize that ordinary language is vaguer and more flexible than my analyses indicate, I am confident that I have accurately described the essential features of the concepts under discussion.

To the general reader, the most important chapter will probably be the one that answers the question "Why should one be moral?" I believe that this chapter will enable parents to answer this question in a manner far superior to the way in which they now generally answer it. I think the chapters on moral ideals, on virtue and vice and on morality and society may also serve to clarify general thinking about these matters. The heart of the book, Chapters 5 and 6, in which I provide the justification of the moral rules, seems to me to be of equal interest to professional philosophers and to the general reader.

The primary task of this book is to provide an analysis of some important concepts and to show the relationship between them. However, an almost equally important task is to persuade the reader to take a certain attitude toward morality. Though these tasks are distinct I feel that it is important to pursue them together rather than separately. I grant it is of little general interest to determine the proper analysis of concepts, even such important ones as morality, reason, good, and evil. However, it is extremely difficult to persuade people to act in a certain way if they cannot see the connection between the proposed way of acting and ways of acting to which they are accustomed. By providing an analysis of the concepts of good, evil, reason, and morality, I can more effectively persuade the general reader to accept my proposals. Also, the very fact that the analyses that I offer can be useful in persuading people to act in certain ways seems to me to provide some evidence in favor of the correctness of the analyses.

Though I regard my two tasks as closely connected, I do not think that failure in one assures failure in the other. It may be that the misuse of the concepts of good, evil, reason, and morality by philosophers, psychologists, and well-intentioned moralists, both political and religious, has so degraded them that my analyses do not seem cogent. I do not think the degradation of these concepts has gone so far, but if it has, I can hope that I have done something to make possible their eventual upgrading. The lack of clear concepts of good, evil, reason, and morality is a serious matter. It makes it difficult, if not impossible, to obtain agreement on important matters even among men of good will. However, even if one does not think I have provided a correct account of good, evil, reason, and morality, I still think it possible that I may succeed in my second task. There is no doubt that all readers of this book wish to avoid what I call evils. Thus I can still hope to persuade them to take a certain public attitude toward what I call the moral rules. Further, I can still hope to provide those readers who are men of good will with a guide to conduct that will be of some value in their personal life.

Moral philosophy should be understandable to the intelligent general reader. A book on moral philosophy understandable only by professional moral philosophers is a bad book on moral philosophy. However, a book addressed only to the intelligent general reader would tend to avoid those philosophical problems that have traditionally concerned moral philosophers. While it would have an impact, it would be subject to criticism that would make it worthless in the long run. I intend this book not only to be immediately convincing, but also to stand up in the long run.

Even though I am concerned with the traditional problems of moral philosophy, it is quite likely that I will be understood more easily by the general reader than by the professional philosopher. It would not be surprising if the general reader found that I say nothing but what is obvious. He may indeed wonder what all the fuss is about. There are times when I feel this way myself. But good philosophy often seems simple after it has been done. The greater difficulty that professional philosophers may have in understanding what I say is due to their having tried to think out these problems for themselves. It is much easier to accept someone else's thinking on a matter you have not thought about than on a matter that you have thought about. Though I expect quicker acceptance from the general reader than from the professional philosopher, I consider ultimate acceptance by the latter a more important test.

Highly critical remarks about the ethical theories of previous philosophers should not be taken as evidence that I consider them worthless. On the contrary, I have learned very much from the writings of other moral philosophers, both classical and contemporary. Only philosophical accounts have been criticized because non-philosophical accounts of morality, with rare exceptions, deserve to be no more than what they usually are, topics of cocktail-party conversation. However, I would not have written this book if I did not consider all previous accounts of morality to be seriously inadequate. Usually this inadequacy is the result of oversimplification. On my account, morality is not simple. Any attempt to describe my view as a simple variation of a classical ethical theory will lead one to overlook some significant distinctions. The inadequacy of an attempt to assimilate my account of morality to a classical view should be apparent from the fact that it is equally plausible to assimilate it to the view of the utilitarians and to the view of Kant. It would be a mistake to regard my view as simply a form of negative utilitarianism (with the ultimate principle being the minimization of evil rather than the maximization of good) or as a variation on Kant (though we both regard the moral rules as those rules which rational men would will to be universal laws). Both of these accounts would oversimplify my theory and hence be inadequate.

Uncritical use of technical terms often results in the overlooking of significant distinctions. I have avoided technical terms as far as possible, but some technical terms were required. One of the most important is "publicly advocate," which replaces the term "universalize," which philosophers since Kant have employed unsuccessfully. The misuse of ordinary words is also a source of great confusion. "Principles," "obligation," and "duty" are three words commonly misused. I do not use the first two at all, and I try to distinguish my use of the third from the general philosophical use as clearly as possible. In general I have tried very hard to use words in their ordinary sense. Ordinary language when used carefully seems to me to embody most of the essential distinctions. However, I do not regard ordinary language as sacred, and when an essential distinction was not marked by the language, I have not hesitated to mark it myself. The most important of these distinctions is dividing *rational* into *required by reason* and *allowed by reason*.

Since I regard the inadequacy of all previous ethical theories to be the result of neglecting some significant distinction or of misusing language, it seemed pointless to enter into any detailed discussion of other views. My criticism of other philosophers is accordingly limited to pointing out how their misuse of language or their failure to make some significant distinction led them astray. I owe much more to other philosophers than my brief comments would indicate. My debts to John Rawls, Kurt Baier, and Marcus Singer are greater than they seem. Students of Aristotle, Kant, and Mill will realize how much I owe to these men. But by far my greatest debt is to the works of Thomas Hobbes, the great seventeenth-century English moral and political philosopher. I hope, in the not too distant future, to show that Hobbes, properly understood, is the best classical moral philosopher.*

I also owe much to the students at Dartmouth College, to whom I have been teaching ethics for the last eight years. Their refusal to accept the jargon that generally passes for moral philosophy forced me to think out these matters for myself. Especially valuable was an undergraduate seminar using the first version of this book, in which I received many important criticisms. This version of the book is much improved, in substance as well as in clarity and style, because of the criticisms I received from the students at The Johns Hopkins University in my graduate seminar "The Moral Rules." I have also benefited from the criticisms of Dan Clouser and his students at Carleton. Also helpful were my sister Ilene Wolosin, and my colleagues, especially Tim Duggan and Don Rosenberg. I owe a special debt of gratitude, however, to Larry Stern, the only person with whom I discussed this book while I was writing the first version. His comments, criticisms, questions, and encouragement were far more valuable than he realizes. Were it not for my discussions with him, it is very doubtful that I would have written several of the chapters.

I am grateful to the Faculty Research Committee of Dartmouth

*See my introduction to *Man and Citizen* by Thomas Hobbes (1972).

College for providing me with funds to have the first two versions of this book typed. And for additional funds to have the first version reproduced for use in my seminar. These funds removed one of those obstacles that stand in the way of those who, like myself, find it difficult to act rationally when forced to spend their own money for scholarly purposes. A Fellowship from the National Endowment for the Humanities, awarded in order to enable me to work on expanding my account of rationality and applying it to problems in the philosophy of psychology, also made it possible for me to devote more time to improving the final version of this book. Thus I owe them thanks not only for helping me to start on that future book, but also for helping me to finish the present one. I am also grateful to Mrs. Jennie Wells, who typed the first two versions of this book and who helped prepare them for reproduction. When I recall the state of the typescripts I gave her, her excellent typing seems to me to be not only a demonstration of her many skills, but also a testimony to her temperance and fortitude. Her untimely death of a heart attack was one of those natural evils that defy all attempts at justification.

It is one of the most important aims of this book to show that if morality is limited to its proper sphere, then one can expect almost complete agreement among rational men on all questions of morality. In this sense, and in this sense only, I should like to make of morality a science.

PREFACE TO THE TORCHBOOK EDITION

I have used the publication of this Torchbook edition to make some changes in the text. There have been no significant philosophical changes, but I hope that I have removed some minor inconsistencies. For example, though I hold that rational action is more basic than rational belief and rational desire, I had said that irrational actions included those that were based on irrational beliefs and desires. The most significant change in the text is a new paragraph on page 37 in which I provide the fullest account of an irrational action. I hope, by this and other related changes, to make it clear that rational action is indeed basic.

It is usually taken as so obvious that no one ever ought to act irrationally, that it is not explicitly stated. Indeed, I did not explicitly make this statement myself in the hardcover edition. However, my entire account of reason was designed so that on the account of irrational action that I provide, no one whom we would consider responsible for his actions would ever think that he ought to act irrationally. Any account of reason that does not have this as a consequence seems to me to be clearly inadequate. For then it would be possible to show someone that a given action is irrational and yet still leave it an open question whether he ought to do it or not. The much discussed gap between "is" and "ought" resulted from the lack of an adequate concept of reason.

The other concept that needed to be clarified was that of public advocacy. Though I have made some changes in the text, I decided that it would be easier to make some remarks in this preface than to reword all of the places in the text that might otherwise require it. On page 92 I say, "When all rational men would publicly advocate the violation I say that it is required by public reason or that reason publicly requires it. If a violation is required by public reason, then all rational men publicly advocate disobeying the rule in this situation." What is wrong with these statements is that they do not make clear that I am only talking about those rational men who accept the conditions of public advocacy. (It was also wrong to use the phrase "rational men," and in this preface I shall use "rational person" instead.) These passages can be taken in such a way so as to conclude that a rational person must take a public attitude. There were passages in the earlier edition where I seemed to draw this conclusion myself. But a rational person need not be willing to publicly advocate anything, unless, of course, he makes genuine moral judgments and not merely judgments of moral matters. For willingness to publicly advocate is essential for the kind of impartiality that one must have when making moral judgments. But a rational person need not make moral judgments, and hence need not take any public attitude.

Thus in all of those places in the text where I say that all rational men would, will, or must publicly advocate something, this means that all rational persons, *if they are publicly advocating,* would, will or must publicly advocate that thing. This reading of "all rational persons publicly advocate" does not, as far as I can see, require any other changes in the text, so that I regard it more as a clarification than as a change of meaning. However, this lack of clarity caused (and was partly caused by) my unclarity about the relationship between reason and morality. Though I was quite clear that reason did not require one to act morally, I was not completely clear that reason did not always require one to make moral judgments. I sometimes talked as if a rational person who was immoral was necessarily a hypocrite. But this is not true. In appropriate circumstances, none of the judgments of a rational person need be moral judgments and one may completely disavow even any pretence at impartiality.

Once one realizes that a rational person need not take a public attitude, the question arises "Why should one?" This was a question that should have been raised in Chapter 10. The question can be put in the following way. "Why should my judgments of moral matters be ones that I would publicly advocate?" Asking why one should be impartial in moral matters is not a senseless question, when "should" is given the appropriate sense. It certainly is not always in one's self-interest or in the interests of those one cares for to be impartial in these matters. That one's judgments will not be genuine moral judgments if one is not impartial simply prompts the question, "Why should my judgments of moral matters be moral judgments?" It is a simple matter to transform this question into "Why should I make *moral* judgments?" If we are talking about sincere judgments, viz., ones that will affect one's behavior, we can see that this question is very similar to the question "Why should I be moral?" If we do not take the judgments as sincere, then the question becomes similar to "Why should I seem moral?" I have given my answers to both of these questions in Chapter 10.

That reason does not require impartiality is contrary to the hopes of most moral philosophers, including myself. Except for the moral skeptics, all moral philosophers have tried to show that reason supports morality. But if one has an account of reason with sufficient force to result in every person responsible for his actions agreeing that no one ever ought to act irrationally, then reason will not require one to support morality except in the hypothetical way that I have described in this book. If reason is impartial in the way required by public advocacy, then it must support morality. But though it is allowed by reason to be impartial, it is not required. Further, it is doubtful that one will be impartial in moral matters unless he has sufficient concern for all involved. Public reason determines what morality is, but concern for others, not reason, determines if one acts morally.

Though I make a sharp distinction between what is required by the moral rules and what is encouraged by the moral ideals (a similar distinction is made by Mill in Chapter 5 of *Utilitarianism*), I admit that there are individual cases where it seems that we are required to act on the moral ideals. I suggest on page 123 that in such cases we may say that the person has a duty to act. I think we should say that a person has a duty to act, i.e., that the action is required, rather than merely encouraged, by morality, only when we think failure to do it should make him liable to punishment. This is very close to saying that whatever is required by morality should be enforced by law (ignoring the practical difficulties involved in such enforcement). Thus though I agree that we ought to help those in need, I deny that we have a general duty to do so. For a rational person would not want the moral ideals in their full generality to be enforced by law (if an enforceable law could even be formulated). Of course, it is possible to favor a law requiring positive action to prevent or relieve the suffering of evil in specific circumstances, but these circumstances would have to be carefully formulated before rational persons would publicly advocate that such action be required by morality. Only consideration of the liability to punishment makes possible the distinction between what is required by morality and what is encouraged by it.

It does not seem too much for morality to require that one have enough concern for all that one does not harm anyone. It does seem too much for it to require that one's concern for oneself and those one loves be no greater than one's concern for all others. This supports my view that one is required to obey the moral rules, but is only encouraged to follow the moral ideals. But even though I distinguish between what is required and what is encouraged by morality, anyone who finds the answers I provide for being moral, persuasive, will almost certainly be morally good as well. My fundamental answer to "Why should one be moral?" is "Because you will cause someone to suffer evil if you are not." My answer to the question "Why should one be morally good?" is "Because you will prevent someone from suffering evil if you are." Thus I do not see that anyone who accepts my account of morality will be dissuaded from doing morally good actions and content himself with merely being moral.

Though morality does not require equal concern for all, it does encourage such concern. Thus it might be useful to explain what I mean by equal concern. This may also explain why I maintain that no rational person will publicly advocate that any individual cause any significant evil simply to promote good, without the consent of the person who will suffer the evil. These topics are connected because publicly advocating is advocating an attitude like one that would be advocated by a person with equal concern for all mankind. I think of equal concern on the following model, that of parents with several children all of whom they love equally. Suppose that all but one of the children have a plan to embarrass that one in order to provide themselves with some fun and excitement. (Notice that it makes no difference how many children will enjoy the embarrassment of their sibling or how much they will enjoy it). No parent who loves each of the children equally would allow this scheme to be carried through. Also, though such parents might allow one child to give up some of his opportunities in order to increase the already adequate opportunities of the others, they would never allow the others to force him to do so. Only if one child was considerably better off than the rest might they force him to give up something to aid his less fortunate brothers and sisters. And only if his brothers and sisters were actually suffering while he had more than he needed, would they necessarily force him to share what he had with them. My claim that no one would publicly advocate the causing of evil simply to promote good rests upon this model of public advocacy, and equal concern.

Having explained what I mean by "equal concern," and how this affects the understanding of public advocacy, I must now admit that public advocacy only requires that one have this concern for other rational persons, or those who were once rational (for a rational person must be concerned with how he will be treated if he ceases to be rational). It does not forbid concern for nonrational beings, but it does not require concern for them either. Thus one's views on the treatment of animals, on abortion, and even on infanticide, may depend on the concern that one has for animals, unborn children, and infants. Also since equal concern is not required, one may have some concern for animals, yet not enough to hold that they be fully protected by the moral rules. I would expect that in any civilized society rational persons would be fully concerned with infants, so that they would be accorded the full protection of the moral rules. With regard to unborn children, concern for them seems to increase as the time of birth comes closer.

Insofar as the abortion issue is a matter of rational disagreement, the issue turns on two considerations. One is an empirical consideration; "What effect will allowing abortion have on the way rational persons treat one another?" Insofar as one's view on abortion is determined by this consideration, it will be relevant to determine if e.g., allowing abortion does result in less concern for all human life. The second is not an empirical matter, but turns on the degree of concern one has for unborn children. If one is as concerned with unborn children as with their prospective mothers, he will publicly advocate that no abortion be allowed, not even to save the life of the mother, just as we do not allow one innocent person to be killed in order to save another. If one is seriously concerned, but not equally concerned, he will publicly advocate that abortion be allowed only to prevent the death of the mother or where there is serious risk of her suffering other evils. As one's concern decreases he will allow abortion for less and less important reasons, till, if one has no concern at all, he will allow abortion on demand, or simply because the mother wants it. Much of the discussion of abortion involves the attempt to get people to increase or decrease their concern for the unborn child. I have nothing to add to this discussion here.

There is a temptation in writing this preface to attempt to deal with all of the issues that have been raised by readers of the hardcover edition. I have been fortunate that several people have pointed out problems in that edition which I have been able to meet by some small change in the text, plus discussion in this preface. I have been helped by my colleagues Ron Green, Victor Menza, and Jim Martin. Huntington Terrell and his students at Colgate were extremely helpful. And again I have benefited from my students here at Dartmouth. I realize that I have not answered all of their objections, but it is doubtful that I could do this even if I had unlimited time and space. Peggy Sanders was very helpful in making the corrections in the text as well as in preparing this preface. Georgina Johnston's index for this edition was also quite helpful and should enable readers of this edition to discover more easily any remaining inconsistencies.

PREFACE TO THE SECOND TORCHBOOK EDITION

I have used the second printing of this Torchbook edition to make some more changes in the text. Almost all of these changes are related to the change in the statement of the moral attitude. Originally this attitude was formulated as follows: "Everyone is always to obey the rule except when he would publicly advocate violating it. Anyone who violates the rule when he would not publicly advocate such a violation may be punished." It has been pointed out to me by Frank Gramlich in personal correspondence that stated in this way not all rational persons would publicly take the moral attitude toward the moral rules. For it would commit a rational person to urging someone to obey a rule whenever that person would not publicly advocate violation, even if the person doing the urging would publicly advocate violation. I have therefore changed the formulation of the moral attitude by substituting "could" for "would" in both places that "would" occurred in the original formulation. I have also made other changes in the text in order to make them consistent with the revised formulation.

This change in my account of the moral attitude also eliminates the problem pointed out by Ted Bond in his critical notice of my book in *Dialogue*, vol. XII (1973), no. 3 that what is moral for one person to do is immoral for another person in exactly the same circumstances, even when they share the same beliefs. For though rational persons with the same beliefs may differ in what they *would* publicly advocate, they do not differ in what they *could* publicly advocate. What a rational person *would* publicly advocate is determined in part by his ranking of the various goods and evils, but this ranking of goods and evils plays no role in determining what he *could* publicly advocate. Thus what one rational person *would* publicly advocate, all rational persons *could* publicly advocate, for if his ranking of the goods and evils is allowed by reason then all rational persons could, consistent with their being rational, have the same rankings.

This point emphasizes the formal, as opposed to empirical, character of what I say about rational persons. When I say that *all* rational persons would do such and such, or that reason requires it, the latter expression is perhaps the less misleading expression. For I mean that not doing such and such is incompatible with the account of rationality that I have offered. Likewise, saying that *no* rational person would do such and such or that reason prohibits it, means that doing such and such is incompatible with my account of rationality. And finally, saying that *some* rational persons would do such and such, or that reason allows doing it, means that neither doing it nor not doing it is incompatible with my account of rationality. When I talk about what some, all, or no rational persons would publicly advocate, this is to be understood in the same formal fashion. All of this makes even more clear how central my account of reason is to the entire book.

Let me now point out what I think are some consequences of the new formulation. It now turns out that although it is moral, i.e. not immoral (for I use "moral" and "immoral" in a way parallel to my use of "rational" and "irrational"), for one to violate a moral rule merely if one *could* publicly advocate such a violation, it is not necessary that one *would* do so. Thus it is not necessarily immoral to go against one's conscience, i.e. act contrary to what one would publicly advocate; it is immoral only if one could not publicly advocate that violation. Given that it is not necessarily immoral to go against one's conscience, we can understand, more sympathetically, those who claim that we should not put our consciences above the law. If we limit their claim to those cases where people's consciences differ, so that some rational persons would publicly advocate obeying the law, it is a very plausible claim. I do not say that all rational persons would agree with the claim, only that some would. Furthermore, so interpreted it is compatible with the view that morality is above the law. One could hold that when all rational persons would publicly advocate violating the law then it should be disobeyed, but when some rational persons would publicly advocate obedience, then one should obey even if he himself would publicly advocate violating the law.

Since it is not necessarily immoral to go against one's conscience, we may be at a loss for the appropriate way to describe someone who violates a moral rule toward which he could publicly advocate violation, but, in fact, would publicly advocate non-violation. One is tempted to call such a man hypocritical, but if he has never made his views on the matter known to others, this seems a misuse of "hypocritical." Cases like this may provide a proper use for the term "inauthentic." But if we take "authentic" to be properly used of a man who always follows his own conscience, then, as pointed out in the previous paragraph, there will be some rational persons who prefer people to be inauthentic sometimes. Of course, in the situations where you did not want a person to follow his own conscience, you would probably not call him "authentic" if he did, but rather something like "stubborn." However, there seems to be no doubt that in general we would prefer people who were "authentic" to those who were not, for in general those who do what they *would* not publicly advocate will be more likely to do what they *could* not publicly advocate.

The fact that what is moral, i.e. not immoral, is what one could publicly advocate, not necessarily what one would publicly advocate, has as an important consequence the notion of moral tolerance. When we realize that even though the moral position taken by another is not one that we *would* publicly advocate, because we have a different ranking of the goods and evils, it is one we *could* publicly advocate, we will not ascribe to him either a lack of knowledge of the facts of the case, or a lack of moral sensitivity or insight. This does not require us to regard it as indifferent which of the two views is held, but it does limit the ways which we will regard as acceptable in trying to change the other's views or to prevent their being acted upon. It is moral intolerance as well as selfishness that Hobbes recognized as making a Leviathan necessary.

Next, a point of some theoretical interest. Many moral philosophers have held, either implicitly or explicitly, that if all the facts are known, every moral question has a unique answer. For example, the utilitarians held that which of the alternatives open to us we should take was determined by its tendency to promote the general happiness. And insofar as there was agreement on the facts, then everyone would agree that A was the right alternative or that B was or that it was indifferent which was chosen. And in saying that it was indifferent they strongly suggested that all people who looked at the issue in the appropriate way would be indifferent to which action was performed. The very strong hold this unanimity view still has on philosophers can be seen by noting that one of the strongest critics of utilitarianism, John Rawls, holds the very same position. I do not accept this position. I allow for some unresolvable moral disputes. This is a direct consequence of my position that even in moral matters not all rational men would publicly advocate the same course of action. However, at the same time, I do not accept the view that all moral disputes may be unresolvable as R.M. Hare does. This is a direct consequence of my position that, especially in moral matters, there are some courses of action that no rational person could publicly advocate. This was always the view of the matter that I had taken in the chapter on Moral Judgments, but my misstatement of the moral attitude showed that I was not as clear about it as I should have been.

One remark about reasons. On pages 33–39 I define reasons as beliefs which can make acting on an irrational desire rational. I still think that this definition is correct, but in the discussion of reasons I concentrate so exclusively on situations in which a reason is offered in order to justify acting on an irrational desire that my definition may be misinterpreted. It may be thought that a belief is a reason only if it is, in fact, offered in order to justify what would otherwise be an irrational action. This is not my intent at all. If a belief is such that in some situation it *can* justify what would otherwise be an irrational action, it is a reason and may with complete propriety be offered as a reason for doing something which even without that reason it would not be irrational to do. For example, I can provide a reason for going for a walk, namely, that it is good for one's health, even though there is no need for a reason to go for a walk.

I am very grateful to Ted Bond and Frank Gramlich for forcing me to reconsider the points I have discussed in this preface. The resulting changes seem to me not only to increase the consistency of my position but also to have several beneficial consequences. Some of these I have already discussed; one that I have not is an aesthetic satisfaction from seeing a fuller parallelism between rationality and morality. I do not know whether what I regard as the increased elegance of my view does anything toward increasing its adequacy, but whether it does so or not I must admit that I enjoy it simply for its own sake.

THE MORAL RULES

CHAPTER 1

MORALITY

WHAT IS MORALITY? This question seems as if it could be answered by any intelligent man. It seems that way until one actually tries to answer it. When one does this, a funny thing happens. One finds that if he starts by saying "Morality is . . . ," nothing he says afterward seems to be quite right. Of course one can say clever things like "Morality is simply the expression of the demands of the superego." But this kind of clever remark does not enable one to understand what morality is. The superego makes many demands which are not moral demands. Which of its demands are the moral ones? If one tries to give an answer to this question, it soon becomes clear that morality cannot be equated with the demands of the superego. In fact, it eventually becomes clear that talk about the superego is completely irrelevant in determining what morality is. And so it goes with any answer that one initially proposes.

Part of the difficulty is that "morality" is an unusual word. We do not use it very much, at least not without some qualification. We do sometimes talk of "Nazi morality," "Christian morality," or of "the morality of the Greeks." But we seldom talk simply of morality all by itself. This is partly due to the widespread belief that there is no such thing as morality per se; there is only this morality and that morality. It is commonly thought that there is no universal morality; no code of conduct that, in some sense, would be adopted by all rational men. But although this belief is widespread, it is false. In this book I shall present an analysis of morality; not of this morality or that morality, but of morality.

I am not the first to provide such an analysis. From Plato on, moral philosophers have attempted to provide such an account of morality. Part of the reason for the widespread disbelief in morality is that no moral philosopher has as yet provided a satisfactory account of it. This is not, of course, the main reason; philosophers are not that influential. The main problem has been that no one has ever adequately distinguished morality from other things. This problem is a result of the fact that no one realizes there is a problem. Everyone thinks that he knows what morality is. Nazi morality is the code of conduct adopted by all true Nazis. Christian morality is the code of conduct adopted by all true Christians. I have talked of morality, or universal morality, as the code of conduct that would be adopted by all rational men. Thus it seems as if everyone, including myself, knows what morality is; it is a code of conduct. But it isn't. It is only a sloppy use of language that has allowed "code of conduct" to be taken as equivalent to "morality" and has allowed such monstrous phrases as "Nazi morality." The Nazi code of conduct was not a moral code; on the contrary, it was grossly immoral. Unless one enjoys talking paradoxically, as far too many people do, one should avoid the use of "morality" which forces one to talk of an immoral morality.

Morality does provide a guide to conduct acceptable to all rational men, but not every guide to conduct acceptable to all rational men is a moral one. Unfortunately no one has distinguished morality from codes of conduct that would be universally adopted. Thus most moral philosophers have spent most of their time trying to discover a code of conduct that all rational men would accept. They mistakenly assumed that finding such a code would be the same as discovering what morality was—even Sidgwick* equated true moral laws with rational Rules of Conduct. And with the usual self-confidence of philosophers they also assumed that if they could not find such a code, then that proved there was no morality. But whether one finds a code that all rational men would accept will depend in large part on the manner in which one looks. If, like Westermarck, one goes from society to society examining the codes of conduct that these societies actually accept,

*Henry Sidgwick was a student of John Stuart Mill and a teacher of G. E. Moore. He is considered by many to be the best of the utilitarian philosophers.

he will probably be struck more by the differences than by the similarities. Although some anthropologists have claimed that the differences often mask essential similarities, the work of anthropologists has generally been used to show that there is no universal morality.

However, philosophers have not been overly concerned with the findings of anthropology. More than two thousand years ago Plato knew that there were important differences in the codes of conduct of different societies. This did not prevent him from trying to formulate a code of conduct that everyone would accept. Plato thought that an analysis of human nature could provide him with the foundation on which to build a universal morality. Today many philosophers try to use the findings of psychoanalysis in the same way. Other philosophers thought that an analysis of reason could provide the foundation for morality. Kant is the outstanding example. But neither Plato nor Kant distinguished between a code of conduct acceptable to all rational men and morality. Although they claim to be concerned with the latter, they really deal with the former. Hence like almost all other moral philosophers, they have taken their task to be the discovery of a code of conduct that all rational men would accept; they simply assumed that this would turn out to be a moral code.

I conceive the task of the moral philosopher quite differently. All agree that moral philosophy is the philosophical study of morality, but I do not believe that this simply involves looking for any code of conduct acceptable to all rational men. For me, the moral rules are central to morality. The moral philosopher ought to be concerned only with that code of conduct of which the moral rules form the core. Although there is some disagreement concerning what counts as a moral rule, no one would deny that rules such as "Don't kill," "Don't steal," and "Don't lie" are moral rules. These rules are the proper object of study for the moral philosopher. His principal tasks are the following: To discover if there is a unique set of characteristics which all or most, including all of the most important, moral rules have in common. If such a unique set can be found, to determine whether it is of such a nature as to justify the attitude generally taken toward the moral rules. And finally: to make clear who is subject to the moral rules and under what circumstances.

In short, the moral philosopher must explain the nature of moral rules, showing their relationship to our conduct and to our judgments, as well as explaining and justifying, if possible, our attitude toward them. He may do some rewording of these rules to make them more precise. He may also show one or more to be superfluous, or to be radically different from the rest, lacking those special characteristics which make moral rules unique. Or he may discover a new rule which shares all of the characteristics of the generally accepted moral rules. But if he is doing moral philosophy, he must deal with these rules. Although he can argue that these rules have no unique set of characteristics which warrant their being distinguished from all other rules and given any special status, he cannot ignore these rules. To do so is to give up moral philosophy for some other, though related, field.

It may not seem a radical proposal to say that moral philosophy must concern itself with the nature and justification of moral rules. Indeed it may seem to be obvious. Moral philosophers, of course, acknowledge the existence of moral rules. However, they seldom, if ever, consider their primary task to be an examination of these rules, showing their role in guiding our conduct or in making moral judgments. Rather, they have taken moral philosophy to be directly concerned with investigating (1) guides to conduct, and (2) moral judgments. This point, though subtle, is of extreme importance. By failing to recognize the central importance of moral rules in the study of moral philosophy, they were often unable to tell when they were no longer doing moral philosophy.

If one ignores the moral rules, then how is one to know which guides to conduct should be studied? A book on etiquette is a guide to conduct, yet it obviously does not treat of moral philosophy. Similarly, in making no reference to moral rules, how is one to know which judgments are moral judgments? Of course, whether they are aware of it or not, philosophers use moral rules in deciding both which guides to conduct they should study and which judgments are moral judgments. But, generally being unaware of what they are doing, they do not do it very well; they often investigate or propose guides to conduct which have nothing to do with morality and discuss judgments which are not moral judgments. And it is not unheard of to find a book, supposedly in ethics, which has almost no connection with morality.

It is not now my concern to show how most classical moral philosophy has erred because of the failure to distinguish morality from general guides to conduct. It would be an interesting undertaking to examine all of the major moral philosophers and show how their failure to make this distinction leads them astray. But this is not the place for it. However, I think it would be valuable to examine at least one philosopher so as to provide some detailed support for my claim. I have chosen to examine the views of John Stuart Mill. This choice is prompted by several considerations. First, all of the relevant re- marks made by Mill are in the first chapter of his popular work *Utilitarianism.* Since this chapter is short (approximately six pages) and easily obtainable, it will be easy for anyone to check whether I am fair or unfair in my comments on it. Second, Mill is a well-known and increasingly respected moral philosopher, so that any confusions found in his writings are likely to be widespread. Third, Mill himself is somewhat concerned with this same problem, so that I cannot be accused of attacking someone on an issue which is not his concern. Fourth, Mill writes in English and clearly enough, so that there is no great problem in interpreting his remarks. When he is unclear, this is due to a confusion of his thought, not of his language. Fifth, utilitarian- ism is, and promises to remain, one of the most popular of ethical theories, and Mill is one of its principal spokesmen. Thus simply showing where Mill goes wrong at the very start of his system is itself of considerable value.

In the very first paragraph Mill maintains: "From the dawn of philosophy, the question concerning the *summum bonum*, or, what is the same thing, concerning the foundation of morality, has been ac- counted the main problem in speculative thought. . . ." In this seem- ingly innocent sentence, we can already see the seeds of confusion. In a paradigm case of a philosophical mistake, Mill has made an impor- tant philosophical claim, without even realizing that he was making any claim at all.* Without any argument, Mill claims that the question concerning the *summum bonum*, or greatest good, is the same as the question concerning the foundation of morality. But this claim, though it is a common one, is quite doubtful.

The following passage strongly suggests that Mill correctly regards the question concerning the foundation of morality as a question of how to provide support for the moral rules.

"The intuitive, no less than what may be termed the inductive

---

*This mistake is sometimes made using the phrases "in other words," "that is to say," or simply "i.e."; I call it the fallacy of *assumed equivalence.*

school of ethics, insists on the necessity of general laws. They both accept that the morality of an individual action is not a question of direct perception, but of the application of a law to an individual case. They recognize also, to a great extent, the same moral laws; but differ as to their evidence, and the source from which they derive their authority."

But it is far from obvious that the *summum bonum* provides a foundation for moral rules. We might discover that the *summum bonum* does not provide us either with evidence or a source of authority for the moral rules. It is just as plausible that a foundation for morality is provided by discovering what helps one avoid the *summum malum*, or greatest evil, as Hobbes maintains. Hobbes denies that there is a *summum bonum*, and most contemporary philosophers agree with him. Yet Hobbes, and even philosophers who do not acknowledge either a *summum bonum* or a *summum malum*, are not thereby forced to abandon all efforts to provide a justification for the moral rules. Thus right at the start Mill equates one of the proper tasks of moral philosophy, providing support for the moral rules, with a task, determining the *summum bonum*, whose relevance to morality is not at all clear.

Although Mill was not completely aware of it, he was not primarily doing what I call moral philosophy. Rather, he was providing a new general guide to conduct. It is interesting and important to note that Mill has been criticized precisely because his guide to conduct can conflict with the guide provided by the moral rules. It allows inflicting a small but significant amount of unwanted pain on one person to provide a great deal of pleasure for many others. Yet the critics do not fully realize the significance of their criticism. Although they see that Mill's utilitarianism is inadequate, they do not see why. They do not see that utilitarianism is not primarily concerned with providing a justification for obeying the moral rules, but offers an alternative guide to conduct.

Mill himself criticizes all previous moral philosophers for their failure to provide support for the moral rules. He says: "They either assume the ordinary precepts of morals as of *a priori* authority, or they lay down as the common groundwork of those maxims, some generality much less obviously authoritative than the maxims themselves, and which has never succeeded in gaining popular acceptance." (Ironically this seems a perfect criticism of utilitarianism.) He criticizes Kant for offering the categorical imperative: "So act, that the rule on which thou actest would admit of being adopted as a law by all rational beings," as "the origin and ground of moral obligation." For he holds that Kant "fails, almost grotesquely, to show that there would be any contradiction, any logical (not to say physical) impossibility, in the adoption by all rational beings of the most outrageously immoral rules of conduct." Whether Mill's criticism of Kant is fair or not, it shows that Mill criticized previous philosophers for the same reason that later philosophers criticized him: namely, the principle used to support the moral rules does not necessarily do so, but is, in fact, capable of supporting conduct contrary to that demanded by morality.

Like Mill, most moral philosophers began by trying to see what support, if any, could be given to the moral rules. However, also like Mill, they soon lost sight of their original task. Once they found a principle, or set of principles, they forgot that the point of the principle was to provide support for the moral rules. But their original search was initiated for a principle that would do this. Thus it is not surprising that the application of the principle results in a guide to conduct which resembles to a greater or lesser degree the guide provided by the moral rules. Although it is barely evident in the works of some moral philosophers, what makes us regard their works as moral philosophy is the connection their principles have, or seem to have, with the moral rules. All of the classical moral philosophers who offered guides to conduct thought that they were providing a justification for morality. Success in this endeavor was the criterion by which they judged the systems of other moral philosophers.

Although this criterion is used by almost everyone, its significance is not appreciated. Moral philosophers continue to offer guides to conduct in the vain hope that these will coincide exactly with the guide provided by the moral rules. But the task of the moral philosopher is not to offer his own guide to conduct, especially as this cannot differ in any significant way from that offered by the moral rules. His task is to explain and justify, if possible, the guide that is offered by the moral rules. The mistaken view that moral philosophers should offer general guides to conduct arises from the fact that, like Mill, most moral philosophers are not aware of the distinction between offering a general guide of their own and justifying the one provided by the moral rules. But let one stray sufficiently far from the moral rules, as Nietzsche does, and suspicion immediately arises whether this is a genuine case of moral philosophy. Hedonism, egoism, and stoicism are more correctly regarded as general guides to conduct or philosophies of life rather than moral philosophies. They are generally unconcerned with justifying or showing the lack of justification of the moral rules as a guide to conduct.

As a consequence of many factors, not including a realization of the point I have been making, some moral philosophers stopped offering general guides to conduct and started analyzing moral judgments. In part this was due to the sense of futility which came from looking at such a long succession of general guides to conduct, all of them inadequate in varying degrees. But since these moral philosophers did not realize that this inadequacy was due to the failure to recognize the central importance of the moral rules in moral philosophy, their analyses of moral judgments were doomed to a similar inadequacy. In fact, since moral rules are more closely connected to general guides to conduct than they are to the making of judgments, most of the analyses of moral judgments were further from an adequate moral philosophy than were the general guides to conduct. For if one does not realize the crucial importance of moral rules, it is impossible to distinguish moral judgments from other kinds of judgments, and the likelihood of even coming close is exceedingly remote. Thus much of the discussion of the nature of moral judgments is almost completely irrelevant to moral philosophy, though it has its own intrinsic interest.

The man who did the most to start moral philosophers on the investigation of the nature of moral judgments was G. E. Moore. His apparent clarity, at least about the task of the moral philosopher, resulted in making it almost impossible for one to distinguish moral judgments from nonmoral ones. Accepting Mill's identification of the study of the foundations of morality with the study of the nature of goodness, he stated his initial task to be an investigation of the meaning of the word "good." As a consequence of a number of considerations, including cogent criticisms of previous accounts of the meaning of "good" and a theory of meaning which he carried to fantastic lengths, he concluded that the adjective "good," in its basic sense, referred to a nonnatural property. Thus for him, a statement of the form "X is good," when it does not mean "X is a means to something good," means that X has a certain nonnatural property.

Those statements which Moore says are his concern as a moral philosopher are statements attributing this nonnatural property of goodness to an object. Why Moore called goodness a nonnatural property is a complex issue which is not relevant to our discussion. For Moore's primary concern was to show that all men agree on what things are intrinsically good. The point that was seized on by later philosophers, however, was Moore's assertion that moral judgments are statements of fact, though admittedly of a queer sort of fact. Although everyone disputed Moore's claim that moral judgments are statements of fact, no one seemed to question Moore's claim, which he never argued for, that all statements of the form "X is good" are moral judgments. Thus right at the beginning, the examination of the nature of moral judgments was presented with an insuperable obstacle by the very man who started the examination. This obstacle has not yet been overcome.

As an indication of how remote from moral philosophy these discussions of moral judgments became, one need only cite the supposedly important distinction between the emotive theory of ethics and the subjective theory. According to the emotive theory, moral judgments are merely expressions of our feelings, just as "ugh" is an expression of our feelings. Thus it supposedly makes no more sense to ask if a moral judgment is true than if "ugh" is true. This theory was presented as a great advance over the naive subjective theory (which it is not clear that anyone ever held), viz., that moral judgments are statements about our feelings. Thus, on the subjective view, moral judgments are thought to be a disguised form of autobiographical statements, i.e., a report about our feelings toward something or somebody. The difference between these two theories is that emotivism views moral judgments as *expressions* of our feelings, subjectivism as *statements about* them.

It shows something about the state of moral philosophy that this difference was thought to be a crucial one. I admit that there are differences between these two theories. According to the subjectivist moral judgments can be true or false, while according to the emotivist they can be neither. But, as was rarely noted, according to the emotivists moral judgments can be either sincere or insincere. Thus, the difference between the two views is as great as the difference between holding your stomach and groaning, and saying "My stomach hurts." The latter can be true or false, the former only genuine or fake.

This is not to deny that the emotive theory was important, if only in leading to the rediscovery that not all uses of language can be classified as true or false. The emotive theory paved the way for many more sophisticated attempts to describe the nature of moral judgments. The names indicate fairly clearly what the view was, e.g., "the imperative theory," "the commending theory." There were also the obvious modifications, e.g., the emotive-imperative view. No doubt a more satisfactory understanding of language has generally emerged from all this. I want to deny none of this; I am only maintaining that the connection between these theories and moral philosophy is extremely remote. Neither the emotivists nor the subjectivists had any way of distinguishing moral judgments from other kinds of judgments. In fact, they seemed to deny that there was any significant distinction to be made. Thus neither could provide any help in discovering the nature of moral judgments. It was puzzling that anyone should have ever distinguished a certain class of judgments from all others and given them a special name.

This puzzle is primarily due to the unexamined premise that moral judgments can be distinguished from other judgments by examining the words that appear in the judgment. Thus statements which include the words "good," "bad," "right," "wrong," "should," or "ought" are examined, as if a proper analysis of these words would clarify the nature of moral judgments. It was too obvious to be completely neglected (though many tried hard) that most statements including these words had nothing to do with morality. So there were attempts by some philosophers to distinguish moral judgments from other judgments using the same words. The most common was to stress the fact that moral judgments had some quality of universalizability. It was never completely clear what this amounted to, but insofar as one could find out what was meant, it turned out that all value judgments had this same quality. All those who attempted to illuminate the nature of moral judgments by comparing them with other uses of language failed to do so, and for the same reason. They provided no way to distinguish moral judgments from nonmoral judgments. Their failure was not due to the crudity of the theories that they proposed. The most sophisticated theory—viz., that moral judgments are in some respects like statements of fact, in some respects like expressions of emotion, and in some respects like commands—is no better than its cruder predecessors in distinguishing moral judgments from nonmoral ones. All linguistic analyses of moral judgments fail because moral judgments are not distinguished from other judgments by their form, or by their function, but by their content.

The importance of content in distinguishing moral judgments from nonmoral judgments also points to the inadequacy of theories which seek to explain moral judgments by appealing to moral emotions or moral feelings. What emotions or feelings are moral? Suppose one attempts to characterize moral emotions without reference to the subject matter toward which one feels these emotions, but simply by means of introspection. The possibility arises that one could have this feeling toward anything, or perhaps toward nothing at all. Thus I could just be walking down the street and all of a sudden have a moral feeling, and if I express that feeling I have made a moral judgment. But this is obviously absurd. Nor if I get that feeling toward a mosquito that has just stung my child, which is more plausible, have I made a moral judgment on that mosquito when I express my emotion. The substitution of attitude for emotion does not alter the case one bit. Nor is it any better if I am willing, indeed eager, to universalize my judgment, whatever that means.

It is quite possible that introspectively we sometimes have the same feelings toward a person who does an immoral action as we have toward a child or animal who does something harmful. The word "attitude" is so vague that one cannot be sure whether it is possible to have the same attitude toward the two cases. But if having an attitude toward something does not involve having certain beliefs about it, then one could have the same attitude toward a disobedient dog as toward an immoral man. If having an attitude involves having certain beliefs, then distinguishing a moral attitude from a nonmoral one will require a specification of the beliefs required for a moral attitude. Further, it will be the beliefs that will determine whether the attitude is a moral one or not. We can only be said to make a moral judgment about something if we believe that something to have certain characteristics. At least some of these characteristics must be objective; i.e., they must be characteristics of that thing which are independent of any attitude we take toward it. We cannot make a moral judgment of a stone, of a plant, or even of an animal. Moral judgments can only be made of men, and not even of all of them.

One cannot be clear about the nature of moral judgments without being clear about their scope. What is subject to moral judgment? This is a question that seems not to have been given sufficient weight by any of the philosophers who discuss the nature of moral judgments. It rules out any view of moral judgments which would allow moral judgments to be made of things that are not subject to moral judgments. It thus rules out almost all, if not all, of the various accounts of moral judgments that have commonly been offered; viz., that moral judgments are expressions of emotion, statements of emotion, commands, commendations, and so forth. None of these accounts ensures that moral judgments can be made only of things that are subject to moral judgments. This is not to deny that when we make a moral judgment we may be expressing our feelings, giving a command, commending, or condemning. But when we have said this, we have done nothing to distinguish moral judgments from other kinds of judgments.

It should now be clear that no attempt to distinguish moral from nonmoral judgments can be made without taking into account the subject matter of the judgment. This is so obvious as to seem hardly worth saying. Yet it is surprising how many accounts of moral judgments have been given without mentioning the content of the judgment at all. It has already been pointed out that moral judgments are limited to men. Not all men, however, are subject to moral judgment, but only those having certain characteristics. Of a person having all of the necessary characteristics, we can make moral judgments of his actions, intentions, motives, character traits, or simply about the person in general. Of course, not all his actions, intentions, motives, and character traits are subject to moral judgments; some of them fall outside the limits of morality.

Thus there are two relatively distinct kinds of limitations on moral judgments to be discussed. First, moral judgments are limited to the actions, intentions, etc., of people who have certain characteristics. Second, moral judgments are limited to a rather small class of the actions, intentions, etc., of these people. A discussion of the first of these limitations largely overlaps with a discussion of what are commonly known as excuses. Excuses generally consist of showing that

one either does not have, or did not have, one or more of the characteristics that are necessary before one can be subject to moral judgments.

What are the characteristics a person must have before his actions,
intentions, etc., are subject to moral judgment? Since animals are not
subject to moral judgments, at least some of the characteristics that
one must have in order to be subject to moral judgments will be
characteristics that animals do not have. One of the distinguishing
features of man is his knowledge of very general facts. Thus it is not
surprising that one of the characteristics that a man must have to be
subject to moral rules is knowledge of a very general sort. A man must
know that men are mortal, that they can be killed by other men, and
that they do not normally want to be killed. He must know that one
man can inflict pain on or disable another man, and that men do not
normally want to be inflicted with pain or disabled. He must also know
that one man can deprive another man of freedom, opportunity, or
pleasure, and that men do not normally want to be deprived of these
things. Obviously if one knew some of these things, but not others, he
would be subject to some moral judgments and not others. Children
are therefore not subject to some moral judgments, even though they
are subject to others. A certain minimal intelligence and knowledge
is required for one to be subject to moral judgment. Someone lacking
this minimal knowledge lies outside the sphere of morality.

One must also know the effects his behavior is likely to have on
others. There is no dispute among philosophers, or even among non-
philosophers, that lack of this knowledge can be a matter of degree.
In some cases lack of knowledge renders the person totally exempt
from moral judgment, but not always. For example, sometimes a person does not know, but should have made an effort to find out, driving
regulations in a foreign country. Here we may feel that he is responsible to some degree for an accident, though perhaps not as much as a
native driver would be. And the degree of responsibility will depend,
in part, on such seemingly unrelated factors as how close to the border
it was, how many warnings or reminders there were, how many for-
eigners (the percentage) fail to find out the regulations, etc. Although
we feel he should have found out, how much we hold him responsible
will depend in part on how actual men behave. It would be unreasona-
ble to expect a man to know something if no one with similar knowl-

edge and intelligence given that same opportunity knows it. Whether a man could have been expected to know the likely consequences of his action will sometimes be an undecidable question. Hence, it will also sometimes be undecidable whether or how much he should be subject to moral judgment.

One also needs the ability to will.* A person who cannot will to do other than what he does, no matter what reasonable incentives are offered, is not subject to moral judgment. Such a person does not really have a will. For to have a will is to be able to will to do or to refrain from doing many kinds of actions. It is not clear whether animals and very young children do have the ability to will. It is clear that moral judgments cannot be made of the actions (if this is the appropriate word) of those persons who do not have the ability to will. Although a person must have the ability to will before he is subject to moral judgment, not only actions which are willed, intentional actions, are subject to moral judgment. If a person has the ability to will, then his unintentional actions may also be subject to moral judgments. Even his failure to act, negligence, may be the proper subject of moral judgment. Thus I am not limiting moral judgments to actions which are done intentionally. Also, in order to be subject to moral judgments, a person must be rational. But since rationality is the subject of the next chapter, I shall say nothing further about it here.

Sometimes when I say "S ought to have done X" I am making a moral judgment. If in response to my remark someone points out that S did not have the ability to will to do X, I do not count his remark as a moral judgment. I think this does not violate our ordinary thought about the matter. But since his judgment is incompatible with mine, it may seem odd that my statement is a moral judgment and his is not. To avoid seeming arbitrary in excluding statements about excuses as moral judgments I propose the following. Statements about excuses concern matters presupposed by moral judgments. The response that S did not have the ability to will to do X is not a contradiction of my judgment that S ought to have done X, but a denial of one of its presuppositions. In making my judgment, I presupposed the person had the ability to will. By showing that my presupposition was false,

---

*For further clarification of this concept see "Voluntary Abilities" by T. Duggan and B. Gert, *American Philosophical Quarterly*, April 1967. Reprinted in *The Nature of Human Action* edited by Myles Brand.

he forces me to withdraw my judgment. Thus I do not deny the close relation between moral judgments and statements about excuses; in fact, I wish to emphasize them. I only refuse to call these kinds of judgments moral judgments.

Excuses are generally offered when one is trying to claim exemption from moral judgment. Obviously this occurs almost invariably when the moral judgment would be unfavorable. If one claims exemption from a favorable moral judgment, this is not ordinarily called an excuse. Yet in both cases, one may cite the same kind of facts, namely that when doing the action in question, he did not have at least one of the characteristics necessary before his actions could be subject to moral judgment. Failure to know the consequences of his action, either because he lacked intelligence and knowledge (which he could not have been expected to have) or because he had no reasonable opportunity, exempts him from both favorable and unfavorable moral judgments. Someone shouts, unaware that his shouting will distract a child and cause an accident. If he could not have been expected to know this, he should not be subjected to moral judgment. Nor, of course, should he be subject to moral judgment if in the same circumstances his shouting helps to avert a tragedy. Nor is any action that is involuntary subject to moral judgment, unfavorable or otherwise. A pyromaniac is not subject to moral judgment for starting fires, nor a kleptomaniac for stealing. The importance of excuses stems from the fact that moral judgments are primarily made of actions.

We have already stated that for an action to be subject to moral judgment, it must have been done by a person who had certain characteristics. If moral judgments were made only of intentional actions, showing which intentional actions were subject to moral judgments would complete the discussion of the scope of morality. But as we have already pointed out, moral judgments are also made of unintentional actions, even of the failure to act. We also make moral judgments of intentions, motives, character traits, even of the person as a whole. But these all depend ultimately on our moral judgments about actions. We generally do not make moral judgments of intentions unless they have not been carried out. If someone does what he intended to do, we make a moral judgment of his action; we do not make a separate moral judgment of his intention. But sometimes we do not carry out our intentions. Only where there is no action to make a moral judgment of, or the action is not the one intended, do we make moral judgments of intentions. Obviously, our judgment of the intention is closely related to the judgment we would have made if the action had been carried out. If the intention was not carried out because of circumstances not in the control of the agent, we may judge the intention exactly as we would have judged the action. If the failure to carry out the intention was due to the agent, we judge not only the intention, but also judge his failure to carry it out. Moral judgments of intentions are so closely connected with those of actions that there is no need to discuss them any further.

Moral judgments of motives are slightly more complex. Sometimes they are indistinguishable from judgments of intentions; sometimes they are more like judgments of character. We make favorable or unfavorable moral judgments of motives insofar as we think that the motive leads to certain kinds of action. Although a particular action is not subject to moral judgment, we may think that the motive for the action is one that is likely to lead to actions which are subject to moral judgment. Our moral judgment of a character trait also depends on the moral judgment of the actions that we think are likely to issue from it. Our general moral judgment of a person is very similar, though obviously more complex, as people have many different character traits, which do not always occur together.

I shall talk primarily about actions and the moral judgments that we make of these. I intend everything I say about our moral judgments of action to apply, with fairly obvious modifications, to the moral judgments we make of the failure to act, intentions, motives, character traits, and people as a whole. Thus, in discussing the further limitations of moral judgments, I shall only attempt to show how moral judgments are limited to certain of our actions and not attempt to show how this limits our moral judgments of intentions, motives, etc. That there are further limits to moral judgments than that they be about the actions of a person with certain characteristics should be clear. Even if I had all of the required characteristics, I would not be subject to a moral judgment for putting on my right shoe before my left—at least not in anything like normal circumstances. Not only is the scope of moral judgments limited to actions performed by persons with certain characteristics, it is also limited to a very small number of the actions done by people of this sort.

Which actions are subject to moral judgment? The simplest answer is: those that are covered by some moral rule or moral ideal. However, this answer, which is largely correct, is not yet of much use. It will not be of much use until we know what the moral rules and moral ideals are. But, of course, we do know some moral rules: "Don't kill," "Don't lie," "Don't steal." And we do know some moral ideals: "Aid the suffering," "Help the needy." So that the answer is not completely useless. But in order to be completely clear about the scope of moral judgments, we must be clear about the moral rules and moral ideals. These matters will be taken up in later chapters, but it is already clear that not all actions are covered by the moral rules or moral ideals. Thus a moral judgment cannot be adequately described as an expression of emotion, a statement about a property, a command, a statement about feelings or attitudes, or as a piece of advice. For all of these can be made of actions that are connected in no way with either moral rules or moral ideals. Simply the realization of the limited scope of moral judgments is sufficient to make clear the inadequacy of almost all previous accounts of moral judgments.

CHAPTER 2

REASON

THE CONCEPT of reason plays an extremely important role not only in moral philosophy, but in almost all other areas of philosophy as well. It also plays an important role in all the social sciences, particularly political science, sociology, and psychology. It is of crucial significance in psychiatry. It is therefore surprising that there has been relatively little work on this concept. Philosophers and others have generally used the concept of reason, and the related concept of justification, as if these concepts were understood by all. But, as will become evident, these concepts are almost universally misunderstood. The general low esteem into which reason has fallen in many circles is due primarily to this misunderstanding. Although a clear account of the concept of reason has a value far beyond allowing for a justification of morality, I shall generally limit myself to discussing those features of reason which are relevant to morality.

Reason, like morality, is primarily concerned with actions. What is basic is the distinction between rational actions and irrational ones. Understanding irrational actions is required for understanding irrational beliefs and desires, as well as the concept of an irrational man. Although it will be necessary to discuss irrational beliefs and desires, I shall have very little to say about distinguishing rational men from irrational men; at least since Freud it has been commonly held that this is a matter of degree. All of us act irrationally some of the time. How serious one's irrational actions have to be before he is considered irrational is a matter of responsibility standards (p. 183). I am now primarily concerned with providing an account of reason such that everyone will agree that the actions I describe as irrational, or prohibited by reason, are actions that they would call irrational, crazy, nutty, idiotic, stupid, or silly. Which of these terms one uses will depend on how serious one thinks it is, on how much it counts against the person's being rational. Whenever I am in doubt as to whether an action is rational or irrational, I shall call it rational. Thus it is quite likely that I shall call some actions rational which others would prefer to call irrational. This disagreement will be unimportant unless one holds that any sacrifice for others is irrational. I am primarily concerned that I call no action irrational that anyone would prefer to call rational.

Newborn babies do not act either rationally or irrationally, nor do animals. When we do consider their actions as being rational or irrational, it is only because of their similarity to actions of some as yet unspecified class of beings. It is tempting to describe this class simply as the class of all adult human beings. But this is obviously inadequate. It excludes older children, whose actions are often called rational or irrational, and it includes adults who are so severely mentally retarded that we do not regard them as acting either rationally or irrationally. Hobbes regarded the class of persons as all those who can speak a language. This seems to me to be largely correct. However, it is not clear how much one must be able to say and understand before one can be said to speak a language. Thus more must be said.

A person who believes that he is made of glass, and can be easily shattered, shows by this very belief that he is sufficiently intelligent to be labeled irrational. For his belief shows that he knows that glass is the kind of substance that can be easily shattered. General knowledge of this kind is sufficient to show that a person is intelligent enough to be described as irrational. This leads to the somewhat paradoxical-sounding conclusion that one must have at least a certain minimal knowledge and intelligence in order to be irrational.

I shall say that a person's actions can be judged rational or irrational only if he has sufficient knowledge and intelligence to hold an irrational belief. I shall call a belief irrational if and only if (1) it is held by a person with sufficient knowledge and intelligence to know that it is false, (2) it is inconsistent with a great number of things he knows to be true, and (3) this inconsistency is apparent to almost all people with similar intelligence and knowledge. Thus an irrational belief must not merely be a false belief, not even an obviously false belief, but an obviously false belief held by a person who has sufficient intelligence and knowledge to know that it is false. I call such a belief irrational because holding it generally leads to what I call irrational actions.

Thus to say of any belief that it is irrational is to say something very strong about it, much stronger than saying that one would be mistaken if he held that belief. There are many beliefs which are mistaken and yet not of a kind to lead one to say that they are irrational beliefs. For example, it is a mistake to believe that Oswald did not participate in the assassination of President Kennedy; but this is not an irrational belief. It would be irrational to believe that Kennedy was not assassinated. It is hard to formulate precisely the difference between the two cases. It is not sufficient to say that there is overwhelming or conclusive evidence that Kennedy was assassinated. It can be claimed, with some justification, that there is overwhelming or conclusive evidence that Oswald participated in the assassination. Nor is it sufficient to talk of our knowing the former and only believing the latter. For, again, it could be claimed that we know that Oswald participated in the assassination; that it had been proved beyond the shadow of a doubt. Nonetheless there does seem to be an important difference between the two beliefs. We feel that rational men can disagree about whether Oswald participated in the assassination, but that it would be irrational for anyone to deny that Kennedy was assassinated.

Of course, the above discussion has an implicit limitation; generally speaking, it is limited to American adults. It would not be irrational for someone in Communist China to believe that Kennedy was not assassinated, but that the whole thing was faked. In general, when one talks of an irrational belief, he has in mind some limited group of people for whom it would be irrational to accept that belief. It is irrational for adults to believe in Santa Claus; it is not irrational for children to believe in him. Thus before one can talk simply of irrational beliefs, he must make clear what group of people he has in mind. Here there is a choice. One can try to specify some intelligent and highly educated class, e.g., readers of this book, and thereby have the opportunity of talking of a great number of irrational beliefs. By specifying this class one could list as irrational beliefs the belief that the earth is flat, that the book of Genesis is literally true, that walking under a ladder brings bad luck, etc. This is a tempting choice, for I am primarily interested in persuading readers of this book that a certain attitude toward the moral rules is required by reason.

However, it is necessary to be able to speak of irrational beliefs without excluding anyone who is subject to the moral rules. It would be of little value to say that certain beliefs about the moral rules were required by reason, if this did not mean the reason of all those who were subject to the moral rules. Thus when I talk about irrational beliefs, I shall mean beliefs which would be irrational to anyone with enough knowledge and intelligence to be subject to the moral rules.

There are several beliefs or doubts or attitudes that would be considered irrational by all who make up the wide class I am considering. Prominent among these are the beliefs that are put forward by philosophical skeptics. The philosophical skeptic puts forward these beliefs in order to force us to examine more carefully the opposing or commonsense views. But if someone were actually to believe the propositions put forward by the skeptic, he would be irrational. Those beliefs include the following: that we can never know, or even be reasonably sure, about what will happen in the future; that we can never know what the effects of an action will be; that we can know nothing about the world outside of our immediate sensations; that we cannot even know if there is such a world; in particular, that we cannot know if there are any other people in the world. Barring extraordinary conditions, any man with sufficient intelligence to be subject to moral judgment would be irrational to accept any of the beliefs listed above. It is important to note that in this list of irrational beliefs, there are none that are in the slightest degree plausible as genuine beliefs, i.e., beliefs that, if relevant, would affect our actions.

All beliefs that are not irrational to everyone with sufficient intelligence to be subject to the moral rules, I shall call rational beliefs. But it should be clear that not all rational beliefs are on a par. There will be some rational beliefs that anyone (when I say anyone from now on, I mean anyone with sufficient knowledge and intelligence to be subject to moral judgment) would be irrational not to believe. I shall call this kind of rational belief a belief required by reason. One kind of belief required by reason is a general belief, i.e., a belief which makes no reference to any particular person, group, place, or time, which is not known to all rational men. One group of these general beliefs consists of the beliefs that the previously listed irrational beliefs are false. There is a simple logical relation between irrational beliefs—or beliefs prohibited by reason—and beliefs required by reason. If any belief is required by reason, then to hold that this belief is false is prohibited by reason or irrational. If any belief is prohibited by reason, then to hold that this belief is false is required by reason.

But not all rational beliefs are required by reason. There are some beliefs that I shall describe as allowed by reason. This class of beliefs, which are neither irrational nor required by reason, probably contains the largest number of beliefs. All those beliefs which someone intelligent enough to be subject to moral judgment could believe to be either true or false and not be considered irrational for so doing are beliefs allowed by reason. Of course, it will be irrational for some people to hold the beliefs that I call allowed by reason. Readers of this book would be irrational to believe the earth is flat. Nonetheless I call this belief one that is allowed by reason rather than one prohibited by reason because it would not be irrational for someone in the wide class I am concerned with to believe this.

Another kind of belief required by reason is a personal belief, i.e., a belief about oneself. However, even most of my beliefs about myself which I would be irrational to doubt are only beliefs allowed by reason, for some other rational man would not be irrational to deny them about himself. Only those personal beliefs which all rational men must have about themselves are beliefs required by reason. These personal beliefs that are required by reason include the following: "I am mortal," "I can suffer pain," "I can be disabled," "I can be deprived of freedom or opportunity," and "I can be deprived of pleasure." Beliefs required by reason must be beliefs that all rational men hold. Thus it should be clear that only a small number of rational beliefs are required by reason.

Closely related to the personal beliefs required by reason are some positive general beliefs that are required by reason. If we rule out extraordinary circumstances, we can list some general beliefs that any man intelligent enough to be subject to moral judgment would be irrational not to believe. There is no point in attempting to make a complete list of such beliefs. I shall now list only those which are immediately relevant to the present task: Men are mortal, they can be killed by other men, and they do not generally wish to be killed. One man can inflict pain on another or disable him; men do not generally wish to have pain inflicted on them or to be disabled. Men generally wish to have the freedom and opportunity to satisfy their desires, and it is possible for some men to deprive others of their freedom or opportunity. Finally, men do not want to be deprived of pleasure, but they can be so deprived by the actions of other men. These beliefs do not seem beyond the grasp of any man intelligent enough to be subject to moral judgment. We can imagine circumstances in which one could come to believe that some person or group of persons were not mortal, nor subject to pain or disability. Nonetheless, in normal circumstances, it would be irrational for anyone to deny any of the beliefs listed above.

In my analysis of reason action is central. It is primarily and basically actions that are judged rational and irrational. This does not mean that rationality and irrationality are incorrectly applied to beliefs. I have just given a fairly detailed account of what a rational belief is, and what an irrational one is. But on my analysis, these beliefs are called rational or irrational because of their connection with rational and irrational actions. Just as, according to Aristotle, health is primarily and basically a property of persons, and all other things that are called healthy are called healthy because of their relationship to a healthy person; e.g., a healthy complexion is a sign of a healthy person. One could give a rather complete description of a healthy complexion, so that it could be recognized without ever mentioning a healthy person. But if one did not know the connection between a healthy complexion and a healthy person, he would not understand why such a complexion was called healthy. If he knew of the connection but thought "healthy complexion" more fundamental than "healthy person," he would be even more confused. For then he could not understand why some foods were called healthy when they had no connection with one's complexion. In a similar manner if one ignores the connection between rational beliefs and rational action, he will not understand why some beliefs are called irrational and other beliefs rational. Also if one takes rational belief to be more fundamental than rational action, he will not understand why we sometimes talk of irrational desires, when this has no connection to beliefs.

Hume was the philosopher who did the most to spread the confusion. He regarded reason to be primarily and fundamentally concerned with beliefs. He held that, considered apart from beliefs, actions were neither rational nor irrational. However, he thought that if actions were related to beliefs in some way they could be regarded as rational or irrational. He held that all actions based on mistaken beliefs were irrational actions and that all actions based on true beliefs were rational actions. He said: "It is not contrary to reason for me to choose my total ruin to prevent the least uneasiness of an Indian, or person wholly unknown to me. It is as little contrary to reason to prefer even my own acknowledged lesser good to my greater, and have a more ardent affection for the former than the latter." Thus, according to Hume, no matter what one did, if it was not based on a mistaken belief, one was acting rationally. It should be clear that this account of reason is not merely inadequate, it is totally false and misleading.

It is impossible to defend Hume's account of reason as it stands, but some philosophers have attempted to defend what they consider a slightly modified Humean view. If you ask them "Why is it rational to act on true beliefs?" they do not answer as a strict following of Hume would require, viz., "That is just what is meant by acting rationally." What they generally say is, "Acting on true beliefs generally results in maximizing satisfaction of one's desires." But what if one now asks, "Why is it rational to do that which generally results in maximizing satisfaction of one's desires?" Here one is likely to get the answer, "But everyone just does want to do that which he believes will result in maximizing satisfaction of his desires." But this answer is false. Some people do not want to do that which they believe will result in maximizing satisfaction of their desires, at least if these words are used in their normal sense. Well, they might reply, "But anyone who does not want this is crazy." But this is just the point. Defining rational action as action based on true beliefs is plausible only because one assumes that people always act rationally in some more basic sense. But once one recognizes that a person can act irrationally even though he has no false beliefs, then defining rational action in terms of beliefs loses its plausibility.

The most popular way in which Hume's account has been modified is to maintain that rational action is action compatible with maximum satisfaction of desires. Note, however, that this modification completely changes Hume's view of reason. For Hume reason has no goal —that is, it is rational to act in any way one desires; all that reason requires is that one act on true beliefs. It may seem only a slight change to require that one not act in any way one desires, but limit oneself to acting in ways not incompatible with maximum satisfaction of desires. But the change is indeed drastic, for now reason has a goal —maximum satisfaction of desires—and one can act contrary to this goal even though one has no false beliefs. Thus reason is no longer limited to beliefs, and rational action can no longer be defined in terms of beliefs. Indeed, one now regards true beliefs as rational primarily because of their connection with attaining the goal of reason, the maximum satisfaction of desires.

It is important to recognize that even on this rather minimal account of the goal of reason, rational action is more basic than rational belief. Rational belief becomes a means for rational action. Thus the view developed that while reason was concerned with the means, desires set the ends. But this is very misleading; it is reason that requires maximum satisfaction of desires. On this view, reason is not the slave of the passions, if that means it is the slave of each and every passion. Reason is the slave of the passions only when they are considered as forming a system. Hume meant reason to be a slave to the passions in the first sense; most followers of Hume, in the second. There is, as I have shown, an extraordinary difference between the two views. Hume's view has no plausibility; the view of his followers is extremely persuasive.

On their account, as well as on Hume's, there is no passion or desire which reason prohibits us from attempting to satisfy simply because we want to. But unlike Hume, they maintain that reason does prohibit us from acting so as to satisfy a desire when so acting conflicts with maximum satisfaction of desires. If acting to satisfy one desire conflicts with satisfying that which we regard as a greater or more important desire, then acting on that desire is irrational. Considered by itself, no desire is irrational. If there is no conflict with some more important desire, it is never irrational to act solely in order to satisfy any desire. Further, each individual decides for himself which desires he considers most important. Reason serves only as a means for harmonizing our desires. Thus, on this view, all desires are allowed by reason; none is either prohibited or required.

This view is extremely persuasive, primarily because the vast majority of our desires are neither required nor prohibited by reason.

Reason allows one to desire to eat an orange or not to desire to. It is rational to want to go to a concert, and it is also rational to want to stay home. Especially when considering such a wide class of people as all those intelligent enough to be subject to moral judgment, it seems that it will be impossible to find any desire that is not allowed by reason. Diversity of desires seems so complete that to say that any desire is prohibited by reason must be arbitrary. Generally we do say that a desire is irrational to act on only when the person acting knows that so acting would result in the sacrifice of some more important desire. Whether a man who likes to drink but dislikes the hangover he always gets is irrational or not depends on whether he considers the desire to avoid the hangover significantly more important than the desire to drink. If he does, then he is irrational in acting on his desire to drink; if he does not, he is not irrational. But the desire to drink is, in either case, not an irrational desire. If it is irrational to act on it, it is because it conflicts with some more important desire. A person is not irrational if he acts simply in order to satisfy his desire to drink.

It is a problem on this account of the rationality of desires when we decide which of a set of desires is most important. Of course, sometimes a person may act on a desire, knowing full well at the time that it is irrational; that he is sacrificing or risking that which is much more important to him. But what of the more common case, where at the moment of action the lesser desire seems the greater. The pleasure of drinking seems to be worth the misery of the hangover. Of course, the next day one does not think so. When confronted with the same situation again, is it rational to drink? Here one can see that simply to say that the person himself decides which is the more important desire is not enough. Is it what the person feels at the moment of acting, when in the grip of one desire? Is it later when he realizes what satisfaction of that desire has cost? Faced with this problem, the most promising solution has been to talk of his considered judgment in a "cool moment." He is the judge of the relative weight of his desires, but he must judge their weight in a moment of reflection when he is not in the grip of either desire. When he does not particularly want to drink, nor is suffering from the aftereffects of drinking, he must decide if drinking is worth the hangover it causes. What he decides then determines whether or not it is rational for him to drink. If on careful reflection he decides that it is worth it, he is not irrational to drink.

Of course, he may decide that there is not enough difference between the two desires to make either choice irrational. Just as with beliefs, it does not follow that in a conflict between two incompatible desires one must be irrational. There must be a significant difference between the two desires before satisfying one rather than the other can be called irrational. On this account, each man decides for himself which desire is the rational one for him to satisfy. This account leaves open the possibility that men may often act irrationally, for they can sacrifice one desire to another when in a cool moment they consider the former significantly more important than the latter. But the final court of appeal for the rationality of acting on any desire is what that particular man would decide in a cool moment. It is not per se irrational to act so as to satisfy any desire.

For those who hold the view I have been describing, an irrational desire would be defined as follows: A desire is irrational if and only if one knows that acting on that desire will result in his failing to satisfy some desire or set of desires which in a cool moment he has decided is significantly more important. The following example should show the inadequacy of the "cool moment" definition of an irrational desire.

A man all of a sudden has the desire to kill himself. At first it is not an important desire. From time to time he considers various ways in which he might kill himself. But he has other desires which, in a cool moment, he considers more important than this desire; so being rational, he does not act on this desire. As time passes, however, the desire to kill himself becomes more and more important. Finally there comes a time when, even in a cool moment, he decides that the desire to kill himself is more important than any of his other desires, more important even than all of them put together. At this moment, according to the "cool moment" definition, it becomes rational for him to kill himself. Immediately the objection comes to mind: he cannot have decided this in a cool moment. The very fact that he takes the desire to kill himself as more important than all the rest of his desires put together shows that the decision was not made in a cool moment. But this objection is self-defeating. We cannot use the fact that he regards certain desires as more important than others as conclusive evidence that he cannot have done so in a cool moment. If we do, then there is no point in limiting irrational desires to those which conflict with desires we considered more important in a cool moment.

The absurdity of taking what is decided in a cool moment as decisive for the rationality of acting on a certain desire comes out even more clearly in the following example. A man decides in a cool moment that his desire to kill himself in the most painful possible way is his most important desire. It is not his only desire, but he thinks it more important than all of his other desires. Among his other desires is a desire to go to a psychiatrist and see if he can be cured (notice how natural this word is) of this desire. He talks to his friend the philosopher, stating his situation, and asking for advice. The philosopher who accepts the "cool moment" definition of irrational desire must tell him that he would be irrational to go to a psychiatrist. For if he goes to a psychiatrist this will result in the sacrifice of some desire, viz., the desire to kill himself, which in a cool moment he considers more important. Thus it is clear that the plausibility of the "cool moment" definition of irrational desire depends on overlooking the existence of what I shall call irrational desires. A desire that it is always irrational to act on simply in order to satisfy it is what I call an irrational desire.

It is not arbitrary to regard some desires as irrational. We do in fact do this. There are limits to what desires we consider it rational to act on. This does not mean that we can simply list a number of desires and say that it is always irrational to act on them. One can imagine reasons for acting on almost any desire which would make that action rational. Although we would consider it irrational for a man to want to cut off his arms just to see what he looked like with no arms, it would not be irrational for him to want to have his arms amputated if he thought that by so doing he would save his life. That certain desires are irrational only means that it is irrational to act simply in order to satisfy these desires. It is not being claimed that to act on these desires is always irrational, nor even usually irrational, for we usually do have reasons for acting on these desires. Indeed, if we are acting rationally we must have reasons for acting on these desires.

We can, as with beliefs, provide a list of desires that it would be irrational for anyone (with sufficient intelligence to be subject to moral judgment) to act on simply in order to satisfy them. The desire to be killed is irrational. Unless one has some reason, it is irrational to act on this desire. Even if, in a cool moment, one decides that he would like to be killed more than he would like to do anything else, we would not say he was rational if he acted on this desire. This does not mean it is always irrational to kill oneself; one may have a reason for doing this. Being killed may be the only way to escape constant severe pain. But to do this for no reason, simply because one desires to be killed, is irrational. There may be some dispute as to what constitutes an adequate reason for killing oneself—that is, a reason sufficient to make the action rational; but there can be no dispute that one needs some reason. It is not enough simply to desire to do so. Thus the desire to be killed or to kill oneself is quite different from most of our desires. If we desire to wear pink shirts, we need have no reason, and acting on this desire will not be irrational. Thus even if we have not decided what is an adequate reason for killing oneself, we still can distinguish the desire to kill oneself from most other desires.

Similarly, the desire to have pain inflicted on oneself is irrational. Of course, there are reasons that can make acting on this desire rational. Further, in the case of being inflicted with pain, there is the troublesome case of the masochist. Is the masochist irrational when he has pain inflicted on himself? I am not sure what to say here, but in keeping with the policy of not calling anything irrational unless there is no doubt about the matter, I shall allow masochism to be rational. This does not conflict with the view that the desire to have pain inflicted on oneself is irrational. For, as has already been noted, it is not irrational to act on an irrational desire if one has a reason. The masochist has a reason; he enjoys having pain inflicted on him. Thus I allow masochism as rational if the masochist has pain inflicted on himself because he enjoys it. If he does not enjoy it, if he simply wants pain inflicted, then he is irrational.

I am aware that there are important logical relations between pain, pleasure or enjoyment, and desires or wants. But I do not think that the relationship is as intimate as is generally maintained. Someone who wants pain inflicted on himself and does not enjoy it can usually be distinguished from someone who wants it inflicted because he does enjoy it. The criteria for pleasure and desire are quite distinct. What gives one pleasure is what makes one smile. Smiling is a criterion of pleasure in the same way that wincing is a criterion of pain. The basic criterion of desire is action. We generally decide what a man wants by seeing what he tries to get. Contrary to the popular view, the natural pattern is not for satisfaction of desire to result in pleasure, though, of course, it often does. What satisfaction of desire usually does is to prevent displeasure. When someone fails to satisfy a desire, he is generally displeased; the criterion for this is frowning. When one is displeased even after satisfying his desire, he may say, "I thought that this was what I wanted." This is what leads us to talk of false or mistaken desires. Complete clarification of the relations between pain, pleasure, displeasure, and desire is an important and difficult task; luckily it is not the task of this book.

I have discussed the relations between pain, pleasure, and desire in order to support my claim that the masochist may have a reason for desiring pain to be inflicted on himself. The reason being that he believes that he will enjoy it. Of course there are other reasons for wanting to have pain inflicted on oneself, e.g., one may believe that it is necessary to cure a disease that threatens his life. But this does not at all count against the view that to desire pain for no reason is irrational. It is not enough to make it rational simply to want pain. Thus the desire for pain, like the desire for death, is an irrational desire.

The desire to be disabled is also an irrational desire, which is not to deny that in some circumstances it would be rational to act so as to disable oneself. All that is being maintained is that for someone to want to be disabled for no reason is irrational. This is not to solve the problem of what will count as an adequate reason, but simply to maintain that "I want to" is not enough. This makes it significantly different from most of our desires, for which "I want to" is enough. Here, again, it does not make any difference if we want this in a cool moment. To say "I've thought it over, and what I want to do is to disable myself" is not sufficient to make it rational. On the contrary, if one has this desire in a cool moment, one is likely to be considered more irrational than someone who has it in a fit of anger at being so clumsy.

Almost identical remarks can be made about the desire to restrict one's freedom or opportunity. Although it is understandable that a person angered by his failure to make anything of his opportunities might wish to restrict them, that does not make it rational. And, again, were one to desire this after reflection, this would make it more irrational, not less. Again, this must not be taken to mean that there are no circumstances in which it would be rational to restrict one's freedom or opportunities. Someone with insight into his character might conclude that he will never get his book written if he does not put himself in a situation which severely limits his freedom or opportunity to do anything else. But, as with the other irrational desires, the desire to restrict one's freedom or opportunity needs to be justified if acting on it is not to be considered irrational.

Finally, someone who wants to deprive himself of pleasure is irrational. If someone enjoys eating peaches, then to deprive himself of the pleasure of eating them is irrational. Of course, in this case also there will be reasons that will obviously make it rational to deprive oneself of a particular pleasure. Continued enjoyment may be harmful to one's health, may conflict with the development of one's abilities, etc. Nonetheless, like other irrational desires, the desire to deprive oneself of pleasure requires a reason or acting on it is acting irrationally.

I have admitted that it is not always irrational to act on an irrational desire, that it is possible to justify such action. I must therefore explain the concept of justification. To justify an action is to show that it is rational. (Moral justification consists in showing an action to be moral; this will be discussed in Chapters 5 and 6.) Normally all that is necessary is to show that the action is allowed by reason. Thus normally we have to justify our actions only when they seem irrational. However, in philosophical discussions, justification often involves showing that what is being justified is required by reason. This involves limiting beliefs to those required by reason. When I attempt to provide a justification for the moral rules, I shall attempt to justify them in the philosophical sense, i.e., to show that they are required by reason. However, in this discussion, I am concerned only with justifying an action in the normal sense, which consists in showing that it is allowed by reason. This is done by providing a reason for the action.

Reasons for acting are certain beliefs. The belief that having my right arm cut off will save my life is a reason for having my arm cut off. In the discussion of irrational desires, several of these kinds of beliefs were mentioned. Beliefs that my action will decrease my chances of dying, of suffering pain, of being disabled, or of losing freedom, opportunity, or pleasure count as reasons. These beliefs are reasons because they can make acting on an irrational desire rational. Other reasons are beliefs that my action will increase my abilities, freedom, opportunity, or pleasure. These also can serve to justify acting on an irrational desire.

They can also justify other actions that would be irrational if one did not have a reason. For it should be clear that there are other ways of acting irrationally in addition to acting on an irrational desire. It is irrational to act on any desire simply because one wants to when one believes that acting in this way will significantly increase one's chances of dying, suffering pain, being disabled, or being deprived of freedom, opportunity, or pleasure. Someone who wants to wash his hands and acts on this desire even when he knows that doing so will significantly increase his chances of being hurt or disabled or of dying, etc., is acting irrationally. This kind of person we call a compulsive hand washer. In general, we regard someone as compulsive, or as acting irrationally, when he has no reason for acting on certain desires knowing that his action significantly increases his chances of being hurt or disabled or of dying, etc.

Knowing what counts as a reason for acting does not solve the problem of what counts as an adequate reason. A reason adequate to justify one action may not be adequate to justify another. Clearly it would be irrational, in anything like normal circumstances, to act on an irrational desire to win a bet of one cent. However, I do not think it is necessary to go into this kind of detail. All that I wish to make clear is that one needs some reason in order to justify acting on an irrational desire or on any desire that one believes significantly increases one's chances of suffering certain consequences. If this is granted, there should be no philosophical problem in determining what will count as an adequate reason for acting in any of these ways. Clearly one will need a stronger reason for wanting to be killed than for wanting to be deprived of some pleasure. This can be seen from the fact that it would be rational to deprive oneself of any pleasure in order to avoid dying, but it would be irrational to die in order to avoid being deprived of some pleasure. Thus though acting on an irrational desire because one enjoys doing so is acting on a reason; if the consequences are serious enough, it is not an adequate reason.

Since a reason is that which can make acting on an irrational desire rational, simply wanting something cannot be a reason. For we have seen that merely wanting to act on an irrational desire is not enough to make it rational. Although there is a sense of "reason" in which "wanting" does provide a reason, this sense of a reason has nothing to do with justification; it simply explains one's actions. I shall always use "a reason" to mean a belief that can justify acting on an irrational desire. Whether someone actually holds the belief or not is irrelevant to its being a reason. When I talk of "a motive," I mean a belief that at the time of deliberating or acting the agent regards as, and which is part of, an acceptable explanation for his doing the action. Everything I call a reason can serve as a motive for a rational man. But some reasons may, in fact, never serve as motives for some rational men. Further, some motives are not reasons. The belief that someone will be harmed by my action may be a motive for doing it; i.e., it may be sincerely offered and provide an acceptable explanation for doing it. But it is not a reason; it cannot make acting on an irrational desire rational.

I usually need no reason for doing those things I want to do. If I want to see the place where Kennedy was assassinated, I do not need a reason. If someone asks me why I want to see it, my reply "I simply want to" may be taken in several ways. It may explain my action by ruling out any motives for it, i.e., that I have any beliefs that I would regard as explaining why I want to see it. It may also be taken as denying that I need a reason for wanting to see it. It cannot provide a reason (justification) for my going to see the place. Philosophers have not distinguished clearly enough between beliefs which can justify actions (reasons) and beliefs which do explain them (motives). Further, they have not clearly distinguished wanting from either of these. That I want to do something is neither a reason for doing it nor my motive for doing it. Of course, I seldom need a reason for doing what I want to, and if I want to do something I do not normally need a motive to explain my doing it. My wanting to do something may explain why I do it, but it can never justify my doing it. But of course, acting as one wants to act seldom needs justification, even though it sometimes does. It may be that part of the confusion concerning wanting is due to a failure to distinguish it from liking or enjoying. My belief that I would enjoy doing something is a reason and can be a motive for doing it.

Of course, there are reasons for believing as well as reasons for acting. A reason for believing is a belief that can make holding an irrational belief rational. We have already listed several irrational beliefs; there are many others, but they play no role in this book. Although reasons for believing also play no role in this book, it may be worthwhile to mention a few. The belief that I see a bird is a reason for believing that there is a bird where I see it to be. The belief that I remember taking an aspirin is a reason for believing that I took an aspirin. The belief that a proposition is entailed by something I know is a reason for believing the proposition. Much of philosophy has consisted in giving reasons for holding irrational beliefs. In more normal cases reasons are beliefs that are offered in order to persuade a rational man to accept some further belief. The justification of induction, or of deduction, cannot possibly be provided until an adequate account of reason as applied to beliefs has been developed and related to the more basic sense of reason as applied to action. However, since reasons for believing do not play an important role in moral philosophy, I shall limit all further discussion of reasons to reasons for acting.

The exact relationship between death, pain, and disability and loss of freedom, opportunity, and pleasure cannot be determined in the abstract. Some pain is so severe it would not be irrational to want to die in order to escape from it. However, there are also lesser degrees from which we would consider avoidance by death to be irrational. Death has no degrees. It seems never to be irrational to want not to die, even when it is rational to want to. Although it may sometimes be allowed by reason to want to die, it never seems required by reason. This means that it is never irrational to want to live even though there may be circumstances, e.g., terminal cancer, when it would not be irrational to want to die. In general, most of our actual decisions are those in which it would be rational to act in either way.

We almost always have adequate reasons for acting in ways that would be irrational if we did not have such reasons. This accounts for some of the plausibility of the "cool moment" account of rationality. The "cool moment" account emphasizes that each man determines the rational way for him to act. Since most of our desires are rational, this is generally true. But as we have already made clear, there are limits. A man cannot decide on his own that it is rational for him to kill himself in the most painful possible fashion simply because he wants to do it. There are some ways of acting that are irrational no matter what the man himself thinks about it.

An action is irrational in the basic sense if it is an intentional action of a person with sufficient knowledge and intelligence to know the foreseeable consequences of that action, when these include significantly increased risk of his suffering death, pain, disability, loss of freedom or opportunity, or loss of pleasure (as well as the frustration of what he considers in a cool moment to be his more important rational desires) and the person does not have an adequate reason for the action. It is not necessary that the person actually believe the consequences to be of the kind listed above, only that almost all people with similar knowledge and intelligence would believe them to be so. On the "cool moment" account it is irrational to act on a desire only when one believes that this will significantly decrease his chances of acting on some other desires that he considers significantly more important and it does not even require that the more important desires be rational ones.

I have listed five irrational desires: the desire to be killed, to be caused pain, to be disabled, to be deprived of freedom or opportunity, and to be deprived of pleasure. Someone might ask, "Why do you call these desires irrational?" My answer is, "Because they are." We just do regard anyone who acts on any one of these desires simply because he wants to as acting irrationally. This answer may seem unsatisfying. One would like an answer with a more self-evident ring to it. Thus one might prefer to say that these desires are irrational since acting on them simply because one wants to is acting contrary to one's selfinterest for no reason. One might argue as follows: to act contrary to one's self-interest for no reason is to act irrationally. To act on certain desires simply because one wants to is to act contrary to one's selfinterest for no reason. Therefore to act on these desires simply because one wants to is irrational. And these kinds of desires I call irrational desires.

I have also listed a number of beliefs that count as reasons. I have said that beliefs that acting in a certain way will decrease one's chances of dying, suffering pain, being disabled, being deprived of freedom, opportunity, or pleasure, or will increase one's chances of obtaining more ability, freedom, opportunity, or pleasure are reasons. Again one might ask, "Why are these reasons?" My answer is the same as above. They simply are. We just do believe that having one of these beliefs can make it rational to act in a way that would be irrational if we did not have such a belief. We can, if we wish, relate all of these reasons to self-interest. Thus we can say that the belief that acting in a certain way is in one's self-interest is a reason for acting in that way. The beliefs listed above are all beliefs that acting in a certain way are in one's self-interest. Therefore the beliefs listed above are reasons for acting in a certain way. Although some may find that the concept of self-interest makes what I say more self-evident, I do not. The concept of self-interest, if it is not to be intolerably vague, must be explained by referring to what I have called irrational desires and reasons.

On the account given so far, irrational desires are desires that are contrary to one's self-interest, and reasons are beliefs that something is in one's self-interest. If man is considered in isolation, as if he existed all by himself on a desert island, then this account would be adequate. Thus rationality is often equated with rational self-interest. This false equation is furthered by the fact that it is always rational to act in one's self-interest. But from the fact that it is always allowed by reason to act in one's self-interest, it does not follow that reason always prohibits acting contrary to one's self-interest. However, if nothing other than one's self-interest is involved, then reason does prohibit acting contrary to one's self-interest. Thus, when considering man in isolation, reason prohibits acting on any desire that results in the sacrifice of one's self-interest or of some more important desires.

However, man is generally not in isolation. He is usually found in the company of others. Considering man in the company of others forces one to enlarge the concept of reason. It is not irrational to deprive oneself of some pleasure if one believes that one will thereby save someone else's life, relieve someone else's pain, prevent someone else being disabled, allow someone else to regain his freedom, or even prevent someone else being deprived of pleasure. It is thus not only some benefit to oneself that makes it rational to deprive oneself of some pleasure, it is also rational to do this in order to benefit someone else. Of course, it is also rational not to deprive oneself of pleasure for the sake of someone else. All that is being claimed here is that a reason is not limited to a belief that the action is in one's own interest. It is also allowed by reason to act contrary to one's self-interest in order to benefit others.

What is wrong with considering man in isolation is that one is likely to overlook the fact that the belief that one will benefit someone else is a reason for acting. By considering man in isolation, one is tempted to conclude that all reasons relate to one's own interest. But we do not consider irrational a person who gives his life in the attempt to save others, let alone one who gives his time or money for the benefit of others. Rationality cannot therefore be equated with rational self-interest. The belief that one will benefit someone else may be as adequate a reason as the belief that one will benefit oneself. Some parents sacrifice their own interests in order to benefit their children; other parents do not. Neither choice counts against their rationality. As we have seen before, in a choice between exclusive alternatives, it often happens that both alternatives are allowed by reason; neither is required by it. It is rational to prefer one's own interests to those of anyone else; it is also rational to prefer to benefit another at some expense to oneself. It is not irrational to sacrifice the interests of others to benefit oneself. There is, as far as I can see, no warrant for saying that reason requires benefiting others. It is, of course, allowed by reason to benefit others, but this is a much weaker and, I think, uncontroversial claim.

We have now seen that a reason for acting in a certain way need not be a belief that acting in this way will benefit oneself; it can also be a belief that acting in this way will benefit someone else. Thus rationality cannot be equated with rational self-interest. A man is not irrational if he acts in a way that he knows is contrary to his self-interest if he believes that acting in this way will benefit someone else. I have defined a reason as that which can make acting on an irrational desire rational. I am now pointing out that beliefs to the effect that acting in a certain way will benefit either myself or someone else are reasons. Further, I think that these kinds of beliefs are the only reasons. Nothing else can justify acting on an irrational desire. It must be kept in mind that what I count as benefiting someone includes decreasing his chances of dying, suffering pain, being disabled, of being deprived of freedom, opportunity, or pleasure and increasing his chances of obtaining more ability, freedom, opportunity, or pleasure. Anything else which seems to count as a reason for acting is so only because it involves the reasons listed above. If anyone shows that there is some reason which does not involve these reasons, I shall have been proved wrong.

Having shown that reasons include not only beliefs that one's action is in one's own self-interest, but also beliefs that it is in the interest of someone else, there is a temptation to expand the concept of an irrational desire. I have limited irrational desires to those desires to act contrary to one's own self-interest. Someone may plausibly claim that it is irrational to desire to kill, inflict pain on, disable, restrict the freedom or opportunity of, or deprive of pleasure of anyone, and not merely oneself, for no reason. One need not be claiming very much by calling these desires irrational. One can agree that it is not irrational to want to do any of these things if he believes that he will benefit himself, or even derive some pleasure from doing them. Thus, one need not consider a sadist, i.e., one who gets pleasure from inflicting pain on others, as irrational. Like the masochist, who gets pleasure from being inflicted with pain, the sadist is unusual—although perhaps not so unusual as we might think, when we consider how many people enjoy boxing, how many laugh at accidents.

We are now trying to decide whether it is irrational to act on a desire to harm others simply because one wants to; i.e., whether the desire to harm others is an irrational desire. It is very tempting to say this, for we do talk of senseless killing. People who simply act on their desire to kill others do seem to be irrational. The student who, from the tower of the University of Texas, shot and killed all the people he could was certainly irrational. And since he seems to have done this simply because he wanted to, it is tempting to conclude that anyone who acts on a desire to kill others simply because he wants to is acting irrationally. But it is not clear that we consider the student to have acted irrationally simply because he acted on his desire to harm others. He was intelligent enough to know that his action was one that significantly increased his own chances of being harmed. Thus he may be considered irrational for the same reason that a compulsive hand washer is considered irrational, viz., acting without a reason on a desire which he knew would significantly increase his own chances of being harmed. Therefore we need not conclude that the desire to harm people is any more irrational than the desire to wash one's hands. It is irrational to act on this desire only when one believes that so acting will significantly increase his own chances of being harmed.

However, it does not seem plausible to say that the desire to harm others is like the desire to wash one's hands, both being allowed by reason except when acting on them increases one's own chances of being harmed. I think it does not seem plausible because as a matter of fact those who act on a desire to harm others simply because they want to are generally irrational. In almost any society someone who harms another increases his chances of being harmed himself. Thus if one has no reason for harming another, one usually is acting on a desire which one knows increases his own chances of being harmed. Acting in this way without a reason is acting irrationally.

However, as long as one takes care that he does not harm himself, it seems perfectly rational to act on a desire to harm someone, e.g., for revenge, even if one has no reason. But if the desire for revenge is so strong that it leads one to act in such a way that he seriously harms himself in order to carry out the revenge, then such action is irrational. So revenge which harms oneself is irrational, whereas revenge which does not is allowed by reason. If this is the case, then acting on the desire to harm another simply because one wants to is not an irrational desire. To harm someone because he has made you angry is usually irrational, not because one needs a reason for harming others, but because one knows he is increasing his own chances of being harmed. Envy, at least in some mild form, is almost universal. Although we do not admire the man who seeks to harm those he envies, if he does it without harming himself, we do not regard him as acting irrationally.

Thus there are serious objections to placing on equal footing desires to harm oneself and desires to harm others. One could be rational and be completely indifferent to other people. Although it would be irrational for me to cut off my own arm just because I felt like doing it, it need not be irrational for me to cut off the arm of another just because I felt like doing it. It would, of course, be monstrous of anyone to do that, but it would not be irrational. I should certainly like to exclude such an action as irrational, but I do not see how I can legitimately do so. If one is completely indifferent to other people, regarding their likes and dislikes as no more significant than the life of plants, it does not seem irrational for one to do the most monstrous acts simply because he wants to do them. It is not irrational to pull up some flowers simply because one feels like doing so. Similarly, if no harm to oneself is to result, it is not irrational to harm someone simply because one feels like doing so.

This conclusion seems to support those that want to make rationality essentially a matter of self-interest. For it is not claimed that a person can be rational and be completely indifferent to whether he himself is harmed. To point out that indifference is not the same as a positive desire to harm seems of little significance. One can be indifferent to flowers and yet sometimes simply feel like pulling one up. Similarly one can be indifferent to people, and yet sometimes simply feel like harming one.

Nonetheless, rationality does not become completely a matter of self-interest. It is still true that it is rational to sacrifice oneself to benefit others. It is irrational to sacrifice oneself to harm others. And here we can make a distinction between the sadist and the person who simply desires to harm others. For the sadist it may be rational to make some sacrifice to harm others, for he gets pleasure from so doing, and this pleasure may outweigh the sacrifice he makes. But for the person who gets no pleasure from harming others, it is irrational to make any sacrifice to do so.

Causing harm to others never, by itself, makes rational an action that would otherwise be irrational; whereas helping others, by itself, can make an action that would otherwise be irrational, rational. If by depriving myself of some pleasure, I enable others to enjoy themselves, what would be an irrational action becomes rational. Moreover, though it may not be irrational simply to harm others, it is irrational to do so if one thereby harms oneself, and gets no pleasure or benefit. We arrive at a concept of rational action which gives prominence to self-interest. We agree that one needs no reason to act on any desires, except one which would sacrifice greater desires or is contrary to one's self-interest. We thus regard it as allowed by reason for a man to harm others simply because he feels like doing so. We modify this essentially egoistic account of reason only in the following way: it is not irrational to help others even if one thereby harms oneself.

Thus rationality does not imply concern for the welfare of others, especially when this conflicts with one's own welfare. It does not even seem to exclude what we generally call "senseless killing." Nonetheless it is important to see that when one's own interest conflicts with the interests of others, it is allowed by reason to act according to one's own interest or to sacrifice one's interest to others. Reason does not offer the guide to conduct that either those who equate it with rational self-interest or those who equate it with morality assign it. This account of rationality makes clear that reason does not provide the support to morality that it is sometimes claimed to do. Yet, despite appearances, it is not the enemy of morality that it has also sometimes been claimed to be.

I have attempted to provide an account of reason such that there would be complete agreement on everything I call irrational, or prohibited by reason. I realize that many people would prefer that some of what I say is allowed by reason be classified as irrational. I do not deny that good cases can be made for calling sadism, masochism, and the desire to harm others irrational. However, I do not want to exclude from the category of rationality anything which anyone can plausibly want to include. To call something rational, or allowed by reason, is in no way whatsoever to praise it. I realize that "rational" is often used as a word of praise, but I do not use it in this way. Only when I say that something is required by reason do I mean to commend it. There are those who wish to make a sharp distinction between facts and values, between the descriptive and the prescriptive. This account of reason shows that when dealing with rational men such a sharp distinction cannot be made. This will become even more evident from the following discussion of good and evil.

CHAPTER 3

GOOD AND EVIL

In most discussions of good and evil, good re-
ceives most of the attention. Indeed, sometimes evil is completely
ignored, almost as if it didn't exist. Some theologians have even explicitly claimed that evil does not really exist. This view is, I believe, a
central tenet of one branch of Christianity. Nonetheless, I do not think
it necessary to defend the claim that there is evil in the world. Unfortunately, there is far too much evil, not all of it caused by man, though
he is increasing his share consistently. In this chapter I shall provide
not only a list of things which are good and of those which are evil,
but also a definition of good and evil. My discussion will differ from
most others in that evil rather than good will receive the most attention. This is not done from a desire to be different. There is considerably more agreement on what is evil than on what is good. Further, evil
plays a much more important role in moral philosophy than good
does.

There is little doubt about some of the things that are evil. Theologians through the centuries have recognized that there is at least a
seeming inconsistency between the view that there is an all-knowing,
all-powerful, and completely benevolent God and the existence of so
much pain and suffering. The so-called "problem of evil" is the problem of trying to show that there is no inconsistency involved in believing in such a God when there is so much evil in the world. There is
no disagreement among theologians about what counts as evil. Even

those who deny the existence of evil agree about the sorts of things whose existence they are denying. They are agreed that if there really is pain, then there really is evil. But some of them are prepared to assert that there really is no pain; or that pain is not really something positive, but is a kind of privation. I shall not go into these theological subtleties. Pain is an evil. No rational man has any doubts on this matter.

However, to say that pain is an evil is not to say that pain never serves a useful purpose. Often the feeling of pain provides a warning that the body needs medical attention. If we did not feel pain, then we might not seek the necessary medical attention, and might even die. This fact about the function of pain is sometimes used in an attempt to solve the problem of evil. Thus it is sometimes claimed that this is the best of all possible worlds, and all the evil in it is necessary evil. But even if that is so, necessary evil is evil. I am not now concerned with showing the futility of all solutions to the problem of evil. I am only providing an account of evil. Pain is an evil. To use the fact that pain helps us to avoid death as a point in favor of pain only shows that death is generally considered an even greater evil than pain.

That death and pain are evils does not seem to be a matter on which rational men can disagree. In the previous chapter we pointed out that it was irrational to act on a desire for pain or death simply because one wanted to. Since desires for death and pain are irrational desires and since death and pain are evils, it is very plausible to conclude that whatever is the object of an irrational desire is an evil. Indeed I shall attempt to show that an evil can be defined as the object of an irrational desire. This definition of evil provides us with a list of evils: death, pain, disability, loss of freedom or opportunity, and loss of pleasure. All of these things are generally regarded as evils. No rational man insofar as he is rational (this phrase is always to be understood when I talk of rational men) desires any evil for himself, without a reason. That there are circumstances in which people—even rational people—desire death, pain, or disability does nothing whatever to discredit the view that these things are undesirable or evils.

Some people are color blind, and there are conditions in which even normal people will not see yellow things as yellow. But this does not discredit the view that some things really are yellow. We determine whether a given object is really yellow or not by making sure that it is in normal conditions. Then we make sure that those who are going to decide have normal vision. Normal conditions are generally those in which we usually see that object or perhaps most things. Normal vision is determined by relatively simple tests in which, in normal conditions, a person demonstrates his ability to discriminate between yellow objects and those of another color. Although it would be pointless to define "yellow" as the color which people with normal vision in normal conditions call "yellow," it would not be obviously wrong to do so. The objectivity of yellow is maintained by the proviso "people with normal vision in normal conditions." If there is a color which these people in normal conditions cannot agree is yellow or not yellow, we then must say that the concept of yellow is to that extent vague. This color cannot be said either to be or not to be yellow. But in most cases, most people in normal conditions agree on whether or not something is yellow. Thus the concept of yellow is a useful one, and an objective one, i.e., one which a person can apply sincerely but mistakenly.

The concept of evil is as objective as the concept of yellow. Further, the concept of evil is even more precise than the concept of yellow. This should not be surprising. It is much more important to be precise about what is evil than about what is yellow. All rational men want to avoid evil; they need have no particular concern about yellow. Defining an evil as the object of an irrational desire provides an objective account of evil, and yet not one which is independent of man. The definition makes it clear that evil is generally avoided by rational men. But we must remember that as a rational man, one need only seek to avoid evil for himself. If we forget this, we create the paradoxes that have plagued philosophers from the time of Plato. No rational man chooses an evil for himself unless he has a reason. But some rational man may choose to inflict evils on others, even without a reason. Indeed, an increasing amount of evil in the world is caused by some men inflicting evil on others. However, not all evil in the world is caused by the actions of men. Floods, earthquakes, and disease still cause a significant amount.

Having defined an evil as the object of an irrational desire, it is tempting to define a good as the object of a rational desire. But if we mean by a rational desire one that is allowed by reason, we cannot expect agreement among all rational men. For a desire that is allowed by reason need not be one that all rational men have. Nonetheless we can see the plausibility of a definition of a good as that which is the object of a rational desire. On this account, what is good for one man need not be good for another, and indeed what is good for a man at one time need not be good for him at some later time. There is, no doubt, a common use of good in which each man calls good whatever is the object of his desire. However, I am now concerned with a concept of good such that all rational men agree on what is good. Since agreement on what is evil stems from the fact that no rational man desires it, we might try to reach agreement on good by defining it as what is desired by all rational men. But is there anything that is desired by all rational men? Of the plausible candidates, pleasure is probably the most plausible. But a rational man need not desire pleasure, at least not if desiring implies willing to make some effort to get.

Are there no desires that are required by reason? Is there no desire such that if one is a rational man, one must act on this desire unless he has a reason for not doing so? I think that there are, but that these desires cannot be used to define what is good. For the only desires that are required by reason are the desires to avoid evil. A rational man not only cannot desire evil, he must also desire to avoid it. He cannot be indifferent to whether or not he suffers evil. There is a problem in deciding how much effort he must make in order to avoid an evil, but if he is rational he must make some effort to avoid suffering any significant amount of evil. Unless, of course, he has a reason for not making such an effort. So defining good as the object of those desires which are required by reason would lead to the conclusion that good is the absence of evil. This is not a worthless conclusion. It is at least as worthwhile as defining evil as the absence of good. However, it seems inadequate. More things are good than the absence of evil.

A definition of positive goods cannot be achieved by equating good with what all rational men desire. However, though the absence of evil is the only thing which all rational men desire, there are many other things which no rational man would avoid without a reason. We can therefore define a good as that which no rational man will avoid without a reason. Given this definition, we can list all of those things which are normally regarded as goods. Freedom, opportunity, and pleasure are obviously goods by this definition, for to avoid these things without a reason would be to deprive oneself of freedom, opportunity, or pleasure without a reason. Voluntary abilities, which include physical and mental abilities and the ability to will, are also goods. To avoid these is equivalent to disabling oneself, an irrational action if one has no reason.

That there are other goods can be shown very simply. Health is a good, for to avoid health for no reason is to increase one's chances of dying, suffering pain, or being disabled, which is irrational. Wealth is a good, for to avoid it is to deprive oneself of freedom or opportunity. The same is true of knowledge. This is not to deny that health, wealth, and knowledge can be desired for their own sake. But whether one desires them or not, they are goods, things which no rational man will avoid without a reason. Many other goods, such as friendship, could be listed if my primary purpose were to compile a complete list of all good things. But such is not my primary purpose. I want to provide an understanding of the concepts of good and evil.

It should be clear that many things are neither good nor evil. All things which are not the objects of irrational desires, but which it is also not irrational to avoid, are neither good nor evil. Sticks and stones are neither good nor evil; neither is taking a walk or believing in God. Some people like to collect stones; others have no interest in doing this. Some people want to believe in God; others do not. These things are neither inherently good nor inherently evil. Only those things are inherently evil which all rational men want to avoid; only those things are inherently good which no rational man wants to avoid. I shall call those things that are inherently good, personal goods; and those that are inherently evil, personal evils. Anything else regarded as good or evil is so regarded because it involves a personal good or a personal evil.

I use the phrases "personal good" and "personal evil" to emphasize that a good is what no rational man wants to avoid for himself personally; an evil what all rational men want to avoid for themselves personally. Although there is some connection between what I call personal goods and what philosophers have traditionally called intrinsic goods, the terms are not synonymous. Only pleasure is unambiguously an intrinsic good, though freedom, ability, health, knowledge, and friendship have also been considered intrinsic goods. However, wealth has always been considered an instrumental rather than an intrinsic good.

Philosophers have generally not discussed intrinsic evils, though it is generally acknowledged that pain is an intrinsic evil. I have found the concept of intrinsic goods and intrinsic evils too confused to make clear. Thus I have abandoned it in favor of the new concept of personal goods and personal evils.

Philosophers have called that which causes a personal good an instrumental good, and that which causes a personal evil an instrumental evil. But depending on circumstances the very same thing may be both an instrumental good and an instrumental evil. Thus I have also abandoned the concepts of instrumental goods and instrumental evils, replacing them by what I call social goods and social evils. A social good is something that by its very nature increases personal good or decreases personal evil. A social evil does just the opposite. Clearly the greatest social evil is war, especially nuclear war. The greatest social good is peace. Slums are a great social evil. Education and medicine are social goods. I use the phrases "social good" and "social evil" to emphasize that most of the things that by their very nature affect the personal goods and evils are social in character. To be sure, earthquakes, floods, and hurricanes often cause great personal evil. But these things do not necessarily affect man. Some hurricanes, floods, and earthquakes affect no one. This is not true of war and slums. When earthquakes, floods, or hurricanes cause great personal evil, we call it a disaster or a tragedy. But war and slums always cause personal evil, so that we can say that they are evils by their very nature. The only social evil that is not clearly social in character is disease. However, the cure for this evil, medicine, is appropriately called a social good.

We now have an account of good and evil such that though neither is defined in terms of the other, they are logically related to each other in the appropriate way. Evil is what all rational men will avoid unless they have a reason. Good is what no rational man will avoid unless he has a reason. Thus nothing can be both good and evil.

The list of personal and social goods and evils is a list of kinds of things that by their very nature are good or evil. This does not depend on the opinion of any person or group of persons, but is an objective matter. I am not maintaining that every use of the words "good" and "evil" is objective. As noted earlier, there is a common use of "good" and "evil" in which they are simply used by a person to express his likes and dislikes. But even this use can be best understood as parasitical of the objective use, as I shall attempt to show shortly. It is the objective sense of good and evil with which most classical philosophers have been concerned. That sense is also the important one in moral philosophy.

This account of good and evil can easily be extended to provide an account of better and worse. One alternative is better than another if all rational men would choose it over the other, unless they had some reason for not doing so. Thus it is better to have a thousand dollars than to have only a hundred. It is better to have an opportunity to choose between five alternatives than to have the opportunity to choose between only two of them. One alternative is worse than another if no rational man would choose it over the other unless he had some reason. Thus it is worse to be disabled for two months than to be disabled for only two weeks. It is worse to be deprived of freedom for ten years than to be deprived of it for only five. On this account, it is perfectly understandable how one can be confronted with a choice of two evils, one of them worse than the other. It is also understandable how one can be confronted with two goods, one of them better than the other. It also follows from these definitions that when confronted with two alternatives, one good, the other evil, the former is always better than the latter; the latter is always worse than the former.

Of course, all rational men will not always agree which of two evils is worse, or which of two goods is better. Rational men, when confronted with choosing between increasing wealth and increasing knowledge, will not always agree, especially since both wealth and knowledge have degrees. Thus it is pointless to talk of knowledge being better than wealth, or vice versa. Similarly there will not be complete agreement among all rational men about which is worse, pain or loss of freedom. Obviously there are degrees of pain, to escape from which all rational men will choose some loss of freedom. But we cannot expect complete agreement where different kinds of evils are involved. Death is usually the worst evil, for all rational men are prepared to suffer some degree of the other evils in order to avoid death. However, there are degrees of the other evils which result in reason allowing one to choose death.

In a memorable phrase, John Stuart Mill maintained that "it is better to be Socrates dissatisfied than a fool satisfied." Mill tried to support this by claiming that the pleasure of Socrates was of a higher quality than the pleasure of a fool. But he did this only because he held that pleasure was the only good. Freed from this mistaken view, we can see that what Mill really thought was that the goods of knowledge and ability, especially mental ability, were better than pleasure. Although my personal preference is the same as Mill's, I am forced to admit that it is merely a personal preference. All rational men need not prefer knowledge to pleasure. Indeed very few actually do. But since those who do are generally those who read philosophy, it is not surprising that Mill's view has met with what seems like general approval. One must be very careful in doing philosophy not to mistake agreement among philosophers for agreement among all rational men. That the life of the mind has been considered by philosophers as the best life shows only that philosophers prefer the life of the mind. This is not surprising; one would not expect them to be philosophers if they did not. Men who do not prefer the life of the mind seldom write books extolling their way of life as the best. Reason does not require emphasizing any one of the goods over the others, but allows each man to make his own choice.

This account of good and evil enables us to understand how one evil can be worse than another, or one good better than another. But it also makes clear that there will not always be agreement about which of two evils is worse, or which of two goods is better. Thus it should not be surprising that there may be nothing which all rational men will agree is the worst of all possible evils, or the best of all possible goods. That there are several different kinds of goods and evils—not just pleasure and pain, as the utilitarians maintain—has some important consequences. It means that two people, both rational and both agreeing about all the facts, even when they are concerned with the same people, may advocate different courses of action. This can happen because they may place a different weight on the goods and evils involved. One may may regard a certain amount of loss of freedom as worse than a certain amount of pain, while another man may regard the pain as worse. Reason allows choosing either way. Thus there is not always a best decision.

The fact that when confronted with two evils or two goods, reason often allows one to choose either, has had an extraordinary effect on some philosophers. They have concluded that presented with any two alternatives, even if one is good and the other evil, reason cannot decide between them. This is obviously absurd. When confronted with a choice between a good and an evil, reason requires choosing the good and prohibits choosing the evil. There are even many cases where one is confronted with two goods or two evils, and where one choice is required by reason, the other prohibited by it. There seems to be a strange view that holds that if reason does not provide a complete guide, then it does not provide any guide at all.

It should now be clear that though all rational men agree on what is good and evil, they do not always agree on what is better and worse. Thus there is no danger that by accepting reason as one's guide, one thereby forfeits his freedom of choice. Reason prohibits doing only those things which no rational man would choose to do. There are very few actual decisions to be made in which reason requires one alternative over the other. No rational man feels that a decision is called for when one alternative results in evil for everyone including himself, and the other results in good for everyone including himself. In those cases where rational men genuinely feel that a decision is called for, reason always allows either alternative. A man dying of terminal cancer must decide if he wants to be kept alive or not. Reason allows him either choice. A talented young man must choose between medical research and a well-paying private practice. Again, reason allows either choice. But that there is no agreement among all rational men on the relative importance of the various goods and evils does not show that there is no agreement on what is good and evil. Indeed, agreement concerning good and evil is presupposed in the daily lives even of those philosophers who have explicitly denied the possibility of such agreement.

This analysis of good and evil can be extended to particular things, like tools, by specifying the interests and qualifications of rational men. A good tool is one that all qualified rational men would select when choosing the tool for its normal use, unless they had a reason not to. ("Qualified," "normal use" and the "unless" clause should be understood from now on.) A bad tool is one that all rational men would try to avoid. One tool is better than another if all rational men would prefer it. Thus two tools can be good, but one better; two tools can be bad, but one better; and naturally if one tool is good and the other bad, the former is better than the latter. This analysis works not only for tools, but also for anything that has a standard function or purpose, e.g., sports equipment. It even works for athletes, as we take their purpose to be to win. Good athletes are those who are likely to win or help their team to win.

However, a tool may have several characteristics that are relevant to how it performs. So it may not always be possible to decide which one of a set of tools is best. Each of them might be better in one characteristic, with no way of deciding which combination is best. All informed rational men may agree that A, B, and C are good tools, and that D, E, and F are bad ones. Further A and B may be preferred to C. Nonetheless there may be no agreement on whether A or B is better. Thus it is not to be expected that even when judging purely functional items, there will always be agreement among all informed rational men. But the lack of complete agreement does not mean that there will not be substantial agreement. There is no agreement about whether Ted Williams, Stan Musial, or Willie Mays was the best baseball player. This does not mean that there is no agreement that all three of them are better than 99 percent of all baseball players, past or present. The lack of complete agreement affects the objectivity of these judgments as little as the fact that normal people sometimes disagree about whether an object is yellow affects the objectivity of these judgments.

In this regard, aesthetic judgments differ radically from judgments of functional items. I do not mean to deny the objectivity of aesthetic judgments. In judging such things as paintings, music, novels, or poems, all qualified rational men who accept the same standards will undoubtedly reach substantial agreement. However, since works of art have no "normal function," qualified rational men may not accept the same standards. This leads to the view that each work of art should be judged by the standards appropriate to it. This is not anarchy, for the appropriate standards will be determined by the "purpose" of the work of art. If it is designed simply to entertain, then it should be judged by how well it does that. It is also relevant to determine for whom the work of art is intended. A children's book should not be judged by the same standards as a novel for intellectuals. As long as aesthetic judgments are confined to judging a work of art on its own terms, that is, in light of what the artist meant to do, I see no reason why aesthetic judgments should not be as objective as any other kind of value judgment.

However, when one says that certain kinds of paintings or music are better than others, then one reaches an area where judgment rapidly deteriorates into expression of preference. It is natural for sophisticated composers to scorn popular music as inferior. Popular music can be composed with much less knowledge of music than is required to compose serious contemporary music. But it does not follow that one who can compose good serious contemporary music can also compose good popular music. Nor does it follow that because something is more difficult to do, the result should be judged superior to something less difficult to do. I realize that the designation "great" is not appropriate to those works of art designed merely to entertain. I also wish to encourage works of art which are designed for more than entertainment. But I see no useful purpose in comparing works of art which have different purposes. Nor do I see how one can expect to reach agreement on the standard by which all qualified rational men are to judge.

All judgments using the terms "good," "bad," "better," and "worse" must be made on the basis of standards. These standards will always be related to the purposes of the things being judged. Sometimes this relationship will be indirect, as in the case of judging dogs. Dogs used to have certain functions; certain forms were characteristically associated with good performance of those functions. Standards for judging dogs developed using these forms as a basis. It must, however, be admitted that many standards are now almost completely conventional, the function that originally generated the standards having long been forgotten. Although all judgments using "good" must be made on the basis of standards, this is more a comment on the concept of judgment than on the use of the term "good." For "good" is often used not in making judgments, but in expressing one's likes, just as "bad" is often used to express one's dislikes. Thus in calling a movie bad, I may not be making a judgment of the movie at all, but simply expressing my dislike of it. Similarly when I say that a meal was good, I may simply mean I liked it and be using no standard at all. But even this use of "good" and "bad" is best understood when related to the objective sense of these terms. Since pleasure is good, it is most natural to call that which gives me pleasure "good." This use of "good" resembles what philosophers have called "instrumentally good," a terminology I have rejected because of its misleading consequences.

It may be that it was concentration on the use of "good" and "bad" as expressing one's likes and dislikes that led philosophers to deny the objectivity of good and evil. It cannot be denied that what gives one man pleasure may not give pleasure to another. Indeed what gives pleasure to a man at one time may not give him pleasure at some future time. But when we recognize that it is because a thing gives him pleasure that a man calls it good, we will see that the objectivity of good and evil underlies the seemingly subjective use of these terms. It is extraordinarily odd that though many have denied the objectivity of good and evil, almost no one has challenged the objectivity of the concepts of reward and punishment.

Examination of punishment and reward provides further evidence for the present account of good and evil. Punishment necessarily involves the infliction of an evil; though, of course, not all infliction of evil is punishment. A full account of punishment must include an account of the relationship between the person inflicting the evil and the person who suffers it. It must also include an account of the reason for inflicting the evil. I am not here concerned with providing a complete account of punishment. I am concerned only with the relationship between punishment and evil.

All of the evils that I have mentioned have been used as punishments. Death is usually regarded as the most severe punishment, reinforcing the view that death is usually the worst evil. The infliction of pain used to be a much more common punishment than it now is, and in minor form is still used by parents. Since it admits of degrees, one cannot say that infliction of pain is more or less severe than other types of punishment. There are degrees of pain that may make death seem the lesser punishment, but some pain may be so light that one prefers it to any other punishment. Disabling has also been used as a punishment, e.g., pickpockets used to have their hands cut off.

The most common punishment is deprivation of freedom. There are many reasons for this. There can be fairly precise gradations in the amount of punishment. The longer one is deprived of freedom the greater the punishment. This kind of punishment is also the easiest to administer, partly for the reason mentioned above. It also allows for greater flexibility than other punishments, a point I shall discuss later. The mildest form of punishment is generally deprivation of pleasure.

This kind of punishment is usually restricted to children. One can also be punished by being deprived of an opportunity. This is sometimes difficult to distinguish from a punishment involving deprivation of freedom or pleasure. But there are some clear cases; for example, being expelled from a school for cheating is a punishment involving deprivation of opportunity.

All punishments involve one or more of the evils mentioned above. If one does not think that a person has suffered one of these evils, then he does not think that the person has been punished. The suffering of these evils is so closely connected with punishment that even if a person suffers one of them through natural causes he is sometimes said to have been punished. Since being punished involves suffering some evil, it seems to follow that no one wants to be punished. But it cannot be denied that some people do sometimes voluntarily confess their crimes and willingly submit to punishment. I do not claim that all of these people are acting irrationally, and thus I seem faced with an inconsistency. But the inconsistency is only apparent. Those people who want to be punished for their actions, if they are not irrational, have some reason for wanting this. The reasons may differ, but they fall into two broad categories. One is psychological. Due to conditions we need not investigate here, some people feel extraordinarily uncomfortable when they are not punished when they think they deserve punishment. Thus they submit to punishment in order to relieve themselves of these unpleasant feelings. The other reason I shall call moral. It is impossible to make this reason completely clear without being clear about the concept of morality. All that I can say now is that some people seek to be punished because they believe it is the morally right thing to do. Generally, but not necessarily, one who has this kind of reason will also have the psychological reason.

Punishment is not for the benefit of the punished. The fact that some people seek punishment for psychological reasons only shows that punishment may benefit the one being punished, not that this is why we punish them. Confusion on this point may have led Plato to talk of punishment being for the benefit of the one punished. His view does not seem very plausible. It is hard to see how death can benefit anyone. Being made to suffer pain or disablement can benefit one only insofar as it convinces him to act in ways that will not lead to further punishment. Generally, being deprived of freedom, opportunity, or pleasure benefits one only in this very limited fashion. But though punishment itself is not for the benefit of the one punished, it is sometimes possible to benefit someone while he is being punished. This is not possible with all punishments. It is not possible with death. It is very unlikely with pain and disabling, and is also unlikely with the deprivation of opportunity or pleasure. But depriving one of freedom is perfectly compatible with doing other things for his benefit.

Rehabilitation of criminals is not a replacement for punishment. It is something that can go on during punishment. It is commonly held that one of the reasons for punishing is to deter the person being punished from repeating the action. Death, of course, does more than this, but all other evils may serve to deter the person from committing a punishable action. However, the word "deter" leads one to think that this must be done by scaring the person. This is often expressed by such a saying as "This will put the fear of God in him" or "This will teach him to respect the law." But though we talk of deterring a person from committing a punishable action, we are not primarily concerned with scaring him. We wish to influence him so that he will, in fact, not commit another such action. Fear may be a deterrent, but it need not be the best way to prevent future punishable action. Deprivation of freedom, or imprisonment, is the punishment that allows the most flexibility in preventing future punishable action. Deprivation of freedom by itself serves as a deterrent, but it can be combined with rehabilitation so as to decrease further the chances of one's committing a further punishable action. I hope this is one reason that deprivation of freedom has become the most popular form of punishment.

Rewards, like punishments, are used to influence future behavior. Whereas punishment is generally used to deter one from performing actions, rewards are generally used to encourage one to perform actions. To give a person a reward is to give him some good, thus providing him with a reason for doing the kind of action being rewarded. The most common reward is money, for reasons similar to deprivation of freedom being the most common punishment: flexibility, ease of administration, and ability to make fairly precise gradations. It is interesting to note that being deprived of money, as in fines, is often not regarded as a punishment unless it is also regarded as causing one to suffer one of the evils. Reward, like punishment, need not be solely concerned with influencing the behavior of the person rewarded. It may be used to influence others who are in a position to earn such a reward later. As with punishment, there must be some reason for the reward. But all that I am concerned with now is the relationship between rewards and goods. A reward must be the giving of a good.

That rewards are the giving of goods, and punishments the infliction of evils affects the ways in which they can best influence future behavior. If there is a certain kind of action that I never want performed, say, stealing, it will be very difficult to discourage this kind of behavior by means of rewards. Suppose that I try to do this by offering a reward every week to everyone who does not steal. If no one steals, then, of course, there will be no further problem. But what if someone does steal, then what do I do? Deprive him of his reward for that week? But what is the difference between doing this and punishment? One might maintain that depriving of a reward is not punishing. This is normally correct, but when everyone is rewarded and only one deprived of the reward, this is not so clear. However, let us grant that depriving of a reward is not punishment and see what happens. Suppose that one does not care about the reward and continues to steal? What is to be done now? Can one raise the reward for not stealing so high that the stealer will finally prefer to get the reward rather than steal? When dealing with any large group of people in anything like normal circumstances, this seems to be impossible. One certainly cannot increase the reward for the stealer, for this would have the effect of encouraging everyone to steal at least once. Clearly rewards are not suited for enforcing prohibitions. On the other hand, punishment is perfectly suited for this. Evil is inflicted only on the stealer, and can be increased if more discouragement is needed.

Punishment can also be used to encourage certain kinds of behavior. One can inflict evil on everyone who does not act in a certain way; for example, make a public declaration of loyalty. However, rewards might be equally suitable for encouraging this kind of behavior. Partly it would depend on whether one wanted everyone to act in this way and how much one wanted it. If it were not necessary for everyone to declare his loyalty, then rewards and punishment might be equally effective. However, if it were required that everyone do it, punishment would seem somewhat more effective.

Rewards seem best suited for encouraging behavior that one does not require everyone to perform—for example, an act of heroism. It might be possible to encourage acts of heroism by punishing everyone who did not perform one when he had the opportunity, but this seems less suitable than rewarding those who do. There are a number of reasons for this. First, it would lead people to avoid occasions for heroic acts. Second, it would force unnecessary action on occasions where there were several people who could perform the act. Third, given the character of most heroic acts, the punishment would have to be extremely harsh in order to encourage such action on the part of people not naturally inclined to do so. Thus rewards seem most suitable for those kinds of action we would like to encourage but do not wish to require of everyone. For actions we require of everyone, punishment generally seems more suitable than reward. For prohibitions, punishment also seems more suitable than reward.

Another reason why punishment is more suitable than rewards for those cases in which we want universal obedience stems from the difference between good and evil. An evil is that which all rational men seek to avoid. Thus punishment will affect, at least to some degree, all rational men. This is what is required if we seek universal obedience. A good is only that which no rational man will avoid, hence there need be no good which will affect every rational man in the desired way. Some rational men may be completely unmoved by the reward. Hence rewards are most suitably used only in those cases where universal obedience is not required.

This examination of punishment and reward serves to support the analysis of good and evil in several ways. It supports the objectivity of good and evil and provides empirical evidence that what I have listed as goods and evils is in accord with our normal view of the matter. That punishment is a more common way of influencing conduct than reward also supports the view that evil plays a more important role than good in the discussion of rules of conduct. The slight asymmetry between punishment and reward, the former being more suitable for obtaining universal obedience, supports the slight asymmetry in the definitions of good and evil.

This account of good and evil shows that it is a mistake to equate them with pleasure and pain. It is also a mistake to think it indifferent whether one talks of good or of evil. The discussion of moral rules will make it clear that good is much less important than evil. It was the neglect of evil, and the concentration on good, that made it impossible for previous moral philosophers to give an adequate account of moral rules.

CHAPTER 4

MORAL RULES

In THIS CHAPTER I shall try to present a set of
characteristics, or criterion, by which moral rules can be distinguished
from all other rules. This set of characteristics will then be tested by
seeing if it adequately distinguishes between moral rules and all others. The criterion must not exclude any obvious moral rule, nor can
it allow any rule that is clearly not a moral rule to be classified as a
moral one. Thus the criterion is tested for adequacy by seeing if it gives
us the results we want. It would be futile to offer as a criterion of moral
rules one that either excluded "Do not kill" or included "The bishop
may only move diagonally." This is why we must start with what are
ordinarily regarded as moral rules in order to arrive at the original
criterion. We must also start by accepting that some rules are not
moral rules.

The test of the criterion of moral rules is similar to the test given
to axioms in mathematics or logic. We test these axioms by seeing if
they allow theorems that we know to be true, and rule out theorems
that we know to be false. This does not mean that once we have a
criterion for moral rules it will not be of some help in deciding cases
that we were previously unsure of. We may, if the criterion works well
enough, be able to discover or formulate new moral rules, to reword
the old ones, and, further, to eliminate as moral rules some about
which we were previously unclear.

In trying to provide a criterion that distinguishes moral rules from all other rules, we must discover what characteristics a rule must have in order to be a moral rule. We must also discover what characteristics, though often associated with moral rules, are not essential characteristics. In other words, we must see what characteristics one requires a rule to have if one considers it a moral rule, and what characteristics one can deny a rule has, without being forced to deny that the rule is a moral rule.

We are concerned with the logically necessary and sufficient conditions for a rule being a moral rule. A logically necessary condition is one such that if one says that something is a moral rule and denies that it has this condition, this shows he does not understand the concepts involved. A logically sufficient condition is one such that if one says that a rule has this condition but denies that it is a moral rule, this shows that he does not understand the concepts involved.

Of course, there may be no single set of characteristics which distinguish moral rules from all others. Perhaps the necessary characteristics that all moral rules share are not sufficient to make a rule a moral rule. There might be a number of different characteristics, none of them necessary, which, together with the common necessary characteristics, are sufficient to make a rule a moral rule. That there are some necessary characteristics cannot be doubted. Moral rules must be rules which rational men can obey or disobey. We are attempting in this chapter to discover all of the necessary characteristics of moral rules, and to see if there is one set of characteristics which is both necessary and sufficient to make a rule a moral rule. To discover such a set of characteristics would be to discover a criterion of moral rules.

Before we set out our own criterion, it will be worthwhile to investigate some of the other criteria that have been offered to provide a test for moral rules. By examining these, we shall begin to see more clearly what tests a criterion must meet if it is to be accepted as an adequate one. Also, it is important to show that some of the commonly offered criteria are inadequate. It will perhaps make us more willing to accept the view that the criterion for distinguishing moral rules from all other rules is not simple. Hence it may prepare us for the complexities of any criterion that will prove adequate.

One of the more popular criteria offered to distinguish moral rules from others is religious. Moral rules are the rules given to us by God. This criterion suffers from the obvious difficulty that different religions offer us different rules that are supposedly given to us by God. Hence even if it were an adequate criterion, we might never know if it was satisfied. We can never know if the rules which are said to come from God really do so.

But there are even more serious difficulties. It is a consequence of this view that atheists cannot consider anything to be a moral rule. Further, not only atheists, but deists, or anyone who does not believe that God gave men any rules to live by, would also be logically excluded from holding that anything is a moral rule. Also, anyone who doubted that the rule against killing came from God would necessarily have to doubt that it was a moral rule. None of these consequences seems to be true. Hence it cannot be a necessary condition for something being a moral rule that it is a command of God.

The above argument says nothing about the actual origin of moral rules, only that it is not a logically necessary condition for something being a moral rule to be God-given. We can also show that it is not a logically sufficient condition. God gave rules to man which are not moral rules. Even the so-called Ten Commandments, often called the moral laws, from which in loose fashion we take our paradigm cases of moral rules, contain rules which are not moral rules. The Commandment to remember the Sabbath day and to keep it holy is obviously not a moral rule. One who never violated a moral rule would not be immoral if he did not distinguish one day a week from the others. Thus even if we say that moral rules are God-given, this does not provide a criterion for moral rules. For God gave rules other than moral rules, so we still need some criterion to distinguish moral rules from other rules. Hence it is clear that a religious answer is inadequate. God-given provides us with neither a necessary nor a sufficient condition for moral rules. Again it is important to emphasize that this is not to deny that some religions may present all moral rules as God-given; it is only to deny that their being moral rules is determined in any way by their being God-given.

Another simple criterion commonly offered to provide a test for determining what moral rules are is social or cultural. It has been maintained that moral rules are those rules to which a society or culture demands obedience. However, this criterion, which is closely related to a view called ethical relativism, makes it impossible for one to talk simply of moral rules. One must talk of the moral rules of such and such a society. Accepting this criterion would entail that our original question, "What are the characteristics of moral rules?," is out of order. We should have asked, "What are the characteristics of the moral rules of such and such society?" I do not deny that some people, in fact, regard as moral rules those rules to which their society demands obedience. But I also do not deny that some people regard as moral rules those rules which they believe to have been commanded by God. But just as this latter fact does not make God-given either a necessary or a sufficient condition for a moral rule, the former fact does not make being required by society a necessary or sufficient condition for a moral rule.

We now want to know whether being required by one's society is either a logically necessary or a logically sufficient condition for a rule being a moral rule. Can someone maintain that a rule is a moral rule and yet deny that obedience to it is required by his society? If he can do so without our concluding that he doesn't understand what he is talking about, this shows that being required by one's society is not a necessary condition for being a moral rule. Further, if one can maintain that a rule is required by his society and yet is not a moral rule, this will show that being required by society is not a sufficient condition.

The plausibility of regarding being required by one's society as a necessary condition of a moral rule stems from the fact that all civilized societies require obedience to all the moral rules. In fact, this may be a requirement before we call a society civilized. But we can easily imagine a primitive society in which one or more of the moral rules are not enforced. To conclude from this that in this society these rules were not moral rules would simply be a misleading way of repeating that the rules were not enforced. A member of that society who criticized his society for not enforcing certain moral rules would not show that he did not understand the concepts involved. If our own society became so corrupt that certain moral rules were no longer enforced, we would not show lack of understanding if we claimed that the moral rules should be enforced. We think it possible that a rule can be a moral rule and yet obedience not be required by one's society. This would, in fact, serve as a basis for a criticism of one's society. Thus we do not regard being enforced by society as a necessary condition for a rule being a moral rule.

It is almost superfluous to show that being required by society is not a sufficient condition for a moral rule. We are all aware that society requires us to obey rules that are not moral rules. No one maintains that all the laws of a society are moral rules, and yet obedience to laws is required. In fact, we regard some laws as immoral and use this as grounds for holding that the government should no longer enforce them. Hence even if it were a necessary condition for being a moral rule that obedience is required by the society, it would not be a sufficient one. We would still have to distinguish those rules required by society which were moral rules from those which were not.

In addition to the two more or less popular criteria we have discussed, there are some philosophical accounts that should be considered briefly. The first of these is that a moral rule is any rule which any individual maintains should be universally obeyed. This criterion does not even demand that the individual be rational. Thus on this account "Do not walk on the cracks in sidewalks" might be one's only moral rule. Or even worse, "Kill yourself in the most painful fashion possible" might be one's only moral rule. These consequences are so absurd that the fact that moral rules could change constantly on this account seems almost a minor objection. Even if we modify this account by requiring that the individual be rational, it does not help much. "Do not speak any language but English" is a rule that a rational individual could want universally obeyed. This proposed criterion, even as modified, has the effect of denying that there is any distinction between moral rules and all other rules, hence it is obvious that it cannot be an adequate criterion. However, it does something that neither of the popular accounts does: it provides a necessary condition for a moral rule. One cannot maintain that something is a moral rule and deny that he wants it universally obeyed.

Probably the most well-known philosophical criterion for distinguishing moral from other rules is that provided by the utilitarians. This criterion may be stated as follows: Those rules which if universally obeyed would promote the greatest happiness of the greatest number are moral rules. I have already discussed the inadequacy of utilitarianism, so that there is no need to go into great detail here. I shall only note that the rule "Improve your sexual technique" is a rule which if universally followed would undoubtedly increase the pleasure in the world by vast amounts. I do not think, however, that anyone regards it as a moral rule. Thus it is clear that utilitarianism does not provide an adequate criterion for distinguishing moral rules from all other rules.

A more promising criterion for distinguishing moral rules from others is the following: If the consequences of everyone disobeying the rule would be disastrous, then the rule is a moral rule. Certainly the consequences of everyone disobeying the rule against killing, stealing, or lying would be disastrous. So that this criterion includes what we normally consider to be moral rules. It also excludes some rules that we do not consider to be moral rules. It would not be disastrous if no one obeyed the rule "Don't step on the cracks in sidewalks." However, though it includes all of the moral rules, it does not exclude some rules which are clearly not moral rules. "Don't stand on your head all day" is a rule which if disobeyed by everyone would have disastrous consequences. Yet it is not a moral rule. Thus the proposed criterion, though it provides another necessary condition for something being a moral rule, does not adequately distinguish moral rules from all other rules.

The inadequacy of all of the simple criteria discussed above does not prove that there can be no simple adequate criterion, but it does make it seem a reasonable hypothesis. Rather than offering another simple criterion I shall try to find some properties shared by all of the commonly accepted moral rules. The conjunction of these properties will provide part of the criterion for distinguishing moral rules from all other rules. I shall also consider our attitudes toward these rules and see if I can discover that which distinguishes our attitude toward moral rules from our attitude toward all other rules. It is an essential feature of moral rules that certain attitudes are taken toward them. So it is not out of place to have these attitudes as part of the criterion of moral rules.

Perhaps the most common moral rules, ones that would be offered by almost everyone, are the following: "Don't kill," "Don't lie," "Don't steal," and "Don't commit adultery." To this group, many would add the following: "Keep your promise," "Don't cheat," and "Don't cause pain." Undoubtedly others could be added, but there is no need to consider them unless one feels that a rule being left out would invalidate the generalizations that are being drawn from this smaller list. I cannot see that this will be the case with any rule that has anything like general currency as a moral rule. But this is obviously open to test by anyone who cares to do so.*

First, I shall be concerned with what I call formal characteristics. All of these rules are completely universal; they simply say what kind of action is to be avoided or done. In none of these rules is there any reference to any particular person, group, place, or time. This is not an accidental feature of moral rules; it makes clear what is meant by the commonly held view that moral rules are universal. Moral rules are to be obeyed without consideration of person, group, place, or time. Moral rules not only make no reference to person, group, place, or time, with regard to whom, when, and where the rule should be obeyed, they also place no restriction on those who are to obey it. All men, or at least, all rational men (in the sense described in Chapter 2), are required to obey them.

From this, at least two other features of moral rules can be inferred. These rules must be understandable by all rational men, and they must, in general, be capable of being followed or broken by them. The first of these features, that they must be understandable by all rational men, means that understanding moral rules cannot depend on some specialized knowledge known only to some cultures. Any rational man who lives in society must be capable of knowing what it is to follow or to break the rule. Thus the rule concerning the Sabbath cannot be considered a moral rule unless one believes that all men everywhere and at all times had the concept of a week with seven days.

The second feature requires that the rule must be such that men in every society, at any time, might have acted upon it or broken it. It must not concern the kind of action which men at some place or in some time could not have done. All who accept the seven moral rules that I have listed believe that the kinds of actions prohibited by them were real possibilities to all men in all societies at all times. With the exception of adultery, and possibly stealing, it is impossible to imagine a human society in which rational men did not have a chance to commit the kinds of actions prohibited by these moral rules. Killing and causing pain are always possible; and given that any society demands some group activity, cooperation, etc., it is obvious that oppor-

---

*I am not now maintaining that these seven rules are all justified moral rules; that will be discussed in the following two chapters.

tunities to lie, cheat, and break one's word are ubiquitous.

Although adultery and stealing depend upon the institutions of marriage and private property, these institutions are generally thought to be present in every human society. However, any doubt on the matter may seem to invalidate the view that actions prohibited by moral rules must be open to all men everywhere. For it certainly seems odd to say that if one society had no private property, then it would not be morally wrong to steal. Similarly it sounds very odd to say that if one society does not have the institution of marriage, adultery is not immoral. But, of course, that is not what is being said. It is not claimed that no action is immoral if that particular action could not have been performed by any man in any society. All that is being claimed is that a moral rule, or, if you prefer, a basic moral rule, is one that is believed to concern actions open to all men at all times.

Driving while drunk is immoral, but obviously this kind of action was not a possibility to societies with no automobiles. Hence the rule "Don't drive when drunk" is not a moral rule in the sense I am concerned with. However, together with some obvious facts, it is deducible that it is morally wrong to drive while drunk. One such fact is that driving while drunk significantly increases one's chances of killing or harming someone. In the same fashion, even if rules against stealing and adultery are not moral rules, this does not mean that stealing and adultery are not immoral. For, together with some obvious facts, this may be deducible from some moral rule.

From the formal characteristics of moral rules, it is possible to infer some other characteristics. A moral rule is unchanging or unchangeable; discovered rather than invented. A moral rule is not dependent on the will or decision of any man or group of men. These two characteristics are obviously closely connected, for if these rules are unchangeable, they cannot be subject to the will or decision of any man or group of men. Since we think that moral rules applied at all times, then obviously they could not be invented or changed, or subject to the will of anyone, after the time that the first society of rational men existed. Further, since they are understandable to all rational men without special knowledge, i.e., without knowing anything more than any rational man in any society could know, understanding of them could not depend on the will or decision of anyone. Although the moral rules may have been articulated by some one person or group at some period in history, they are regarded as having discovered the moral rules rather than invented them. For if they had invented them, that would entail that before the moral rules were invented they did not exist, and hence they could not have applied to men before that time. Thus moral rules have a status similar to the laws of logic, or of mathematics. No one invents the laws of logic, though the articulation of them, or perhaps the discovery of them, may have taken place at some definite time or times. I do not say that moral rules are like the laws of logic in all respects. However, I do maintain that any account of moral rules which makes them subject to human decision is inadequate.

Even though moral rules are thought to be completely universal in the sense described, it would be misleading to leave it at this. To say that the moral rules are universal means that they apply to all rational men with the voluntary abilities to do the kinds of action prohibited or required by the moral rules. In discussing the scope of morality in Chapter 1, I emphasized that moral rules were limited to this class. Those who either cannot understand the rules or cannot guide their actions by them are not subject to the rules. Now I am pointing out that a moral rule cannot be limited to anything smaller than this class. If a rule applies to any group smaller than the class of all rational men it is not a moral rule. The universality of the moral rules means that unlike almost all other rules they apply to all those who can understand them and can guide their actions accordingly.

It is the claim of some moral fanatics that one ought never to break any moral rule. But this claim has little support even from those who have some relevant views concerning the supernatural. Almost everyone is aware that there may be times when any of these rules can be broken without the person thereby doing anything immoral. Breaking a promise to save a life is not normally regarded by any rational man as being immoral. Hence one further characteristic of the moral rules must be mentioned which is often overlooked: namely, moral rules have exceptions. What this means is that a person who is subject to a moral rule may in some circumstances intentionally break it and not be immoral. Thus universality should not be confused with absoluteness. All moral rules have exceptions.

There is another characteristic of moral rules, one which accounts for quips such as "Everything I like is either illegal, immoral, or fattening." Moral rules may, and often do, conflict with one's desires and interests. This is a characteristic which some philosophers have tried to deny by talking of true desires and real interest, but this view has never been widely accepted. A moral rule may and for many people often does require action contrary to their interests and their desires. Almost everyone would benefit from breaking a particular moral rule on some occasion. I am not saying that most of the time one wants to break or would benefit by breaking a moral rule. I do not think this is true. I am simply admitting what is commonly held, that there are times in the lives of almost everyone when they either want to break, or would benefit from breaking, a moral rule unjustifiably.

In the account of moral rules given so far, nothing of significance has been said about the content of the rules. From what I have said so far, "Break your promises" could be a moral rule. It is universal in the necessary sense, and it can conflict with one's desires or interests. Thus if an adequate account of the characteristics of moral rules is to be given, something which limits the content of the rules must be given. This is a problem which has faced, in different forms, almost all moral philosophers. Many different answers have been given; e.g., moral rules lead to self-realization or to the greatest happiness of the greatest number. But even the most casual look at the seven moral rules listed shows that all of these accounts are inaccurate descriptions. Moral rules do not tell one to promote good, but to avoid causing evil. Thus it is not an accident that all moral rules are, or can be, stated as prohibitions.

The fact that moral rules tell us to avoid causing evil rather than to promote good has some unexpected consequences. For example, the Platonic view of a moral man as one who minds his own business can now be seen to have some plausibility. Of course, what will count as minding one's own business will depend upon the circumstances. A father who neglects his children is not minding his own business, nor is a person who fails to obey the law. However, though it is sometimes contrary to our interests or desires to obey moral rules, generally obedience will not require the doing of some action which it is not one's business to do. Moral rules are therefore not quite so demanding as they are sometimes made out to be. It is not ordinarily a burden to obey them; one can generally do so by doing hardly anything at all.

That moral rules demand only that one avoid causing evil, not that one promote good, has another interesting consequence. It eliminates some rules which philosophers have put forward as moral rules. Consider the rule "Promote pleasure," which the utilitarians would not distinguish from the rule "Don't cause pain," or if they would, would think the distinction of little significance. But some questions that one can ask show that this rule does not have the formal characteristics of moral rules. For example, with regard to the rule "Don't cause pain" and to all other moral rules, the question "When should one obey these rules?" has no clear sense. The answer "Always," followed perhaps by a statement about justified exceptions, is not an answer about time. It would be a joke to answer this question by listing a certain time of day, or year, or even by giving a certain proportion of time, i.e., half of your waking hours. Time, per se, has no relevance to moral rules. There is no certain proportion of time when I need not obey moral rules, nor, certainly, is there any particular time of day or night in which they do not apply.

However, when one considers the rule "Promote pleasure," one sees that questions about time are relevant. The question "When should one obey the rule 'Promote pleasure'?" cannot be answered simply by "Always" even if one then adds a statement about exceptions. When this question is asked of the rule "Promote pleasure," time per se is relevant. One could answer this question quite plausibly by citing a certain proportion of one's time which should be devoted to following it. It would be less plausible, but still understandable, if one listed certain specific times of the day or year when one should obey this rule. It would not be absurd to say that one should obey this rule every Sunday morning. It would be quite plausible to say that one should spend some proportion of his life in following this rule. People have, in fact, said things strikingly like this: viz., spend one hour every day trying to make life more pleasant for those around you.

This last example suggests another important difference between moral rules and the rule "Promote pleasure." With regard to moral rules, insofar as the question "Toward whom should I obey the rule?" makes sense, the answer is obviously "Everyone"—perhaps followed by a list of justified exceptions. This is because moral rules do not generally require positive action, but only the avoidance of certain kinds of actions. Thus if one is not killing, one is not killing anyone, and so on for all other moral rules. When one obeys these rules, there need be no specific individual with regard to whom one is doing so. (Obviously when one is keeping a promise, he is keeping it with regard to an individual, but he is not thereby breaking it with regard to anyone else.)

However, with the rule "Promote pleasure" the question "With regard to whom should one obey the rule?" is a genuine question that is not so easily answered. As noted above, one is sometimes advised to promote the pleasure of those around one. Thus there can be genuine disagreement with regard to whom one should obey this rule. Some may claim that it should be obeyed only with regard to those in one's local community. Others might say that it should be obeyed with regard to everyone in one's country. Still others might say that it should be treated like a moral rule and obeyed with regard to everyone. However, promoting pleasure requires doing something for someone. Unless I am doing something that is actually promoting the pleasure of everyone (a case almost impossible to envisage), I am not obeying the rule with regard to everyone. Whereas with a moral rule, by not acting I usually obey the rule with regard to everyone.

Another point, closely related to the previous one, can be raised to distinguish "Promote pleasure" from moral rules. Moral rules apply to all persons equally. The question "Should you obey the rule more with regard to some than to others?" if it makes sense is obviously answered in the negative. However, when the question is asked of the rule "Promote pleasure," the answer is not obvious. As we have already noted, it could be held that this rule should be followed only with regard to those in one's local community. Thus it is clear that one might modify this view and hold that it should be obeyed more with regard to those in one's local community, even if some regard should be given to those outside. Thus this rule, unlike moral rules, does not demand equal treatment of all, nor does one usually obey it equally with regard to all.

These considerations show that the rule "Promote pleasure" differs from moral rules in some significant ways. Whereas, ignoring the question of exceptions, moral rules are to be obeyed at all times, with regard to everyone equally, the rule "Promote pleasure" does not require obedience at all times with regard to everyone equally. It is not only possible, but relatively easy, for one to obey all moral rules all of the time with regard to everyone equally. It is humanly impossible to obey the rule "Promote pleasure" all of the time with regard to everyone equally. These considerations are all very closely connected to the fact that all moral rules are or can be, with no change in content, stated as prohibitions on actions. Thus keeping these rules at all times with regard to everyone equally is accomplished simply by not breaking them at any time with regard to anyone. But the rule "Promote pleasure" demands positive action, hence the difficulty in following it at all times with regard to everyone equally.

Moral rules require us not to cause evil for anyone; they do not require us to promote the general good. Thus any account of moral rules which characterizes them as leading to the greatest good for the greatest number, or even for the good of everyone alike, will be seriously misleading. It is not the promoting of good but the avoidance of causing evil which is important. Of course, if a rule is for the good of everyone alike, it cannot allow causing evil to anyone; hence the plausibility of regarding moral rules as rules that are for the good of everyone alike. But a rule that would simply promote the good of everyone alike, even one that had the formal characteristics of a moral rule, would not be a moral rule. It is not easy to think up such a rule, but the following seems to fit the description: "Smile when greeting people." This rule seems to meet all of the formal requirements of a moral rule. It can be obeyed or disobeyed by all. It can run counter to one's desires. It mentions no person, group, time, or place. But we would not regard it as a moral rule because of the fact that it requires the promotion of good, not merely the avoidance of causing evil. Thus it should not be thought that limiting the content of moral rules to those that demand avoidance of causing evil rather than promotion of good is a pointless limitation.

It is a universally accepted criticism of utilitarianism that it would allow the infliction of evil—e.g., pain, on one person—in order to promote a great amount of good—e.g., pleasure, for many others. This criticism makes clear that the causing of evil cannot be balanced by the promotion of good. This criticism of utilitarianism depends on there being a morally significant difference between good and evil. This can be seen from the fact that the argument does not seem valid when we substitute preventing evil for promoting good. Suppose we have a plague, which if not stopped will result in countless painful deaths. Suppose, further, that the circumstances are such that only by sacrificing one or more innocent people can we obtain what is necessary to stop the plague. Here, though one might cringe at taking such a step oneself, one would have to admit it was morally justifiable to kill in order to prevent much more evil. Alyosha's answer to Ivan in *The Brothers Karamazov*, that he would not kill one innocent baby in order to produce a perfect world, is not obviously the morally right answer. If one considers the countless number of innocent babies who die in the world today, let alone the other evils suffered by almost all of mankind, it seems as if one would be a moral coward if he failed to take the opportunity offered to Alyosha.

However—and this is extremely important—such an opportunity is not a real one. It should not be confused with the plans of those who advocate the sacrifice of the lives of generations in order to promote a better world in the future. The promotion of good does not justify the infliction of evil; only the prevention of greater evil does that. Thus, not only must one distinguish between promoting good and avoiding causing evil, one must also distinguish between promoting good and preventing evil. This distinction is not as obvious as the previous one. One can avoid causing evil by doing nothing, but both promoting good and preventing evil demand positive action.

Thus in addition to the distinction between good and evil, it is also necessary to distinguish between avoiding causing evil and preventing evil. Since preventing evil demands positive action, it should be clear that moral rules will not demand the preventing of evil. This will be so for the same reasons advanced against considering the rule "Promote pleasure" as a moral rule; viz., one cannot, nor is one required to, obey the rule all of the time with regard to everyone equally. But the prevention of evil can provide a justification for breaking a moral rule, even without the consent of the person who suffers because of the violation of the rule. In this respect the prevention of evil has a moral relevance that the promotion of good does not. The promotion of good cannot justify the violation of a moral rule without the consent of the person who will suffer because of one's violation of the rule. Because moral rules only require that one avoid causing evil, guides to conduct that encourage the prevention of evil cannot be considered as moral rules. But the prevention of evil is obviously a moral matter. Thus I shall call those guides to conduct that encourage the prevention of evil, moral ideals. They will be discussed in more detail in Chapter 7.

Let us make a distinction between acting in accordance with a rule and following it. Acting in accordance with a rule simply means not violating it, and does not require that one even be aware of the rule he is acting in accordance with. Following a rule requires that one consciously guide one's action by the rule. Given this distinction we can express one important difference between moral rules and most other guides to conduct in the following manner. Leaving aside the question of exceptions, one is expected to act in accordance with the moral rules at all times. As already noted, this is usually no great burden. In fact, it would take some considerable effort to violate moral rules more than a small fraction of the time. Most of the time we act in accordance with moral rules without thinking about them at all. One is not required to act in accordance with moral ideals at all times. Nor is one required to act in accordance with those guides to conduct which advocate the promotion of good, what I shall call utilitarian ideals, all of the time. Further, when these ideals, moral and utilitarian, guide our conduct it is usually in such a way that it is more appropriate to say that we follow them rather than that we simply act in accordance with them.

Since moral rules prohibit those actions which are thought to have evil consequences, we can infer that all rational men generally advocate obedience to them; that breaking them is generally condemned. We now have a substantial limitation on the content of moral rules— one which allows us to keep all of the rules we have listed, and which excludes any rule that would obviously not be accepted as a moral rule. Not only rules which advocate the committing of evil action, as "Kill all unbelievers," but also trivial or insignificant rules, such as "Don't cut your hair," are excluded as possible moral rules. Nonetheless, this account does allow some changes in conventional moral rules. A generally accepted moral rule may not have all of the required features, or a rule may be formulated which will have all of them even though it has not generally been listed as a moral rule. Further, it allows rewording the rules to make them more inclusive without sacrificing any of the required features of moral rules.

Most of the characteristics I have listed are purely formal; they simply make clear what is meant by the universality of moral rules, viz., the irrelevance of considerations of person, place, group, or time. Moral rules apply to all and only those who can understand and guide their actions by them, i.e., to all rational men with the relevant voluntary abilities. This makes clear the independence of moral rules from the will or decision of any man or group of men, and entails that moral rules are unchanging. It also guarantees that men without certain features are not subject to moral rules. That there are exceptions to moral rules makes clear that it is impossible to apply them mechanically in deciding what to do or in making moral judgments.

The content of moral rules is determined by the requirement that protection from evil, rather than the promotion of good, is their primary purpose. This leads to the final characteristic of a moral rule. All rational men must advocate obedience to it. Of course, the concept of a rational man is usually not made very clear. Nor is it clear in what manner or with what qualifications all rational men would advocate obedience to moral rules. Nonetheless, though vague, there is no doubt that in order to be a moral rule, all rational men must agree in taking a certain attitude toward it, an attitude that involves the view that it should be universally obeyed, though this is not meant to exclude exceptions.

This rather vague characteristic that all rational men advocate obedience to moral rules is very important. Together with the other characteristics of moral rules, it provides a criterion for distinguishing moral rules from all other guides to conduct. With this characteristic we have not only the necessary conditions for a rule being a moral rule, I think, we also have sufficient conditions. The usefulness of having this set of characteristics to distinguish moral rules from all other rules depends on making suitably precise the last characteristic. In Chapter 2 I tried to present a fairly precise account of a rational man. In the following two chapters I shall try to provide a fairly precise account of the attitude a rational man, so conceived, would take toward moral rules. We shall then see if the rules we have considered in this chapter really are moral rules; i.e., we shall see if they have all of the characteristics that moral rules are believed to have. We shall also see if any other rules have all of these characteristics.

CHAPTER 5

JUSTIFICATION OF THE MORAL RULES— THE FIRST FIVE

WHAT I wish to show in this chapter is that any rational man, using only those beliefs required by reason, would take a quite definite and precise attitude toward certain rules. I do not claim that all these rational men need take identical attitudes toward these rules, but only that there is at least one statable attitude that all of them would adopt. This is sufficient for what I call a justification of the moral rules. This discussion does not depend in any way upon the meaning of the word "moral," nor indeed, on the meaning of any so-called ethical term, e.g., "good," "bad," "right," "wrong," "ought," or "should."

Although I am interested in providing a justification of the moral rules, it may turn out that some commonly accepted moral rules will not be justifiable. Further, some new rules may be formulated, which will be justifiable in the same way as most of the accepted rules. Thus there may be some revision of the ordinary notions of morality. My primary task is to show that there is a certain set of rules toward which all rational men would take a certain attitude. I believe that this attitude is similar, if not identical, to that which people generally take toward the moral rules. One could say these are the basic rules of a rational morality or these are the justified moral rules, or simply the moral rules; I do not care which alternative one chooses.

I have not performed an empirical investigation involving all the rational men in the world. Hence it would seem that I could not reach any significant conclusion about the attitudes of all rational men on any topic, including their attitudes toward certain rules. However, I am concerned with rational men only insofar as they are rational. (If I were concerned with the irrational aspect of rational men, I might as well be concerned with irrational men.) Thus I can employ the conclusions of Chapter 2 on the nature of rationality. There is very little in that chapter which makes it obvious that there are any rules toward which *all* rational men will agree to take a certain attitude. Indeed if we do not specify the beliefs that these rational men have, then there may not be any attitude toward anything that all rational men will agree on. One's attitude is often determined by one's beliefs; and since the beliefs allowed by reason can vary so much, unless we restrict beliefs to those required by reason it is very unlikely that all rational men will have any significant agreement in attitude.

Since I wish to show that reason requires a certain attitude toward the moral rules, it is appropriate to specify the beliefs upon which this attitude is based as those beliefs which are required by reason. Further, only beliefs required by reason are held by all those who are subject to the moral rules. This emphasizes how closely the concept of rationality, in its seemingly haphazard formulation, fits together and makes it possible to formulate an attitude toward the moral rules that all rational men will hold. I wish to show that if a man uses only those beliefs that are required by reason, there is a conceptual or analytic relationship between his being rational and his having a certain attitude toward a particular set of rules. This is an important conclusion, for we have specified what it is to be rational independently of showing anything about one's attitudes toward any rules. But the importance of the conclusion depends on the adequacy of the concept of rationality presented in Chapter 2. Insofar as one regards that analysis as correct, just so far will one acknowledge the importance of the relationship between rationality and taking a certain attitude toward a certain set of rules.

The rules toward which all rational men will share a certain attitude are closely related to the commonly accepted moral rules. Therefore let us start by considering what attitude all rational men would take toward the most important moral rule, "Don't kill." First let us rule out one attitude which they need not hold. Not all rational men would want to obey the rule themselves. This is not to deny that some rational men might want to obey it; it is only to affirm that some rational men might not want to obey it themselves.

At first glance it would seem that they all would want all other people to obey the rule. But, to say this simply, as if all rational men would never wish anyone to be killed, at least not by anyone other than themselves, does not seem correct. One could be perfectly rational and not be concerned with the killing of persons of whom one had no knowledge. One could, consistent with our account of rationality, be rational and not even be concerned with the killing of people of whom one did have knowledge. Thus, if all rational men are to hold an attitude toward the rule, it will not be simply the attitude that all other people should obey the rule.

Consider the following attitude that all rational men might advocate: "All other people ought to obey the rule with regard to me." This seems quite plausible. Rational men are necessarily concerned with their own preservation. However, as we pointed out in Chapter 2, rationality and self-interest are not synonymous. A rational man might be as concerned with the preservation of others as with his own preservation. A man is not irrational if he sacrifices his life to save others; though, of course, he is not irrational if he does not. Nonetheless, though a rational man could sacrifice his life for others, he must also be concerned with his own life. Hence it seems that all rational men would hold this attitude toward the rule.

But it is possible to modify the attitude in a way which does not suggest that a rational man must be concerned only with his own preservation. All rational men might hold this formulation: "All other people should obey the rule with regard to anyone for whom I am concerned, including, of course, myself." Thus if a rational man were concerned only with himself, he would want the rule obeyed only with regard to himself. If he were concerned with his family as well, he would want the rule obeyed with regard to them; if he were concerned with all mankind, he would want it obeyed with regard to everyone. Thus, even though rational men can differ in the breadth of their concern for people, they would all hold that the rule should be obeyed by all others with regard to those for whom they were concerned. This is not to say that all would hold that it ought not to be obeyed by themselves or with regard to those for whom they were not concerned; it is only to say that some might not hold this.

Thus it seems as if we have an attitude toward the rule "Don't kill" which all rational men would hold; "All other people should obey the rule with regard to all persons for whom I am concerned." But though it would seem that all rational men would hold this attitude, some might not. As we pointed out in Chapter 2, there are circumstances in which it is not irrational to want to die, or even to be killed, e.g., when faced with torture or some incurable and extremely painful disease. Thus a rational man might not take such an absolute attitude toward the rule. Let us therefore modify the attitude as follows: "All other people should obey the rule 'Don't kill' with regard to anyone for whom I am concerned, including myself, except when they have a good specific reason for believing that the person has (or would have if he knew the facts) a rational desire not to have the rule obeyed with regard to himself."

Again it must be emphasized that to say that all rational men would take this attitude toward the rule does not mean that there is not some further attitude that some or most rational men might take toward the rule. I am only concerned with the attitude that a rational man must take toward the rule, and so I must be extremely careful not to include anything on which rational men might disagree. It seems that a rational man must want all other people to obey the rule "Don't kill" with regard to anyone for whom he is concerned, except when they have a good specific reason for thinking that the person has a rational desire not to have the rule obeyed with regard to himself. This does not mean that a rational man would necessarily want someone to kill a person for whom he was concerned (including himself) if that person had a rational desire to be killed. It means simply that when someone one cares for has a rational desire to be killed, rational men might differ on whether or not he should be killed. The "except" clause does not mean that all rational men hold that the rule ought not to be obeyed in these cases, but only that they need not hold that it should.

It now seems that we have an attitude which all rational men would take. Certainly it is hard to think of a rational man refusing to take this attitude. However, I think some cases can be found. Suppose someone for whom I am concerned is not concerned for me; in fact, he is going to kill me. Then I would not want someone to obey the rule "Don't kill" with regard to him, if killing him was the only way to keep him from killing me. To one who may object that I should not be concerned for someone who is going to kill me, I present the following example. I am suffering from some disease. I need a transplanted vital organ in order to survive. Someone for whom I am concerned is the only one who has a suitable organ, but to remove it from him would kill him. To take the proposed attitude would force me to die if I could not kill him. For it says that no one else is to break the rule with regard to those for whom I am concerned unless there is a good specific reason for believing that he has a rational desire not to have the rule obeyed with regard to him. But it certainly seems rational for me to want someone to break the rule with regard to this person, even though he may have no rational desire to have the rule broken with regard to himself. This objection seems unanswerable. Let us try to accommodate it by adding the italicized words to the "except" clause: except when they have a good specific reason for believing that *either* that person, *or myself,* has a rational desire that the rule not be obeyed with regard to him. This formulation accommodates the objection and seems to make the attitude one that all rational men would take.

I conclude that all rational men would take the following attitude toward the rule "Don't kill": "I want all other people to obey the rule 'Don't kill' with regard to anyone for whom I am concerned (including myself), except when they have a good specific reason for thinking that either that person or myself (possibly the same) has (or would have if he knew the facts) a rational desire that the rule not be obeyed with regard to him." I do not maintain that there is no other attitude that a rational person would take toward this rule. In fact, I have insisted that there are any number of attitudes that a rational person could take. All that I am maintaining here is that every rational person must take this attitude, not that he would not enlarge upon it. I am not even maintaining that there is no other attitude which all rational men would take (I shall provide one); I am only maintaining that they would all take the attitude as I have formulated it.

Having formulated an attitude that all rational men would take toward the rule "Don't kill," let us see if there are any other rules toward which the same attitude would be taken. It seems plain that the rule "Don't cause pain" is also a rule toward which all rational men would take the same attitude. Pain includes not only physical pain but also various forms of mental suffering. One may object that I have forgotten about sadists and masochists. I admitted in Chapter 2 that sadism and masochism need not be irrational. If one genuinely enjoyed inflicting pain on others or in having others inflict pain on himself, he would be eccentric, but not irrational. Having admitted this, how can I affirm that all rational men, which includes sadists and masochists, would take the required attitude toward the rule "Don't cause pain"? With the sadist, of course, there is no trouble. A rational sadist would want all other people to obey the rule with regard to himself and those people for whom he is concerned. Thus I see no reason why a sadist, if rational, would not take the same attitude toward the rule "Don't cause pain" that all rational men take toward the rule "Don't kill."

There is some greater difficulty with the masochist, the person who enjoys pain. Since he enjoys pain, he would not seem to want others to obey the rule "Don't cause pain" with regard to himself. However, a masochist may have nonmasochistic friends and would take the attitude for their sake. More important, masochists do not enjoy all pain, nor do they enjoy pain in all circumstances. Hence, if rational, he would accept the stated attitude toward the rule "Don't cause pain," for there is the "except" clause. Thus others need not obey the rule toward him when they have a good specific reason for believing that he has a rational desire for them not to obey it. If they know in a particular circumstance that he would enjoy pain, then he is not committed to wanting that they not cause him pain. The masochist can make much greater use of the "except" clause.

It may seem absurd to worry about sadists and masochists. It could be held that one need not provide an attitude that everyone would take. But the point is, sadists and masochists need not be irrational; they may merely be eccentric. As long as they are aware that they are eccentric, i.e., that most people do not generally enjoy being inflicted with pain, then being rational they should take the same attitude as more normal rational men. The importance of seeing this is that it shows that by rational men I do not mean men with a certain basic goodness, or normalcy, or any other vague but suspicious characteristic. Even masochists and sadists, without giving up their sadism or masochism, will, if rational, take the same attitude toward certain rules as more ordinary rational men. This shows that the connection I am making between rationality and certain rules is not one that simply takes the traditional moral problems and makes them problems of rationality.

We have seen that all rational men would take the same attitude toward the rules "Don't kill" and "Don't cause pain." It requires no additional argument to show that all rational men would take this same attitude toward the rule "Don't disable." What is required is to make clear what disabling involves. As I use the term, to disable someone is to take away or diminish any of his voluntary abilities. A voluntary ability is an ability to do a kind of voluntary act. It can be taken away by taking away a physical ability, as would be done by cutting off a man's hands. It can be taken away by taking away a mental ability, as would be done by cutting out certain parts of his brain. It can be taken away by taking away his ability to will, as would be done by brainwashing. To take away one's ability to do any kind of voluntary act is to disable him. As with pain, there are degrees of disability. But no rational man wants to be disabled in any degree unless he has some reason. Thus all rational men would take the same attitude toward the rule "Don't disable" as they took toward the two previous rules.

Once one has accepted the rule against disabling, it immediately becomes apparent that another rule is necessary: namely, a rule prohibiting the limiting of the exercise of one's abilities. In fact, it may often be impossible to decide whether one is being disabled or simply being prevented from exercising one's ability. This is especially true when the disabling, if it is to be called that, is temporary. This is the old question of deciding when one's power is being taken away, and when one's liberty. It is often an undecidable issue, though there are undoubtedly clear-cut cases. That there are many borderline cases— e.g., giving a person drugs in order to prevent his doing something— is not important because we have both rules. Thus even if it can't be decided whether one was being disabled or simply being deprived of the freedom or opportunity to act, it will always be clear that it was one of the two. Hence no ambiguous act will unacceptably be allowed. The rational man will take the same attitude toward the limitation of the exercise of abilities as he would toward the diminishing or removing of them. It is not necessary for him to decide if a given act fits under one or the other of these rules. All that is necessary is that it is clear that it falls under one or the other. The rational man need make no important distinction between someone who wants to cut off his arm and someone who wants to tie it in such a way as to make it permanently unusable.

Although it is clear that all rational men will take the same attitude toward this fourth rule as they did toward the previous three, it is not so clear how one should formulate this rule. What one wants is a rule which prohibits interference with the exercise of one's voluntary abilities—i.e., performing voluntary actions. The problem is to say this in the clearest, most readily understood fashion. The formulation I have decided upon is "Don't deprive of freedom or opportunity." This rule does not have quite the simplicity of the previous three rules; however, it seems preferable to any alternative. Freedom and opportunity are very closely connected. Being deprived of freedom is simply being deprived of an indefinite number of opportunities. Being deprived of an opportunity is simply being deprived of the freedom to do some particular thing. However, when the deprivation is due to coercion, we usually say that the person has been deprived of freedom rather than opportunity. Thus there seems no good reason to have two separate rules concerning freedom and opportunity. (I am probably also influenced by the desire to end up with ten rules.) To deprive someone of freedom, as when you put him in a cell or tie him to a chair, prevents him from doing an indefinite number of things. To deprive someone of an opportunity, as when you do not allow him to participate in a game, prevents him from doing some specific things. How many opportunities one must deprive a person of before one can talk of depriving him of his freedom is a problem that our formulation of the fourth rule enables us to avoid. I do not claim that my account of freedom and opportunity captures exactly what is ordinarily meant by these terms. But taking these terms either in the sense I have described or in their vaguer ordinary sense, there is no doubt that all rational men will take the same attitude toward the rule "Don't deprive of freedom or opportunity" as they did toward the previous three rules.

The final rule toward which all rational men can immediately be seen to take the same attitude as they did toward the previous four rules has often been confused with the second rule, "Don't cause pain." I formulate it: "Don't deprive of pleasure." It could be stated in a number of ways, but there seems to be no good reason not to use "pleasure" or rather "deprive of pleasure" in the official statement. For one thing, this emphasizes that causing pain is not depriving of pleasure or vice versa. To make noise so that someone cannot enjoy a symphony is to deprive of pleasure; it is not to inflict pain. To torture someone is not to deprive of pleasure, but to inflict pain. This makes clear the greater significance of pain; inflicting pain is generally worse than depriving of pleasure. Yet a rational man would take the same attitude toward the rule "Don't deprive of pleasure" as he did toward the previous four rules.

This rule seems somewhat vaguer than the rest, for what gives pleasure to one man may not give pleasure to another. Indeed, what gives pleasure to a man at one time may not give pleasure to him at some other time. But as we pointed out earlier (p. 31), smiling provides us with a criterion of pleasure, so that there is usually no difficulty in knowing what gives a man pleasure, or what he enjoys doing or having done to him. The rule against depriving someone of pleasure tells one not to do that which will make a person stop smiling, unless, of course, one has a good specific reason for thinking that the person wants you to.

Many philosophers have been tempted to regard pleasure as indefinable. Each man supposedly finds out by introspection what pleasure is. But though this may sound plausible for pleasure, and even more plausible for pain, it has the absurd consequence that no one knows what anyone else means when he talks of pleasure or pain. Taking smiling as the basic criterion of pleasure and wincing of pain, we can account for people understanding what others mean by pleasure and pain. To feel pleasure is to feel like smiling; to feel pain is to feel like wincing. It is no accident that pleasure and pain are sometimes called feelings. This account of pleasure and pain also makes understandable how so many diverse things can be pleasing as well as painful. For there are many things that make us feel like smiling and many that make us wince. An ice cream cone, a job well done, the easing of a pain, and a smile from one we love—all give pleasure. And an unexpected insult may make us wince as much as a slap in the face.

Contrasting pleasure with pain is slightly misleading. Though smiling and wincing are usually incompatible, the case of the masochist shows that they are not necessarily so. An equally valid contrast is that between smiling and crying. This contrast lies behind our contrasting happy with sad. However, smiling and crying, like smiling and wincing, can occur together, so that sadness should not be regarded as the best contrast with pleasure. Not surprisingly the opposite of being pleased is being displeased. Smiling and frowning, which is the basic criterion of being displeased, cannot occur together. The second rule, prohibiting causing pain, should be regarded not only as prohibiting making someone wince, but also making him cry, or frown. Anxiety should also be added to the list of things prohibited by the second rule, but I shall not discuss anxiety as it is much too complex.

Even this brief account of pleasure, pain, sadness, and displeasure makes it clear that one need be feeling none of these. One need not feel like smiling, wincing, crying, frowning, nor have any closely related feeling. In fact, the most casual examination of people around me leads me to believe that most people most of the time are neither feeling pleasure nor pain, are neither happy nor sad, are neither enjoying themselves nor being annoyed. This is not to say that they are not in some state which may lead to their having one of the feelings mentioned above. If they are bored, they are very likely to become annoyed. If they are absorbed in some activity so that they are likely to be pleased by their recollection of it, we even say that they are enjoying themselves while they are so absorbed. I realize much more must be said in order to provide an adequately precise account of pleasure and related concepts. But I felt these concepts needed some clarification in order to make the rules in which they figure clear enough to be useful.

The rule against depriving someone of pleasure, and the immediately preceding rule, need one further clarification. What counts as depriving someone of something? I count as depriving a person of something, doing something which causes him to lose that thing. The action may be done intentionally or knowingly, but it may also be done thoughtlessly. Someone who talks loudly during a concert with the result that I can no longer enjoy it is depriving me of pleasure, whether that was his intention or not. But I do not count failing to act as depriving someone of anything unless that failure to act is a violation of one of the second five moral rules (to be discussed in the following chapter). If someone does not give me a ride to the concert, he is not depriving me of the opportunity to hear it unless by not doing so he has violated a moral rule; e.g., he has broken his promise to give me a ride. Thus I do not count failing to act as violating either the rule against depriving of freedom or opportunity or the rule against depriving of pleasure unless such failure violates one of the second five moral rules. Similarly, I do not regard the failure to act as a violation of the rules against killing, causing pain, and disabling, unless such failure is also a violation of one of the second five rules.

We now have five rules toward which all rational men would take a certain attitude. The five rules are:

1. Don't kill.
2. Don't cause pain.
3. Don't disable.
4. Don't deprive of freedom or opportunity.
5. Don't deprive of pleasure.

The attitude that all rational men would take toward these five rules, stated with all the modifications introduced so far, is: "I want all other people to obey the rule with regard to anyone for whom I am concerned (including myself) except when they have a good specific reason for believing that either that person or myself (possibly the same) has (or would have if he knew the facts) a rational desire not to have the rule obeyed with regard to him."

The "except" clause does not imply that all rational men hold that the rule not be obeyed when the clause applies, but only that they need not hold that it should.

It is important to see that the rational man takes the attitude described above toward the five rules in order to protect himself and those he cares for from certain consequences. These consequences—death, pain, disability, loss of freedom or opportunity, and loss of pleasure—are the five evils discussed in Chapter 3. All rational men want to avoid these consequences. The rules can be formulated in order to make this point more obvious:

1. Don't cause death.
2. Don't cause pain.
3. Don't cause disability.

4. Don't cause loss of freedom or opportunity.
5. Don't cause loss of pleasure.

Stated in this way, these rules would still require the same attitude by all rational men. But stated in this way, it becomes clear why the rational man has the specified attitude toward the rules. All rational men take this attitude toward the rules because they all want to protect themselves and those they care about from suffering evil. Realizing that evil can be brought about by the actions of men, they take the specified attitude toward the actions of men. Why reason requires everyone to take the specified attitude toward the five rules under discussion (no matter how stated) is not that rational men somehow simply want others to act according to certain rules. This attitude toward these rules is required by reason because it is an attitude required by those who want to avoid the consequences that all rational men want to avoid.

Thus, there is no queer implicit notion in rationality that requires rational men to want all others to act according to moral rules. Moral rules, at least the ones under discussion, are rules that prohibit causing the kinds of consequences that rational men want to avoid. A rational man wants to avoid these consequences as much when they are brought about by natural causes as when they are brought about by the actions of men. A rational man wants to avoid death, pain, disability, loss of freedom or opportunity, and loss of pleasure, whether these are caused by an avalanche, or a man, or a mosquito. (Thus it is not surprising that in theology the problem of evil arises in those cases where these evils are brought about, not through the action of man, but simply in the course of nature.)

All of these rules can be broken unintentionally; i.e., a person can bring about the consequences that the rules prohibit causing without intending to do so. A drunken driver can break all five rules, even though he has no intention of doing so. The rational man not only seeks to prevent certain intentional action, but also to prevent those kinds of thoughtless actions which would lead to the undesirable consequences. We now understand more fully the attitude a rational man has toward the five rules. He not only wants others to refrain from intentionally disobeying these rules, he also wants them to take care not to break them unintentionally.

But though the attitude described above is one that would be taken by all rational men, it does not seem to be the attitude we think should be taken toward the moral rules. The egocentricity of the attitude must be eliminated. We do not normally say that a moral rule ought to be obeyed only toward those for whom one is concerned. We pointed out in the preceding chapter that a moral rule is one that we feel ought to be obeyed by everyone with regard to everyone. If we cannot show that all rational men will take some attitude toward the rules which includes this feature, then we will have failed to provide a justification of the moral rules. The problem we now face is eliminating the egocentricity of the attitude toward the moral rules while at the same time keeping it an attitude that would be taken by all rational men.

One way of eliminating the egocentricity of the attitude is to add the condition that the attitude be one that it would not be irrational for a man to advocate being adopted by all other rational men. In one sense, the attitude we have described is one that would be adopted by all rational men, i.e., they all want the rules obeyed with regard to those for whom they care. But in a more important sense they do not have the same attitude. Each man is usually concerned with a different group of people. Thus each wants the rules obeyed with regard to a different group. Although there is a sense in which your attitude toward the rules will be the same as mine, you will not be willing to adopt my attitude if you are concerned with a different group of people than I am.

Unless he had a concern for all mankind, it would be irrational for a man to expect all other rational men to share his particular attitude toward the rules. Each rational man will at least demand that the attitude be modified so as to include himself and those for whom he cares. Thus if one wishes to reach agreement among all rational men, he must advocate that the rule be obeyed with regard to all. A rational man also knows that all other rational men want him to obey the rules. Thus insofar as he advocates an attitude that he wishes all other rational men to accept, he must advocate that the rules be obeyed by everyone, including himself. A rational man who wishes to persuade all other rational men to adopt an attitude toward the five rules under discussion cannot advocate any attitude toward the rules except one like that which would be advocated by a rational man who had an equal concern for all mankind.

When an attitude is being advocated in order to reach agreement among all rational men, I shall say that it is being "publicly advocated" and I shall call it a "public attitude." Publicly advocating an attitude does not necessarily require advocating it openly or "out loud." Publicly advocating resembles what some philosophers may have meant by universalizing, but the difference is significant enough to justify introducing the new phrase. One is publicly advocating, in my technical sense, when and only when one regards all rational men as potential listeners and believes that they all could accept the attitude being advocated. There may be a conflict between what one publicly advocates and the attitude that one actually holds—i.e., that one is prepared to act on. In particular, to publicly advocate an attitude toward the moral rules does not entail that one actually wants the rules obeyed in the way that he has publicly advocated. Public advocacy need not be sincere, though of course it may be. Since publicly advocating an attitude is advocating it to all rational men in order to reach agreement, one cannot publicly advocate an attitude that one knew could not be adopted by all rational men. And by all rational men I do not mean merely all rational men now living, but all rational men past, present, and future. Thus when we add the condition that the attitude be one that a man can advocate for adoption by all rational men—i.e., that it be a public attitude—the attitude that will be adopted will be one that would be adopted by a man who had an equal concern for all mankind.

We have now shown that if a man must adopt an attitude that could be agreed upon by all rational men, he will adopt an attitude which will not be egocentric. Since what we wished to do was to eliminate the egocentricity of the attitude, we may now claim to have accomplished our task. However, I think an even stronger conclusion can be reached, or rather, that the same conclusion can be reached without adding the condition that the attitude be one that would not be irrational for a man to advocate that it be adopted by all rational men. We must remember that our rational man uses only those beliefs that are required by reason. This means that he does not use any beliefs about his social position, abilities, wealth, race, religion, or nationality. Every personal and general belief that he holds is one that is held by every other rational man; he differs from other rational men only in his desires, for we have not added the condition that a rational man have only those desires required by reason, but allow any rational desire that is possible using only beliefs required by reason. Thus not all rational men will desire the same goods, and though they all will desire to avoid the same evils, they will not rank them in the same way.

I shall now try to show that simply by limiting their beliefs to those required by reason, all rational men will advocate that the moral rules be obeyed by all with regard to all with no egocentric exceptions. The rational man knows that all rational men wish to avoid suffering any evil unless they have a reason. He also knows that men are prepared to take action so as to avoid suffering any unwanted evil. He is aware that they are prepared to inflict evil on those whom they believe will cause them an unwanted evil. Thus he is aware that to refuse to advocate the attitude toward the moral rules that they be obeyed by all rational men with regard to all is to increase his chances of suffering evil at their hands. Since he increases his chances of suffering evil by not advocating this attitude, and has no reason for not advocating it, I conclude that it would be irrational for him not to advocate it. Thus I conclude that simply limiting a man's beliefs to those required by reason is sufficient to make it required by reason for him to advocate the same attitude toward the moral rules as would be advocated by a man who had an equal concern for all mankind.

We can now see the close connection between the condition that one use only those beliefs that are required by reason and the condition that one advocate an attitude that could be adopted by all rational men. I have tried to show that if one satisfies the first condition, one will necessarily satisfy the second. One might therefore suggest that the definition of "publicly advocate" be changed. It seems as if we can give a simpler definition, viz., what is advocated by a rational man using only those beliefs required by reason. If the argument of the previous paragraph is correct, then this simpler definition entails the more complex one. If this is so, then there is more in the writings of defenders of natural law than they are usually given credit for. For natural law is regarded as that law which is agreeable to the reason of all men. What the defenders of natural law were missing was an adequate account of reason.

I am aware that the condition that one use only those beliefs that are required by reason is an artificial condition. All rational men have numerous beliefs that are only allowed by reason. In fact, these kinds of beliefs make up the overwhelming majority of a man's beliefs. Men who use these beliefs will not necessarily advocate an attitude toward the moral rules similar to that which would be advocated by rational men with an equal concern for all mankind. However, if such men were to be faced with the earlier condition, viz., advocating an attitude that would be understood and could be adopted by all rational men, then they would be forced to advocate this kind of attitude. Thus the original definition of "publicly advocate" entails the second. Thus we can see again how closely related are the condition that one use only those beliefs that are required by reason and the condition that one advocate an attitude that could be adopted by all rational men.

I conclude that the public attitude of all rational men toward the moral rules, no matter which definition of "publicly advocate" one uses, will be one that would be advocated by a rational man with an equal concern for all mankind. Of course a rational man may not adopt any public attitude. The closest to a situation where taking a public attitude is required is signing some document like the United Nations Charter on Human Rights. Nonetheless many people often do claim to be adopting a public attitude. In fact this necessarily occurs when they make moral judgments. For to claim that a judgment is a moral judgment, one must claim that it is a judgment that can be publicly advocated. This is what was meant by most of those who claimed that moral judgments must be universalizable. To say that a moral judgment must be one that can be publicly advocated means that the action must be describable in such a way that all rational men understand the kind of action being described. It also means that the action so described must be one toward which it would not be irrational for any man to take the attitude being advocated. Of course not all judgments that can be publicly advocated are moral judgments, but we can see the relevance of talking about a man's public attitude in discussing morality.

The rational man's public attitude toward the moral rules does not encourage blind obedience to them. On the contrary, it allows that quite often they need not be obeyed. Less often, all rational men may even publicly advocate that they should not be obeyed. Not only are there justified violations of the moral rules, there is even unjustified keeping of them. For a rational man does not have a fetish for neat, uncluttered obedience to rules, but desires, insofar as possible, to avoid the unwanted evil consequences that usually result from violation of the moral rules. But sometimes, violation of a moral rule may result in preventing significantly more evil than is caused by the violation. This possibility must be taken into account in formulating the rational man's public attitude toward the rules.

In Chapter 2 we saw that only those actions which would be irrational if one did not have a reason for them needed to be justified. We also noted that such actions could be justified by providing reasons which showed either that the action was allowed by reason or, less frequently, required by it. In a similar manner, only those actions which would be immoral if one did not have a reason need to be morally justified. Generally these are violations of the moral rules. And such violations can be justified by providing reasons which would result in either some rational men publicly advocating such a violation, or less frequently, all rational men publicly advocating violation. When all rational men would publicly advocate the violation I say that it is required by public reason or that reason publicly requires it. If a violation is required by public reason, then all rational men publicly advocate disobeying the rule in this situation. Obeying the rule is morally unjustified. When rational men differ on whether or not they would publicly advocate the violation I say that it is allowed by public reason or that reason publicly allows it. These kinds of violations cause most of the genuine moral controversy. When no rational man would publicly advocate a violation I say that it is prohibited by public reason or that reason publicly prohibits it. These kinds of violations are morally unjustified.

One kind of violation required by public reason is one in which, with his consent, one inflicts an evil on someone in order to prevent his suffering a significantly greater evil. A kind of violation allowed by public reason is one in which significantly greater evil is prevented by breaking the rule than is caused by the violation, though not for the same persons. A kind of violation prohibited by public reason is one in which the rule is broken in order to promote good for oneself or for someone for whom one is concerned. We want a formulation of a public attitude toward the moral rules that accounts for the different kinds of violations. The following formulation seems to be acceptable: "Everyone is to obey the rule with regard to everyone except when he could publicly advocate violating it." The "except" clause does not mean that all rational men agree that one is not to obey the moral rule when he could publicly advocate violating it, but only that they do not agree that one should obey the rule in this situation.

The public attitude of all rational men will be the stated attitude toward the moral rules, but not all these men will obey the rules as the public attitude requires. Reason, although it publicly requires advocating a certain attitude, does not require adopting this attitude as one's genuine attitude toward the rules. Reason only allows; it does not require acting morally. It would be a mark of a false theory to "prove" that it is irrational to act immorally the most that one can hope to show is that public reason requires a certain attitude toward at least some of the moral rules. But all rational men are aware that agreement in public attitude does not guarantee that no one will violate a moral rule except when he could publicly advocate violating it. The rational man need not be a hypocrite, but all rational men are aware of the possibility of hypocrisy. Awareness of the possibility of unjustified violation of the rules requires us to consider the rational man's attitude toward such violations.

It is clear that he wishes to discourage the breaking of these rules, at least with regard to those for whom he is concerned. He knows, however, that if he is to enlist the support of all other rational men, he must advocate treating in equal fashion all those who unjustifiably break the rules with regard to anyone. Thus, as a rational man trying to persuade all others to obey the rules, he will support measures which will discourage anyone from unjustifiably breaking these rules. If this were his only consideration, he might recommend the harshest measures to be used against anyone unjustifiably breaking the rules. However, he has another consideration: namely, what would happen to those for whom he is concerned if they unjustifiably broke any of the rules. He is publicly advocating that everyone obey the rules with regard to everyone so that others will obey it with regard to those for whom he is concerned. To recommend the harshest possible measures against anyone who broke the rule might result in extremely harsh measures toward someone for whom he is concerned for breaking a rule toward someone for whom he is not at all concerned. This quite possible occurrence, the unjustified breaking of a rule by someone for whom he is concerned, perhaps himself, with regard to someone he cares for not at all, will make a rational man consider taking the most lenient measures toward those who break the rules.

However, the measures adopted must be harsh enough to discourage most serious unjustified violations of the rules, not only intentional ones, but also those done thoughtlessly. The rational man will also be more concerned with preventing those violations of the rules which cause the greatest amount of evil consequences. Hence he will, as a rational man, publicly advocate harsher measures for the violation of the rule against killing than of the rule against the deprivation of pleasure. The harshness of the measures for violations of rules against causing pain, disabling, and deprivation of freedom will vary according to the degree of pain, disability, and loss of freedom. In some cases, the amount of pain, disability, or loss of freedom may demand measures as harsh as that against killing; in others, as little as that against the deprivation of pleasure.

Obviously, the measures adopted to discourage violations of the rules will be the infliction of evil on the violator. The question arises, "What evil?" Perhaps the same one that the violator inflicted on some person. If he killed, let him be killed; if he caused pain, let him have pain inflicted upon him; if he disabled, let him be disabled, etc. Although this formula might appeal to the rational man's aesthetic sense, or sense of fitness of things, it would not necessarily appeal to his reason. The point of inflicting evil on violators is not to establish some fitness, but to prevent further violation of the rules. An eye for an eye may have some appeal, but unless it can be shown that such retribution prevents violations better than some more lenient system, no rational man will accept it. Of two systems that inflict evil on violators and are equally good at discouraging violations, the rational man will choose that which inflicts the lesser evil. For his goals are to have those he cares about protected as much as possible from those he does not care about, and to have as little evil as possible inflicted on those he cares about when they break the rules with regard to those he does not care about.

Given these goals, a rational man can decide between all those sets of evils which discourage violators equally, by picking that which is most lenient; and of all those sets which are equally lenient, by picking that which most discourages violations. Here, of course, a rational man would try to find out what effect different sets of evils in fact have in discouraging future violations. This cannot be known *a priori*.

Further, between a set of evils which is harsher and better at discouraging violations and one which is less harsh and not as good at
discouraging violations, reason allows either choice. One rational man
may prefer the balance one way; another, the other way. It depends
on whether one is more interested in protecting those for whom one
is concerned from having the rule violated with regard to them; or
more interested in having a lesser evil inflicted on those for whom one
is concerned when they break the rules with regard to someone for
whom one is not concerned.

The point of inflicting evils on those who unjustifiably violate the
rules is to discourage future violation of the rules. Thus the rational
man will seek to have punished only those violators who are capable
of guiding their actions by the rules. He will not publicly advocate
inflicting evil on those who violate the rules through no fault of their
own, either through excusable ignorance of the consequences of their
actions or through inability to act according to their knowledge. He
will not publicly advocate inflicting evil in these cases because it will
do nothing to discourage violations, and might necessitate inflicting
evil on those he cared about if they were to violate the rules through
excusable ignorance or inability to act. This is simply a special case
of choosing between two systems which equally discourage violations
but one of which is more lenient than the other.

All rational men will publicly advocate choosing that system of
punishment which provides the most discouragement of violations
with the least infliction of evil on violators. However, some may prefer
greater discouragement of violations even though it involved more
evil being inflicted on violators; others, less evil on violators even
though it resulted in less discouragement of violations. In this possible
disagreement on balance, discouragement of violations would play a
greater role in the violation of the rule against killing, and in more
serious violations of the other rules, than it would play in the violation
of the rule against the deprivation of pleasure and lesser violations of
the other three rules. Further, public reason would prohibit the infliction of evil on those who violated the rule through no fault of their
own.

This seeming digression on the rational man's attitude toward those
who unjustifiably violate the rules provides a necessary ingredient in
the rational man's public attitude toward the moral rules. If one al-

lowed any rule toward which the rational man publicly advocated the attitude described on page 92 as a moral rule, then one would be forced to allow a number of obviously nonmoral rules as moral rules. The rule "Promote pleasure" would be a moral rule, for no rational man would refuse to take the public attitude toward this rule that it should be obeyed by all. So that in order to distinguish this rule from the moral rules, one must add to the rational man's public attitude toward the moral rules, his attitude toward those who unjustifiably violate the rules.

All rational men would publicly advocate that all those who unjustifiably violate the moral rules be liable to punishment. Failure to publicly advocate this would lessen the protection from violations that all rational men desire. We can now state the rational man's public attitude toward each of the moral rules as follows: "Everyone is to obey the rule with regard to everyone except when he |could publicly advocate violating it. Anyone who violates the rule when he could not publicly advocate such a violation may be punished." I call this attitude the moral attitude. Only those rules toward which all rational men would publicly advocate this attitude count as genuine or basic or justifiable moral rules. It is clear that all rational men would publicly advocate the moral attitude toward the five rules discussed in this chapter. Thus we may now be said to have justified five moral rules, or to have shown that at least five rules are justifiable or genuine or basic moral rules.

One of the reasons for including the rational man's public attitude toward unjustified violations into the moral attitude was to exclude the rule "Promote pleasure." Thus it should be no surprise that not all rational men would publicly advocate the moral attitude toward the rule "Promote pleasure." Indeed it is doubtful if any rational man would publicly advocate this attitude. Unlike the five moral rules, this rule cannot possibly be obeyed all of the time. This requires the rational man either to publicly advocate that no one need obey the rule whenever he does not feel like obeying it or else to publicly advocate that he be liable to punishment whenever he did not obey this rule simply because he did not feel like doing so. To do the former would make it pointless to advocate the moral attitude toward the rule; to do the latter would be to increase his chances of suffering evil. Thus I see little likelihood of any rational man publicly advocating the moral attitude toward the rule "Promote pleasure."

Similar arguments can be given to show that "Prevent evil" is also not a moral rule. It is more plausible that some rational men might publicly advocate the moral attitude toward this rule. However, the impossibility of obeying the rule all of the time would make some rational men hesitate to publicly advocate the moral attitude toward it. The increase in the chance of suffering evil through punishment may more than offset the decrease in the chance of suffering evil because of someone acting so as to prevent it. The addition of the rational man's public attitude toward unjustified violations also rules out most rules that can be obeyed all of the time. Although some rational men might publicly advocate the moral attitude toward the rule "Smile when greeting people," many clearly would not. A rational man need not care about being smiled at when he is greeted. All rational men publicly advocate the moral attitude toward the moral rules because all rational men want to avoid the evils that violation of the moral rules causes.

The moral attitude has so far provided us with a test which excludes the rules that we want excluded and includes the rules we want included. Since it serves such an important task, it is worth examining in some more detail. As we have been discussing that part of the attitude which concerns unjustified violations; let us now examine this part of the attitude. I have said that the rational man publicly advocates that unjustified violations *may* be punished. What is the point of the "may"? Why didn't I say that unjustified violations are to be punished? I could indeed have said this. But then I would have needed to qualify this. There may be extreme situations in which punishing unjustified violations would cause significantly more evil than would result from failure to punish. In these cases some rational men might not publicly advocate punishment. This could be true even if punishment is determined in the way that we outlined earlier in the chapter.

The rational man does not publicly advocate that unjustified violations be punished in order to achieve some metaphysical fitness in the nature of things. His public goal is to minimize the amount of evil suffered. Generally this goal will be best served by punishing unjustified violations. But if it is not, the rational man is not committed to punishment. It is primarily for this reason that we say that the rational man publicly advocates that those who unjustifiably violate the rules *may* be punished rather than simply say that they are to be punished.

There are also further reasons. To advocate punishment requires someone to do the punishing. Who this someone should be and how he should go about his job is more properly a subject for political philosophy than for moral philosophy. Some things, however, should be said. First, it will usually be the responsibility of the government to punish. However, setting up a system that results in punishing all unjustified violations may cost more than it is worth. Moreover, parents are generally considered to have the responsibility to punish their children for less serious violations. A parent may know that punishing his child for an unjustified violation will do more harm than good. Thus though the child has put himself in a position where he may be punished, we do not want to assert categorically that he should be. Most of the time I think that children should be punished for unjustified violations, but one must admit that there are times when they should not be. To insist that unjustified violations demand punishment, regardless of the consequences, is to allow one's desire for retribution to overwhelm one's reason.

Since the moral attitude allows one to break the rule when he would publicly advocate breaking it, it is important to examine the circumstances in which a rational man might do this. Publicly advocating anything requires that all rational men be able to understand and to accept what one is advocating. This means that the circumstances in which one can publicly advocate violation of a rule must provide reasons that could be understood and regarded as adequate by all rational men. As noted earlier, sometimes these circumstances will be such that all rational men would publicly advocate violation of the rule. The clearest example of this kind is one in which the person toward whom one is violating the rule has a rational desire that the rule be violated with regard to him. For example, a person wants a rabies shot because he knows that even though it is very painful, failure to have it will result in significantly greater pain, and perhaps in death. In fact, in this example, given the extreme horror of death by rabies, even if the person, because of his fear of present pain, did not want the rabies shot, still public reason would require giving it to him. However, when the evil that a person would suffer if you did not break the rule with regard to him is not indisputably significantly greater than the evil he would suffer if you did, then public reason only allows breaking the rule with regard to him when he does not desire it.

Public reason may also allow violating a moral rule whenever this results in significantly less evil being suffered, even when the evil is shifted from one person to another. However, it must be indisputable that the evil being prevented by the violation is significantly greater than the evil caused. But even when this is the case, rational men may still publicly advocate different courses of action. One man might publicly advocate killing one man in order to save ten others. He might feel that this will decrease the future possibilities of rational men suffering a preventable death. Another man might not publicly advocate violation in this situation. He might feel that a significant decrease in the protection from violations of the rule plus general anxiety due to added uncertainty more than offsets the possible benefit. Thus we can see that even when the evil being caused by violation of the rule is significantly less than that prevented by the violation, there will be some rational men who will not publicly advocate violation of the rule.

Nonetheless, there are extreme cases in which all rational men would agree that even if the evil is to be switched from one person to another, there is a point at which the amount of evil to be prevented by breaking the rule is so much greater than the amount of evil caused by breaking it, that one ought to break it. Thus, if an innocent child contracts some highly dangerous and infectious disease, similar to that which causes plagues, it will be justifiable to deprive him of his liberty, and perhaps his life, in order to keep the plague from spreading. Thus the rational man would publicly advocate some violation of the rules even if not for the benefit of the person with regard to whom the rule was violated. However, he would not do this lightly, and some rational men will demand an extremely high proportion of evil prevented to evil caused before they would publicly advocate violation. Further, all rational men will demand good specific reasons for believing that more evil is being prevented by violating than by obeying the rule.

"Punishment" is also a justifiable violation of the moral rules. Of course, one must be the appropriate person to administer the punishment. There also is a further limitation: namely, more evil should not be inflicted than one would publicly advocate for this kind of violation. Violation of the rules in order to prevent violation of a rule would also be publicly advocated by some rational men—provided, of course, that one had a good specific reason for thinking that a rule was going to be violated. However, one cannot inflict greater evil than would have been inflicted as the punishment for the violation of the rule unless significantly greater evil is being prevented. If these provisions are not met, then I do not see the possibility of any rational men still publicly allowing it. Any violation in order to obtain some good for anyone for whom one is concerned, including oneself, is an unjustifiable violation. No rational man would publicly advocate this kind of violation. Thus all killing and torturing for pleasure or profit is clearly immoral, whereas killing and torturing to prevent greater killing and torturing may sometimes be allowed by public reason.

Thus we now see that rational men may disagree about some violations. So that not all rational men need take precisely the same attitude toward the moral rules and their justifiable violations. However, the disagreements will occur within a larger framework of agreement. But this does not mean that in genuine cases of moral disagreement, taking one side is required by public reason; taking the other, prohibited. For it is very likely that genuine moral disagreements are those that occur within the larger framework, where it is allowed by reason to publicly advocate either alternative. It is here that each individual has to decide for himself what violations he would publicly advocate.

Providing a justification of some violations of the moral rules does not provide a mechanical decision procedure for moral questions. Very few if any genuine moral disputes can be settled by applying this set of justifications to the facts. All that I have attempted to do is to provide a limit to genuine moral disputes; to show that there is a point beyond which rational men can no longer disagree about what morally should be done. Before this point is reached, no application of what has been said will settle the issue. Men must decide on their own what weight they will give to the various considerations. I have only shown what the morally relevant considerations are: the amount of evil to be caused, avoided, or prevented; the rational desires of the people toward whom the rule is to be broken; and the effect that this kind of violation, if allowed, would have. Therefore, I have not provided anything that functions like an ideal observer, or Aristotle's practically wise man, to whom one can take any moral problem and he will pronounce what ought to be done. The cases which can be answered clearly by what I have said are those cases in which most people have had no doubt about what is morally right. Thus I have not only not provided a complete guide to life, I have not even provided a complete guide to the moral life.

I realize that my justification of the moral rules may be considerably weaker than what has been generally sought. I realize that one would have liked to be shown not only that public reason requires taking the moral attitude toward the moral rules, but also that reason requires acting in the way specified by the attitude. I should have liked to be able to show it. In Chapter 10 I shall try to explain why the most one can do is to show that reason allows acting morally, but I shall provide the best reasons I know of for acting in this way. In the present chapter, I have been concerned only with showing that reason publicly requires the moral attitude toward certain rules. It is important not to confuse these two distinct tasks. It is impossible to justify acting morally in as strong a sense as it is to justify publicly taking the moral attitude toward the moral rules.

This chapter has shown that if rational men take a public attitude toward each of a certain set of rules, it will be what I call the moral attitude, which presently goes as follows. "Everyone is to obey the rule with regard to everyone except when he could publicly advocate violating the rule. Anyone who violates the rule when he could not publicly advocate such a violation may be punished." Showing that reason publicly requires the moral attitude toward a moral rule is what I call justifying that moral rule. Further, only those rules toward which reason publicly requires the moral attitude count as moral rules, or justified moral rules. Our discussion of the justification of the moral rules has therefore served a dual function: it has justified our attitude toward some commonly accepted moral rules, and has also furnished us with a criterion for determining if a rule is a justified moral rule. In the following chapter we shall not only see toward what other rules reason publicly requires the moral attitude, we shall also examine the moral attitude in greater detail.

CHAPTER 6

JUSTIFICATION OF
THE MORAL RULES—
THE SECOND FIVE

IN THE LAST CHAPTER we saw that there were five rules toward which all rational men would publicly advocate the moral attitude. These rules—"Don't kill," "Don't cause pain," "Don't disable," "Don't deprive of freedom or opportunity," and "Don't deprive of pleasure"—are five basic rules of any justified morality. However, they are not the only basic rules of a justified morality. In fact, these rules include only two of the original seven moral rules listed in Chapter 4 (p. 65). Three of the basic rules—"Don't disable," "Don't deprive of freedom or opportunity," and "Don't deprive of pleasure" —are thus, in a sense, new moral rules. However, this is not in any way disturbing, for these three rules share all the relevant characteristics of "Don't kill" and "Don't cause pain." Further, though they are not ordinarily mentioned as moral rules, anyone who unjustifiably disabled a person or deprived him of freedom or opportunity or of pleasure would be considered to be acting immorally. So we can say that these three rules were always implicitly moral rules. Indeed we must say this, for moral rules are discovered, not invented; and they are unchanging.

But we have still not discussed five of the seven original moral rules:

"Don't lie," "Keep your promise," "Don't cheat," "Don't commit adultery," and "Don't steal." Are all of these rules justifiable moral rules? Would all rational men take the same public attitude toward these five rules as they did toward the five rules discussed in the last chapter? Are there any other rules that should be added to this group of rules? Should any of these rules be reworded? These are the questions that must be answered in this chapter.

Let us start with the rule "Don't lie." What would be the rational man's attitude toward this rule? Being lied to is not an evil in the way that the consequences of the violation of the first five rules are. No rational man wants to be killed, suffer pain, be disabled, be deprived of freedom or opportunity or of pleasure; but must he have a particular aversion to being lied to? It may be true that most people dislike being lied to most of the time, but why should they? Is there anything in human nature or the social situation of man that makes reason require this aversion? Let us define lying as attempting to deceive by making a false statement. It then becomes clear that reason does not require the aversion to lying because of the manner in which one is being deceived. Being deceived by gestures, even by a true statement made in a certain tone of voice, would not be more acceptable to reason. It is the attempt at deception that is important, not that it is done by making a false statement.

The question we should therefore consider is, "What is the rational man's attitude toward the rule 'Don't deceive'?" Does a rational man wish those he cares for to be protected from deception? Obviously so, for to be deceived generally increases one's chances of suffering evil or lessens one's chances of obtaining those things which one is seeking. Thus by a process that we need not repeat here, we can show that a rational man would take toward the rule "Don't deceive" the same public attitude that he took toward the first five rules.

There may, however, be some doubt upon this point. A blanket condemnation of deception may seem much too strong. But one must remember that the rational man's attitude toward those actions prohibited by the moral rules is never blanket condemnation, but is, on the contrary, modified by exceptions. In the case of deception, one of the exceptions seems to take on added importance, namely that if one has a good specific reason for thinking that a person does not want the rule obeyed with regard to himself, it is not necessarily immoral to break it. We also have as possible exceptions to the prohibition against deception, deception done in order to benefit the deceived. This often takes the form of white lies. Thus we have no condemnation of magicians, for it is clear that their deception is with the consent of and for the pleasure of the deceived. Since exceptions are included in the moral attitude toward the moral rules, it can easily be seen that the rational man would take toward the rule "Don't deceive" the same public attitude as he took toward the previous five rules.

The next rule, "Keep your promise," is unique, so far, in that it is the only one to be stated positively. However, the negative formulation "Don't break your promise" is exactly equivalent, so that there is no need to adjust any of our arguments. This equivalence of negative and positive formulations is not trivial. It is not repeatable with any of the previous rules. I do not know what would be the positive formulation of "Don't deceive," but if we take "Don't lie" as the rule, then "Tell the truth" seems a plausible positive formulation. However, this plausibility is short-lived. For "Tell the truth" demands positive action, whereas "Don't lie" allows one to say nothing. The moral rules prohibit certain kinds of actions. They do not require positive action, except in those cases where there is no difference between requiring action and prohibiting it. There is no difference, except in style, between saying "Keep your promise" and "Don't break your promise." Following either one necessarily involves following the other. (This will also be the case with some of the rules considered later.)

We have already seen that "Tell the truth" does not mean the same as "Don't lie." To make it equivalent one might add the phrase "If you talk," but then it becomes obvious that the point of the rule is to prohibit certain kinds of talk, viz., lies, not to require that one talk. "Don't deprive of pleasure" does not even seem to have a plausible equivalent positive formulation. Both "Prevent the loss of pleasure" and "Promote pleasure" demand positive action in a way that the original negative rule does not. The rule against depriving of freedom or opportunity can be obeyed by doing nothing. The same is not true of any positive formulation, e.g., "Prevent the loss of freedom or opportunity" or "Promote freedom and opportunity." The positive actions taken by countries as well as individuals in order to follow these positive guides should make it quite clear that they require more than does obedience to the original rule. "Don't disable" obviously has the same relationship to "Prevent disabilities" as the previous rules had to their positive formulations. "Don't cause pain" and "Don't kill" obviously require less action than the positive formulations: "Prevent the causing of pain" or "Relieve pain"; and "Prevent killing" or "Preserve life." So that the equivalence of "Keep your promise" to "Don't break your promise" should not be considered trivial.

This peculiar feature of the rule "Keep your promise" stems from the fact that, unlike the other rules considered so far, it applies only to persons who have already entered into some relationship with other people. The previous six rules can be broken with regard to people we may not have come into contact with previously, either directly or indirectly. The rule concerning promises obviously can be broken only with regard to people to whom we have made promises. If we have not made any promises to anyone, then we cannot break this rule. The fact that the rule concerning promises presupposes some action on the part of the person who is subject to the rule has led some philosophers to consider this rule to be significantly different from all of the previous rules. However, I do not see any significant difference between this rule and the one against deception. The action that is presupposed before this rule can be broken is one which any man who is part of a society would have had the opportunity to perform many times.

Some may object that the practice of promising may not be present in every society. They may claim that promising is a formal institution, similar to marriage in the respect that we can imagine a society without such an institution. This claim seems to me to be mistaken. Any society composed of men who are subject to the previous moral rules will have a practice of promising. Every society demands some degree of cooperation among its members, some division of labor, some postponements of rewards. This, in turn, requires some practice whereby society can arrange for this cooperation, division of labor, and postponements of rewards. This practice will necessarily involve what we now call promising or some close equivalent. Thus any man who is part of a society will have the opportunity to make a promise; indeed, it is almost inevitable that he will make some, and so this rule has the required universality.

Although I have talked of the practice of promising, I do not regard promising as involving any elaborate conventions. In any society where people have the ability to express their intentions, they have the ability to make promises. For promising need only involve stating your intention to do something in certain kinds of circumstances. The clearest case is one in which the intention is expressed hypothetically; e.g., "I will do x, if you do y," and we both know that x is an action you want me to do and that y is an action I want you to do. This is merely the clearest example of a statement of intention becoming a promise. Any statement of intention to do x, where doing x will benefit some person and both he and I know that the point of my making the statement to him is to lead him to count on my doing x, may be a promise. A statement of intention in these circumstances will quickly come to have the features that many philosophers have listed as part of the practice of promising.

This account of promising shows how closely related the rule about promising is to the rule concerning deception. It would not be too far wrong to say that the rule concerning deception tells one not to lie about the past or present; the rule concerning promises, not to lie about the future. What is wrong with this account is that it ignores the fact that one can lie about the future and that promises can be broken by some act in the future even if the promise, when given, was sincere. Not only may one change his mind, he may also forget about his promises. Thus there seems good reason to keep the rule concerning promises distinct from the rule concerning deception. This account also makes clear that all rational men would publicly advocate the moral attitude toward the rule "Keep your promise." A rational man would certainly not want those for whom he is concerned to have promises broken with regard to them. For, like deception, the breaking of a promise increases one's chances of suffering evil and lessens his chances of obtaining those things he is seeking. Thus a rational man would take the same public attitude toward the rule "Keep your promise" as he did toward the previous six moral rules.

The next rule to be considered is "Don't cheat." There are several objections to including this rule in a list of basic moral rules. It may be objected that it is unnecessary, that cheating, like lying, is simply a subclass of deception. Or it may be objected that cheating is a special case of breaking one's promise. Both of these objections are plausible. Most cheating, if not all, does involve deception; the question is, "Is this necessarily so?" Also, cheating seems very similar to breaking a promise; seems, in fact, to be the breaking of an implicit promise. In order to reply to these objections, some account of the concept of cheating is necessary.

Cheating, in its basic form, takes place only in voluntary activities with built-in goals, for which there are well-established standards. These standards can be drawn up explicitly, as in games, or simply grow out of custom, as in generally agreed-upon practices in buying or selling. Cheating involves the violation of these standards in order to gain these goals, but not merely this. It is a violation for which the activity includes no explicit penalty except perhaps expulsion from the activity. Cheating usually involves the violation of a rule or standard which it is expected that no one participating in the activity would violate. It is, in this respect, the violation of trust or faith. If this is all that is meant by breaking an implicit promise, then cheating can be considered the breaking of an implicit promise. Further, since cheating is primarily done in order to obtain the built-in goals or benefits of participating in the activity, for it to be successful, one must not let other participants in the activity know of one's cheating. We can see why cheating seems to demand deception. People are not generally going to allow themselves to be cheated.

Although I admit the close connection between cheating and both the breaking of a promise and deception, it still seems desirable to have a separate rule concerning cheating. The notion of an implicit promise is unclear. Promises are always made to a particular person or group of persons. There is a sense of implicit promise in which this is also the case, e.g., the kind of case sometimes characterized by saying "Silence gives consent." Here, one is made an offer and by not refusing implicitly promises to carry out his part of the bargain. But in some cases of cheating there is no particular person or group of persons to whom one implicitly promises anything. One can cheat, never having come into contact with anyone who can claim that an implicit promise was made to him. Cheating is a social rather than personal phenomenon; it is failing to live up to certain standards expected by all who participate in the activity. Thus it seems that cheating ought to be distinguished from the breaking of a promise.

Although cheating generally involves deception, the account given above shows that deception is not essential. Of course, if one fails to live up to the standards expected of him, he generally will try to conceal this from others, especially as he expects to gain some benefit thereby. But we can easily imagine special cases where all of the people participating in the activity are, in an important way, dependent on one person. Then we can imagine this person taking advantage of his position outside of the activity to cheat without even bothering to conceal this from the others. The boss who plays golf with his subordinates may sometimes cheat quite openly. He may not count missed strokes, or he may remove the ball from the rough without taking a penalty. Of course, if he cheats too much, one might say that he is not really participating in *that* activity, e.g., that game. But in a sense, cheating just is "not playing the game," and so this is not a serious objection. One need only notice the reactions of the people being cheated to realize that they do not consider themselves playing a different game.

Thus cheating does not seem to be reducible to either the breaking of a promise or deception, though, as mentioned before, it is possible that all three of them might be considered violations of trust or faith. However, this would be to use "violation of faith" in a very vague sense. I think it preferable to have the rules as precise as possible consistent with reasonable scope. I should note that, as I have explained it, cheating, like deception and the breaking of a promise, is something one may be justified in doing. I mention this explicitly because justified cheating seems almost a contradiction. It may be hard to imagine a case of justified cheating. But, though they may be outlandish, such cases are certainly possible. If I play cards with someone who will kill my family if he wins,* I am certainly justified in cheating him. Thus cheating, though it may seem different from the other kinds of actions prohibited by the rules, is like them in the relevant respects.

The rule against cheating does seem to have one characteristic that none of the other rules have. One cannot break this rule unintentionally. There seems to be no such thing as unintentional cheating. With the first five rules, it is clear that violations can occur unintentionally. To obey these rules one must not merely not break them intentionally, one must also take reasonable care not to break them unintentionally. The same is true with the rule concerning promises; not only intentional breaking of promises is forbidden, but one is required to take

*If he will kill them if he loses, I am not cheating if I let him win.

reasonable care that one does not break a promise unintentionally. One must make some effort not to forget about the promise.

Although unintentional deception does not have a clear application, one can, without too much difficulty, give it one. The rule against deception gets its point from the fact that being deceived generally has bad effects. The rational man is as concerned with natural deception as with man-made deception. Were ice to give the appearance that it would support the weight of a man when it would not, then a rational man would publicly advocate a sign warning of this. A rational man wishes to avoid being deceived by nature as much as by man, for it is the consequences of deception that he wishes to avoid. The rule against deception requires that one take reasonable care not to deceive others; not to do things that would lead someone to believe what is false: e.g., not to pass on gossip which you have no good reason to believe true, not to tell jokes to naive people who might be misled by them.

I admit that there is no such thing as unintentional cheating. However, since cheating is failure to abide by the well-established standards of some voluntary activity in which one is engaging, we can easily describe something that might plausibly be called unintentional cheating. A most plausible case is where one breaks one of the rules unintentionally, discovers it later, but does nothing about it. I do not claim that this is now called unintentional cheating. I am not sure whether it would actually be called either cheating or unintentional. There was no intentional breaking of the rules, yet there was an intentional concealing of a past violation. Obviously this kind of activity would be prohibited by the rule against cheating. Further, one would expect people to take reasonable care that they do not unintentionally violate the rules. For the violation of those rules which would clearly be cheating if intentional generally is against the interests of all the other participants in the activity. Thus the rule against cheating must be understood as requiring reasonable care that one does not violate the rules of any voluntary activity in which one is participating. This, of course, requires that one not enter any activity unless he knows the rules or standards by which it is governed. Although its significance is probably so small as not to warrant calling it a moral matter, the attitude of people toward someone who enters a game not knowing the rules is close to moral condemnation. Expulsion is not unjustified.

The concept of cheating is an extremely interesting and important concept. Investigation of it is very helpful in understanding the nature of morality, for cheating provides in miniature the nature of immoral action. We have already pointed out that cheating in its basic form involves violating the standards of an activity that one is participating in voluntarily in order to gain some advantage over others participating in that activity. (This is why students do not normally regard cheating in school in the same way that they regard cheating in a game. Going to school, except at the more advanced levels, is not a voluntary activity. Nor do students realize, unless they are graded on the curve, that the cheating affects them in a disadvantageous way.) The close parallel between cheating and all immoral action can be seen if we simplify and redefine cheating, using the technical terms we have already introduced. Cheating is participating in a voluntary activity and acting in a way that all rational men participating in that activity would publicly advocate that no one act. This redefinition of cheating shows how closely it parallels immoral action in general. We need only remove from the redefinition any reference to a voluntary activity and we have a general redefinition of immoral action.

This extraordinary parallel between cheating and immoral action helps to explain why cheating seems the paradigm case of an immoral action. Indeed, many philosophers have considered all immoral action to be cases of cheating. Although they are not generally aware of it, all those who make fairness central to morality are using cheating as the model of immoral action. Similarly cheating provided the model of immoral action for the social contract theorists. Their talk of promises, especially implicit promises, is most easily understood when we recall the close connection between cheating and breaking an implicit promise. Also, we can more easily understand their effort to view society as a voluntary association.

However, despite the parallel between cheating and immoral action, using cheating as the model of immoral action has had some bad effects. It has resulted in overemphasis on the notion of consent. This has resulted in the view that one can perform an immoral action only with regard to someone who is participating in some shared activity. Coupled with the view that only people in the same society can participate in a shared activity, the conclusion follows that one can be immoral only with regard to someone in one's own society. This is an argument which leads some people to accept ethical relativism. The immoral consequences of this view come out with great vividness in Chapter 10, section 2 ("The Notion of 'Duty' "), of Stephen Toulmin's book *The Place of Reason in Ethics* (Cambridge, 1949). In considering an island composed of two communities, C_1 and C_2, he seems to hold that nothing the members of C_1 might do to the members of C_2, or vice versa, can be immoral. Another serious fault with using cheating as the model of immorality is the trivialization of morality. Cheating generally results only in the lesser of the evils that the moral rules are designed to prevent. Thus Toulmin holds that morality is designed to prevent "causing to other members of the community some inconvenience, annoyance, and suffering. . . ." There is no mention of death or disability. Although cheating is not the model for all immoral action, there is no doubt that all rational men will take the same attitude toward the rule against cheating as they did toward the previous seven rules. Thus "Don't cheat" becomes the eighth justified moral rule.

The next rule to be discussed is "Don't commit adultery." There was some question whether this rule was a basic moral rule, for it was thought that a society might lack an institution of marriage. If no one in the society is married, then no one can commit adultery, and so the rule would not apply to all people in all societies. But it does not seem that the immorality of adultery depends upon all societies having our institution of marriage. Thus it seems likely that the immorality of adultery does not depend upon there being an independent rule against adultery. I am encouraged to take this view because I do not feel that the practice of adultery by the Eskimos, if it really is a practice, is immoral, whereas I do feel that adultery in our society generally is. It seems to me that adultery in our society is immoral because of the kind of institution of marriage that we have. Given this institution of marriage, adultery is generally immoral, for it involves violating the standards of an activity in which one participated voluntarily. Adultery is a form of cheating. This is, in fact, reflected in our ordinary talk about adultery, as when we say that a man is cheating on his wife. Thus, given the institution of marriage as we have it, it follows that adultery is immoral, for adultery is cheating and cheating is immoral. But as mentioned earlier, cheating can in certain instances be justified.

Further arguments can be made against adultery. It generally involves deceit. It may also be said to involve the breaking of an implicit promise. Although this is true, it is the same kind of thing that can be said against most kinds of cheating. In fact, it supports the view that given the institution of marriage that we now have, adultery is cheating. Nothing in what has been said involves approval or disapproval of our present institution of marriage, but only that given that institution, adultery is generally immoral. It may be argued that this institution should be changed or, perhaps, should be adopted by all societies. This question, luckily, does not fall within the scope of our investigation. However, some points should be made.

The relations between the sexes concern all people in all societies. It seems to be an issue on which there ought to be a moral rule. However, philosophers, in contrast with the general public who often regard morality as concerned solely with sexual matters, have almost completely ignored sexual problems. To say that adultery is immoral because it is cheating may seem to most people a thoroughly implausible answer. Adultery is wrong, they might say, because any sexual relationship between two people who are not married is wrong. Thus they hold that premarital sexual intercourse is also wrong, and this is obviously not a case of cheating. It is here that one hears talk of the new morality. Those who uphold the traditional standards of sexual behavior and those who uphold the new are thought to be having a fundamental moral dispute. This is a mistake. Whatever side one takes on this issue should not affect, in the slightest, one's attitude toward any of the other moral rules we have discussed.

This is an extremely important point and one that cannot be over-emphasized. It is thought by some defenders of the tradition that with sexual freedom comes moral anarchy. It is thought by some defenders of the new morality that since a moral rule against sexual freedom is unjustifiable, no moral rules are justifiable. Both of these positions seem to me to be mistaken and for the same reason. They both think that rules governing sexual behavior are on a par with the basic moral rules. That they are not can easily be seen by trying to formulate an independent moral rule concerning sexual behavior to which all rational men would agree.

Of course, rape and seduction are immoral. But they are immoral not because they are concerned with sexual matters, but because they necessarily involve violation of one of the moral rules. Rape normally involves the infliction of pain, and necessarily the deprivation of freedom. Seduction is, by definition, a case of deception. Thus, in denying that there are any independent moral rules concerning sex, there is no denying that rape and seduction are universally immoral, and that adultery is immoral in any society with an institution of marriage like ours. Whether premarital or postmarital sex is immoral or not depends on the institutions and laws in the society concerning these matters. We are now talking about nonmarital sex between mutually consenting adults. Unless it can be shown that nonmarital sexual relations between consenting adults cause harm to someone, public reason does not prohibit such activity. On the contrary, given that sex can provide some of life's more enjoyable moments, it would seem that the deprivation of this pleasure is itself immoral unless one can show that such deprivation is necessary for avoiding greater evil. Whether this can be shown or not, I do not know, but certainly the burden of proof is on those who seek to deprive anyone of the pleasures of sex.

We have seen that eight basic moral rules can be justified, and we have only one of our original rules (see Chapter 4) left to consider: "Don't steal." It does not require any argument to show that all rational men would take the same attitude toward the rule "Don't steal" as they did toward the previous eight rules. A rational man usually does not want to have anything he owns or anything owned by those he cares for stolen. To steal something from someone generally deprives him of pleasure or opportunity. Thus it follows immediately that all rational men would support the rule against stealing. However, it is just this immediate consequence that is troubling. It seems as if we do not need a rule against stealing. Insofar as stealing results in the deprivation of pleasure or opportunity, no special rule is needed against it. But we can steal from rich men who will not even miss their money, or from companies who will simply add a penny to everyone's bill. In these cases the rule against stealing does not seem to be deducible from the fourth or fifth rule.

Further, like adultery, stealing seems to require something which it is not certain that all societies have: the concept of ownership. Yet it does not seem as if the immorality of stealing would be put in doubt by discovery of a society with no concept of ownership. Thus it seems that the immorality of stealing does not depend on there being an independent rule against stealing.

However, none of the previous eight rules seems to cover all cases of stealing. Thus it seems as if we do need another rule in order to assure that all stealing, when it is done simply to promote the good of oneself or those one cares for, is immoral. Stealing involves taking that which is owned by another. But the concept of ownership depends upon the concept of law. Whether you own something, and under what conditions, is determined by the law. Stealing is not merely taking that which is owned by another, it is taking it unlawfully. Thus every case of stealing will be a case of breaking the law. By including as a basic moral rule, the rule "Obey the law," we can guarantee that stealing is immoral, without having an independent rule against it. There are other reasons for having the rule "Obey the law" as a basic moral rule. We do generally hold that those who break the law simply in order to benefit themselves or those they care for are acting immorally. Including "Obey the law" as a basic moral rule allows us to continue regarding these actions as immoral without making individual laws into moral rules.

But if I am to include "Obey the law" as a basic moral rule, I must give an account of law such that every society has laws. For I have required of a basic moral rule that it be applicable to all men in all societies. I realize that it is impossible to give an adequate account of law in a few paragraphs. It may even be that the condition which I require to be satisfied, viz., that every society have laws, will make it impossible to give an account of law which even hints at the complexities that law has in sophisticated societies. However, all that I wish to provide is a set of characteristics which are sufficient for calling something a law. I realize that in sophisticated societies laws will have characteristics that I do not mention. All I require is that every society have laws in the sense I provide.

Laws are rules, and thus disobeying the law will be similar to cheating. But there are important differences between laws and those rules or standards, the violation of which is cheating. Cheating is the violation of rules of a voluntary activity, one which a member of the society can choose to participate in, or refrain from. In a sense, one chooses to be subject to the rules or standards, the violation of which is cheating. But one cannot always choose to be subject to the law; whether or not one is subject to a law is often determined by the law. This difference between laws and other rules gives rise to another difference. There is often an explicit penalty for violating a law. There is usually no explicit penalty for cheating. A law is a rule which is part of a system of rules which applies to all members of a society, some of which cover members of that society whether they wish to be subject to them or not, and some of which have explicit penalties for violation.

This account says nothing of the origin of laws. Laws are not necessarily those rules which are instituted by authorized legislators. Law, in the sense I have given it, may arise from custom. I have also said nothing about the purpose of laws, though it is trivially true that they are to guide the conduct of those subject to them. One would like to say that laws are for the benefit of society, but this would rule out as laws far too many laws. Even the qualification that laws are believed to be for the benefit of society has too many exceptions to be included in the account of law. But good or bad, laws generally have the result of producing order in society, of allowing greater predictability of the actions of members of the society. Laws enable one to plan his actions with greater assurance.

With this minimal account of law, is it possible to provide a justification for the rule "Obey the law"? This rule, unlike the previous eight rules, presupposes what I shall call a formal political situation. The first six rules apply in what we might call a desert island situation. Coming upon a stranger who is minding his own business, we should neither kill him, cause him pain, nor disable him. Nor should we deprive him of freedom, opportunity, or pleasure. It seems equally clear that we should not deceive him. Obviously we cannot break a promise to a man we have never met, so that the seventh rule presupposes some prior contact. But once a promise has been made, then it ought to be kept. The situation with cheating seems much the same; if appropriate activities evolve, one ought not cheat when participating in them. Thus the first six rules seem to apply even when we have had no prior contact between individuals, and the next two rules demand only what I call an informal social situation.

For each of the first eight rules, the public attitude of the rational man was developed from his aversion to having the rule violated with regard to himself or those he cares for. Each of the first eight rules prohibits something which may be done to me or those I care for. It is not possible to build up the rational man's public attitude toward "Obey the law" in the same fashion that it was built up for the previous rules. Also, the formulation of the moral attitude does not seem appropriate when applied to this rule. This formulation was: "Everyone is to obey the rule with regard to everyone, except when he could publicly advocate violating the rule. Anyone who violates the rule when he could not publicly advocate such a violation may be punished." "Obey the law" creates a problem because one does not disobey the law with regard to anyone, even though someone often suffers some evil because of the breaking of the law.

A similar problem, though not as acute, arises with the rule "Don't cheat." Although generally when one cheats, one cheats someone, it is sometimes impossible to say who, if anyone, has been cheated. Cheating provides a kind of bridge between personal and social moral rules. For violations of the first seven moral rules, there is necessarily some one or more individuals with regard to whom one is breaking the rule. For the eighth rule, this will usually be true, but not necessarily so. Cheating has an impersonal aspect; it is the violation of the standards governing an activity. Violation can occur and yet, even when all the facts are known, it may be impossible to pick out any individual of whom we would want to say he had been cheated. Thus it seems that the present formulation of the moral attitude makes it sometimes inappropriate for the eighth rule, and always inappropriate for the ninth.

However, the first part of the formulation "Everyone is to obey the rule with regard to everyone" can easily be replaced by "Everyone is always to obey the rule." Simply replacing "with regard to everyone" by "always" and changing the word order makes it quite appropriate to take the moral attitude toward the rule "Obey the law." When considering only one society, we can even substitute "law" for "rule" in the moral attitude and then put in particular laws where we had previously put in the moral rules. This parallelism between particular laws and the moral rules is not accidental. Advocating the moral attitude toward a rule is very like advocating that the rule be made a law. The law is often talked of as the embodiment of reason, and particular laws often embody the moral rules. Unfortunately the law is not always the embodiment of reason, and some particular laws may even be contrary to the moral rules.

We now arrive at the important question: Would all rational men take the moral attitude toward the rule "Obey the law"? It seems to me quite clear that they would. We must remember that the moral attitude admits the possibility that disobeying the law can be justified. Thus in taking the moral attitude toward the rule "Obey the law," the rational man is not publicly advocating an end to all civil disobedience. Civil disobedience occurs when one believes that the law is causing significant evil. All that the rational man is publicly advocating by taking the moral attitude toward the rule "Obey the law" is that unless the person could publicly advocate breaking the law, he should obey it. When a person can publicly advocate, rational men may differ in their attitudes. These cases, when the breaking of a moral rule is allowed by public reason, cause problems which cannot be solved by any system, but must be worked out in each particular case.

I have admitted that it is not possible to build up the moral attitude toward the rule "Obey the law" in precisely the way that it was built up for the preceding rules. In trying to show how the attitude can be built up, we shall discover that the previous way of building this attitude was not completely adequate. All rational men know that they and those for whom they care may suffer some evil when the law is broken. Thus all rational men want all others to avoid breaking the law when doing so might cause anyone for whom they were concerned to suffer an evil. In changing this attitude to one that can be publicly advocated, the egocentricity drops out and we seem to have all rational men publicly advocating the moral attitude toward the rule "Obey the law." But all that we have really got so far is a moral attitude toward the rule "Obey the law whenever not doing so might cause anyone to suffer any evil." We do not have the moral attitude toward our original rule. Now, only a moment's reflection will show that the same inadequacy is present in the account of the rules concerning deceit, promises, and cheating. Thus, the problem we have uncovered here is not one that is peculiar to the rule "Obey the law" but affects all the rules considered in this chapter.

We can understand why this problem did not seem to arise in discussing the rules concerning deceit and promises; it seems as if every unjustifiable violation of either of these rules must result in someone suffering some evil or being deprived of some good. But, of course, this is not true. Unjustified deceit may result in my getting some undeserved good, while no one suffers in any way from that particular act. A deathbed promise may be unjustifiably broken even though no one suffers because of it. Unjustified cheating seems so obviously immoral that no one even considers that the moral attitude toward it could not be justified. But unjustified cheating can clearly occur without anyone suffering any evil because of that act. Just think of someone who cheats on the bar exam because it is easier, even though there is no doubt that he could pass if he worked at it. Thus it seems as if the justification of these rules is inadequate in the same way as the justification of the rule "Obey the law."

The inadequacy of the justification became apparent in the discussion of this rule, not merely because it necessitated a change in the wording of the moral attitude. Far more important, I think, is that "Obey the law" does not seem to be a moral rule as clearly as all of the previous rules. We are suspicious of this rule, thus we are more careful in examining its justification. And the suspicions seem to have turned out to be correct. All that we seem to have justified is the rule "Obey the law whenever not doing so might result in anyone suffering any evil." But now it turns out that the justification of our three previous rules suffers from the same inadequacy. If we want to justify these rules as originally formulated, we must show that it is not necessary to put in any qualification about the particular violation resulting in increased chances of someone suffering some evil.

I do not deny that a rational man will sometimes publicly advocate violating each of the last four rules. Nor do I deny that sometimes this will happen when no evil is caused by the particular violation. What I do deny is that simply the fact that the particular violation will not cause anyone to suffer any evil is enough to allow a man to publicly advocate such a violation. Consider a case of cheating. In exams in which everyone's grade and whether he passes or fails is completely independent of what others do on the exam, a person may cheat without his act causing anyone to suffer any evil. However, to publicly advocate cheating in these circumstances would be equivalent to publicly advocating that such exams be eliminated. For the purpose of the exam is to distinguish between those who have the ability tested by the exam and those who do not. Thus only if one is willing to publicly advocate that the activity in which one is participating be abolished can one publicly advocate that people cheat in that activity. But sometimes one is not willing to publicly advocate abolishing the activity; in these cases one cannot publicly advocate violation simply on the grounds that an individual violation causes no harm.

Public advocacy of a violation of a moral rule requires that the violation be describable in a way that is understandable to all rational men. The only things that are relevant in deciding whether to publicly advocate a violation are the amount of evil to be caused, prevented, and avoided; the rational desires of the people affected; and the effect that this kind of violation, if allowed, would have. It is this final consideration which makes it impossible for a rational man to publicly advocate cheating simply on the grounds that the violation will cause no harm. For to publicly advocate that such a violation be considered a justified exception is to publicly advocate that anyone who has good reasons to believe that his particular violation will cause no harm should cheat whenever he wants. But we all know that men are sometimes mistaken in their beliefs about the future, even when they have good reasons for such beliefs. This is especially true when the beliefs concern the consequences of their own actions.

The fallibility of man, his inability to know all the consequences of his actions, is often overlooked in discussing moral rules. But this fallibility is important not only for explaining why a rational man would not publicly advocate cheating simply on the grounds that no one will be hurt by it, but also for explaining why we need any moral rules at all. If all men were omniscient, knew all of the consequences of their actions (if it is even possible that this be known), then they would have no need for rules. A moral man would then simply act so as never to increase the amount of evil in the world. He would be unconcerned whether or not his actions were violations of the moral rules. But men are not omniscient, hence the need for rules. The order and stability provided by the moral rules explain why the moral attitude requires one be able to publicly advocate his violation before it can be considered justified. An increase in the number of unjustified violations of the moral rules is almost always accompanied by a greater amount of evil being suffered by the people involved.

I have shown that the fact that cheating does not cause any harm is by itself not sufficient to allow one to publicly advocate such a violation. But I must show that one would publicly advocate the moral attitude toward the rule against cheating. We now have a situation in which one could not publicly advocate cheating because that would be equivalent to publicly advocating that a valuable activity be abolished. But if we wish to protect this activity, we must discourage people from cheating even when their individual acts of cheating would cause no harm. Discouragement requires liability to punishment, and thus we have shown that the rational man would indeed publicly advocate the moral attitude toward the rule "Don't cheat" without the added qualification.

Does this same argument work with the rule "Obey the law"? It seems to me clear that it does. There is a perfect parallel in the two cases. If the law is a bad one, then the moral attitude may allow one to break it because one might publicly advocate such a violation. But if the law is a good one, then the fact that an individual violation would do no harm is not sufficient to allow one to publicly advocate violation. Indeed, one must publicly advocate that the rule not be violated in this situation. But this results in one publicly advocating the moral attitude toward the rule "Obey the law."

I do not think it is necessary to go through the argument again to show that reason requires publicly advocating the moral attitude toward the rules "Don't deceive" and "Keep your promise," without qualification. The undesirable consequences of the erosion of trust that result from allowing unjustified violations of these two rules is evident to all. Breaking any of the four rules under discussion, when one could not publicly advocate such a violation, is acting immorally. Even if one's particular violation causes no harm, one is generally acting hypocritically. The effect on one's character provides an additional reason for the rational man to publicly advocate the moral attitude toward the four moral rules as originally formulated. I shall discuss this in more detail in Chapter 8, but even without this reason, we have shown that our rules as originally formulated are justified moral rules. Hence we can see that our earlier conclusions were correct even though adequate arguments had not yet been provided.

I have now shown that the rational man would have the same attitude toward the rule "Obey the law" as toward the previous eight rules. Stealing always involves breaking the law. Thus stealing is immoral even though there is no basic moral rule against stealing as such.

For all practical purposes one can treat "Don't steal" as a moral rule. I have not done so for reasons of economy; "Don't steal" can be deduced from the rule "Obey the law." I have attempted to make all the moral rules logically independent of one another. Someone who breaks one of these rules does not necessarily break any of the others, though the breaking of one may always involve the breaking of some other. The rule "Obey the law" does not entail the rule "Don't kill" even though most, if not all, societies have laws against killing. For even if a society did not have a law against killing, it would be immoral to kill, or to break any of the previous moral rules. Thus it should not be thought that this rule, in any way, renders superfluous the previous rules.

We have now considered all of the moral rules listed in Chapter 4 (p. 65). We have seen that all of them can be justified, though not in the same way. Some of them, "Don't kill" and "Don't cause pain," "Keep your promise" and "Don't cheat," are basic moral rules. The rule "Don't lie" was changed to "Don't deceive" to broaden its scope. "Don't steal" was justified in that it could be deduced directly from the basic moral rule "Obey the law." "Don't commit adultery" was the only one that did not have a universal justification, but could be justified in any society with our institution of marriage. Given that institution, the rule against adultery could be deduced from the rule against cheating. In addition to these rules, we discovered three other rules which should be considered basic moral rules. We thus add to the list of basic moral rules, the rules "Don't disable," "Don't deprive of freedom or opportunity," and "Don't deprive of pleasure." We have now arrived at a list of nine basic moral rules. I may be influenced by tradition, but this list does not seem to me to be complete. I believe one more rule is necessary to complete the list. This rule I have formulated as "Do your duty."

This rule provides for those actions in society not covered by the rule "Obey the law," and yet not necessarily falling under any of the previous eight rules. In all societies there is a division of labor. There are many different jobs or offices to be filled, each with specific duties. As I am using the term "duty," duties are primarily connected with jobs, offices, positions, etc. A teacher has certain duties, so does a night watchman; the recording secretary and the treasurer have specified duties that are spelled out by the rules of the organization in which they hold office; a father has duties, and so do children. Some of these duties are specified very precisely; some are extremely vague. Judges and umpires are required to make their decisions impartially; it is their duty to do so. Failure to do so, e.g., to favor one side, is to violate the rule "Do your duty." For it is not only one's duty to do certain things —e.g., a night watchman must make his rounds—but it is also often part of one's duty to do things in a certain way. A judge must not only show up for trial and make decisions; he must also make them impartially.

Although duties, in general, go with offices, jobs, roles, etc., there are some duties that seem more general. Some would say that it is the duty of every citizen to uphold the law. Although it is not incorrect to say this, it is usually said only in very special circumstances. These circumstances are when an appeal is made to a very large number of citizens to obey the law, e.g., to white southerners when the civil rights laws were passed. Here, one does appeal to the duty of a citizen to uphold the law of the land. One who steals, however, is not normally thought of as failing to do his duty, but simply as violating the law. Even where the appeal is made to all citizens to do their duty by obeying the law, it is violation of the law that is condemned. No further reference is usually made to failure to do one's duty as a citizen.

In these contexts, "it is your duty" means little more than "you ought." It is this use which philosophers have taken over when they maintain that we have a duty to obey the moral rules. I do not use the term "duty" in this extended sense. Duty in its basic sense, in which I am using it, is tied to one's role in a society. I think that using "duty" in the extended sense is another reason why some philosophers have been led to accept ethical relativism. Toulmin's discussion of duty referred to earlier (see p. 111) is an excellent sample of this. Also, extending the term "duty" to cover everything that one morally ought to do leaves no term available for formulating a rule equivalent to "Do your duty."

Although duties are generally voluntarily incurred, they are not always so. A soldier who is drafted has no fewer duties than one who enlists. Children have duties to their parents, though these are extremely vague. Duties can arise from circumstances also. In our society, if a child collapses in your arms, you have a duty to seek help.

You cannot simply lay him out on the ground and walk away. This duty cannot simply be called the duty to aid those in distress. For we do not have a duty to send money to those who are starving. It is, of course, morally good to do this, but we have no duty to be morally good. In our society you seem to have a duty when you are already involved, e.g., when the child collapses in your arms; you do not seem to have a duty to get involved. It is sometimes impossible to say whether a person neglected a duty or simply failed to do what was morally good when he had a special opportunity to do so. But there is no general duty to promote good or to prevent evil. This is not to deny that you ought to promote good and prevent evil; it is only to deny that you have a duty to do so.

I am concerned with clarifying what I mean by "duty," for otherwise it may seem that the rule about duty makes some of the previous rules superfluous. We have already seen that it is possible to take the rule "Do your duty" as eliminating the need for the rule "Obey the law." It is also possible to maintain that this rule eliminates the need for the rule "Keep your promise." For it could be maintained that it is your duty to keep your promise. It could also be said that we have a duty to play fairly, and so the rule against cheating is superfluous. It has been maintained that we have a duty to tell the truth, so that the rule against deception might also be eliminated. Thus it might seem that the second five rules could all be reduced to the rule "Do your duty." But as I noted above, I do not wish to use "duty" in such a wide sense.

"Why should I give the book to him?" This question, depending on the circumstances, could be answered by citing several different rules. One obvious answer would be "you promised to give it to him," and the circumstance that makes this reply appropriate is simply the fact that you did promise. We can also imagine circumstances where the appropriate reply is "It is your duty as president of the organization to give the book to the winner of the contest." Sometimes the reply "Because the judge ruled that the book was legally his" is the appropriate one. We can even imagine circumstances in which the reply "Because it would be cheating not to" would be an appropriate reply.

There is no point in trying to reduce all of these replies to "It is your duty," for this reply carries no more weight than the replies that it is supposed to replace. The rules against breaking promises, cheating, and breaking the law are justified as directly as the rule demanding that you do your duty. If one does not see the point of these other rules, there is no reason to believe he will see the point of the rule concerning duty. However, it is one of the standard practices of philosophers to try to reduce the moral rules to a single one, or failing that, at least to some smaller number than is generally accepted. One of the aims of social contract theorists was to reduce the rule "Obey the law" to "Keep your promise." Although had they thought of the rule against cheating, they would have tried to use it instead. But I see no point in reducing the number of rules, especially when doing so makes one stretch the scope of the remaining rules beyond what is generally accepted. Thus I regard "Do your duty" as a basic moral rule that is on a par with the other rules, not one that includes the others within it.

I have not yet shown that all rational men would adopt the moral attitude toward this rule as their public attitude. However this is very easy to do. The reasoning is identical to that used to justify the rule "Obey the law." All rational men know that they, or someone for whom they are concerned, may suffer some evil when someone fails to do his duty. Thus all rational men want all other men to do their duty when their not doing it may cause anyone for whom they are concerned to suffer evil. When this attitude is put in a form that is acceptable to all rational men, it loses its egocentricity. We thus arrive at the moral attitude toward the rule "Do your duty whenever your not doing it may result in someone suffering an evil." Realizing that failing to punish failure to do one's duty simply because that particular act results in no harm to anyone may destroy valuable activities that depend upon general obedience to the rule, the rational man publicly advocates the moral attitude toward the rule "Do your duty." This also applies to the duty that some people have to punish violations of the moral rules. Refusing to carry out this duty when one could not publicly advocate this is itself an immoral act. That one may refuse to do this duty because of compassion simply shows that compassion may lead one to act immorally.

I am aware, in these days of totalitarianism, that doing one's duty has been used to justify the grossest immorality. I am aware that business executives often try to justify immoral company policy, claiming that their duty is to increase profits. But I am not advocating blind devotion to duty; indeed, I am not advocating blind obedience to any of the moral rules. I am merely maintaining what seems to me a completely uncontroversial view, that when the person could not publicly advocate disobeying this or any of the other moral rules, he should obey them. Further, as I have already indicated and will discuss in more detail in Chapter 8, I do not hold that all of these rules are of equal rank. Normally, certain rules, e.g., against killing, take precedence over others.

We now have ten rules:

1. Don't kill.
2. Don't cause pain.
3. Don't disable.
4. Don't deprive of freedom or opportunity.
5. Don't deprive of pleasure.

6. Don't deceive.
7. Keep your promise.
8. Don't cheat.
9. Obey the law.
10. Do your duty.

It should be remembered that I regard the second rule as prohibiting various forms of mental suffering as well as physical pain.

Toward each of these rules, the following public attitude would be taken by all rational men: "Everyone is always to obey the rule except when he could publicly advocate violating it. Anyone who violates the rule when he could not publicly advocate such a violation may be punished." I call this the moral attitude. In Chapter 4 we listed the characteristics that all moral rules are believed to have. Any rule toward which all rational men would publicly advocate the moral attitude has all of these characteristics. Thus by showing that there are some rules toward which all rational men would publicly advocate the moral attitude, we have shown that some rules are genuine moral rules. But we have done more than discover which rules are genuine moral rules. We have shown that all of these characteristics fit together, and that toward any rule that has all of these characteristics public reason requires one to take the moral attitude. We have, in other words, justified the moral rules.

Further, we have tried to make clear when it is morally justifiable to violate the rules, viz., only when one could publicly advocate such a violation. We have discussed the considerations that are relevant in deciding whether to publicly advocate violation. These are the amount of evil to be caused, avoided, and prevented by the violation; the rational desires of the people affected by the violation; and the effect that this kind of violation, if allowed, would have. It must be kept in mind that a publicly advocated violation must be describable in such a way that all rational men could understand the reasons offered for publicly advocating it, and could accept them as adequate.

I should also like to point out again that the "except" clause of the moral attitude does not mean that no rational man publicly advocates punishment for a violation of a moral rule when the person violating the rule could publicly advocate such a violation. Only if the violation is required by public reason would no man publicly advocate punishment. When the violation is only allowed by public reason, then rational men will disagree on whether or not the person should be punished. A rational man need not exempt from liability to punishment even one who has violated a rule because he would publicly advocate such a violation. Evils are ranked in too many diverse ways for all rational men to be willing to permit any publicly advocated violation. This explains why there is sometimes a divergence in moral judgment and legal judgment. We agree that the person has morally justified his violation; but since those in charge of enforcing the law would not have publicly advocated such a violation, they are willing to publicly advocate punishment. Thus they are morally justified in punishing him.

It should be clear from the preceding that in justifying the moral rules, I have not eliminated all moral disagreement. But I have set limits on such disagreement. I was able to set these limits because I have limited my discussion to rational men. It is my account of rationality, plus the replacement of universalizability by public advocacy, that allows me to provide a formal criterion of moral rules which has precisely the content that those opposed to formal criteria usually want. The debate between the formalists and those who demanded content can now be seen to be like most other debates in philosophy. Both parties were partly right, but because both lacked some more basic concept they were unable to reconcile their differences.

The debate between the deontologist and the teleologist can be seen to be resolved in a similar manner. The deontologist is right about the need for rules; the teleologist is right about morality having a point or purpose. The former failed to see that moral rules, like all other rules, must be interpreted, and that a rational man will always interpret them by reference to the point of the rules. The latter failed to see that a rational man, in order to achieve the point of morality, must make use of rules. Once we have the concept of a rational man, we realize the need both for the moral rules and for the moral attitude which tells us how to obey these rules. Thus I hope that the concept of a rational man is not only useful in resolving moral disputes but equally helpful in resolving philosophical disputes about morality.

CHAPTER 7

MORAL IDEALS

ALTHOUGH THE MORAL rules are the most important part of morality, they are not all of it. Morality consists not only of rules, but also of ideals. This has been noted from the very first chapter, but emphasis on the moral rules has been so great that it may very well have been forgotten. In the first chapter we noted that moral judgments are judgments on actions, intentions, etc., using some moral rule or ideal. In the previous two chapters the role of the moral ideals in providing a justification for violating the moral rules was noted. But there has as yet been no detailed discussion of the moral ideals; no attempt to identify them or to distinguish them from other ideals. This shall be done in this chapter.

Just as the moral rules might be summarized as "Don't cause evil" or "Don't do that which will or is likely to cause anyone to suffer evil," so the moral ideals can be summarized as "Prevent evil" or "Do those things that will or are likely to lessen the amount of evil suffered by anyone." Particular moral ideals can be paired with particular moral rules. Substituting "prevent" for "don't" and changing the wording slightly generates a moral ideal from each of the moral rules. "Prevent killing," "Prevent the causing of pain," "Prevent disabling," "Prevent the deprivation of freedom or opportunity," "Prevent the deprivation of pleasure," "Prevent deceit," "Prevent the breaking of promises," "Prevent cheating," "Prevent the breaking of the law," "Prevent the neglect of duty" are all moral ideals. A rational man would publicly advocate that all men follow these ideals, but not that they follow them all of the time. The rational man requires that everyone be careful always to obey the moral rules. The rational man only encourages one to follow the moral ideals.

These moral ideals can be followed in a number of different ways. One way is by teaching people to obey the moral rules. Thus someone who tries to persuade others to obey the moral rules is following the moral ideals, e.g., the writer of this book. But public advocacy of the moral attitude toward the moral rules does not indicate anything about the moral character of the person doing the advocating. Any rational person will publicly advocate obeying the moral rules and following the moral ideals. Nothing I say in this chapter or in any other chapter of this book is a reliable indication of my moral character. This is as it should be, for what I say should be judged entirely on its own merits. If it is claimed that I am preaching rather than doing moral philosophy, my response is that I am preaching what any rational man would preach. That we expect all rational men to preach that men guide their actions by the moral rules and ideals helps to explain the popularity of the maxim "Practice what you preach."

Following the moral ideals merely by preaching that everyone follow the moral rules and ideals, when this preaching requires no sacrifice or risk, as in writing this book, does not count for much. However, there are occasions in which preaching morality does have significant moral worth. Someone who speaks out openly against the immoral action of some powerful person or group of persons is following a moral ideal in a significant way. Someone who urges his country to stop acting in immoral fashion often undergoes significant risk in so doing, and his action deserves moral praise. Even someone who does not undergo any risk but merely devotes a great deal of time to encouraging people to act morally may deserve moral praise. Of course, much depends on the motive for the action, but this needs no special comment here.

The moral ideals which urge preventing the violation of the moral rules may justify violations of the moral rules when the moral ideals which relate directly to the evils would not. This means that rational men may publicly advocate violating a moral rule with regard to someone who is about to break a moral rule even though significantly greater evil will not be prevented by breaking the rule with regard to him. Of course, you must have a good specific reason for believing he will break the rule, and you cannot cause more evil than punishment would unless you are thereby preventing significantly greater evil (see pp. 99 f.). In practical terms this means that it is easier to justify breaking the moral rules with regard to those who are breaking or intend to break the rules themselves than with regard to innocent men.

"Prevent death," "Prevent pain," and "Prevent disability" are three moral ideals which need not be connected with any moral rule. For death, pain, and disability are not always caused by violation of moral rules. In fact, these evils are often not caused by man at all. Natural disasters—floods, earthquakes, tornadoes, and famine—kill, cause pain to, and disable a vast number of people. Those who seek to control these disasters so as to prevent the evil they cause are following moral ideals. Disease is also a cause of much death, pain, and disability. When one is dealing with disease it may sometimes be more appropriate to talk of the moral ideals of "Preserving life," "Relieving pain," and "Lessening disabilities." In former times it was thought that these moral ideals were the primary motives for those who went into the practice of medicine. Thus doctors used to be regarded as among the morally best men.

Although it may not seem as obvious, there are also moral ideals directly connected with the evils that are the concern of the fourth and fifth moral rules: "Prevent the loss of freedom or opportunity" and "Prevent the loss of pleasure." These need not be related to violations of the moral rules. Freedom, opportunity, and pleasure may be lost by the operation of natural causes, as well as by the acts of man. One who seeks to prevent others from losing freedom, opportunity, or pleasure is following a moral ideal, even if the threat of loss comes from natural causes.

An extraordinary amount of evil is neither the result of natural causes, nor of the unjustified violation of moral rules, but stems from social causes. Thus those who work to eradicate slums and poverty are generally following the moral ideals. War, justified or not, causes immense amounts of all of the evils. Those who sincerely work to achieve and preserve peace are almost always acknowledged to be following moral ideals. "Blessed be the peacemakers" is a sentiment shared by all rational men. In fact, since war is one of the greatest single causes of the evils suffered by man, the prevention of war and the preservation of peace must be among the most important goals of those following moral ideals.

Like the moral rules, the moral ideals are concerned with evil rather than good. However, whereas the moral rules require that you not cause anyone to suffer evil, the moral ideals encourage you to prevent or lessen the evil being suffered by anyone. When what we are required to do by the moral rules conflicts with what we are encouraged to do by the moral ideals, we must decide whether our breaking of the rule is justified. We have already pointed out that these cases cannot be decided in the abstract, but that each case must be treated on its own merits. One could maintain that one ought to choose that alternative which, all things considered, results in the least amount of evil being suffered. But if this principle does not require that one be able to publicly advocate violation of a moral rule, it is simply false. If it does require that one be able to publicly advocate one's violation, the principle is superfluous.

Further, the principle is so vague as to be almost totally useless. It does not say what ought to be considered. Should it merely be the evils directly avoided, caused, and prevented? Should it include the effect on the moral character of those involved? Should it include the effect on respect for the rule by others? What is the weight of these various considerations? How does one weigh one kind of evil against another? None of these questions is answered by the general principle. It seems to me best to regard the principle of minimization of evil as a device to remind oneself of the point of morality, rather than as a guide to be rigorously applied to individual cases of moral conflict. Misuse of this principle is what leads to the view that those who violate the second five moral rules but do not intend to cause evil to anyone are amoral rather than immoral.

Because morality is concerned with the minimization of evil it is important to distinguish the moral ideals from all other ideals, particularly utilitarian ones. Only the moral ideals can justify the breaking of a moral rule. A utilitarian ideal, i.e., an ideal which encourages us to promote some good, does not justify the breaking of a moral rule. No one is likely to confuse moral ideals with utilitarian ones when he is concerned with death, pain, or disability. The evils that are the subject of the first three moral rules are obviously also the proper subject of moral ideals. But when one considers the evils that are the subject of the fourth and fifth moral rules, the distinction between moral and utilitarian ideals may not seem so clear. Is there really a distinction between the moral ideals concerning freedom, opportunity, and pleasure and the utilitarian ideals "Increase freedom and opportunity" and "Increase pleasure"? I do not claim that there is an absolutely clear-cut distinction. In fact, it seems to me that increasing the freedom, opportunity, and pleasure of those whom I would call "deprived persons" is following moral rather than utilitarian ideals. I shall have more to say about this in Chapter 11, when dealing with morality and society. Nonetheless, there seems to me to be a difference between preventing or lessening a loss of goods, which count as minimizing evil, and simply promoting good.

In moral considerations one must start with the status quo. The moral rules prohibit changing the status quo by causing evil. The moral ideals encourage changing the status quo by lessening the amount of evil. This is the only change encouraged by morality. It does not discourage promoting good as long as this does not involve violation of the moral rules. But it is not the goal of morality to promote the greatest good for the greatest number. Nor does morality demand that the goods of the earth be equally distributed among all its inhabitants. The moral ideals are not revolutionary—except in those societies where immoral action by those in power is taken for granted, or when there are great numbers of deprived persons. Unfortunately, in the world today there are many societies where the moral ideals are revolutionary.

The moral ideals, like the moral rules, make no mention of person, place, group, or time. As the moral rules require obedience with regard to all men equally, so the moral ideals encourage action with regard to all men equally. This may lead some to the view that in following the moral ideals we must exclude all personal preferences as rigorously as when obeying the moral rules. This is a mistake. Personal preference does not justify violating a moral rule with regard to someone one does not care about in order to follow a moral ideal with regard to someone one does care about. For example, that you love someone cannot justify killing an innocent stranger in order to save her life. But when no violation of the moral rules is involved, one may choose to follow the moral ideals with regard to some group of persons with whom one has some special relationship. The NAACP has no need to justify concentrating its efforts in following the moral ideals toward aiding black Americans. The United Jewish Appeal need not justify concentrating its moral efforts toward aiding other Jews. Nor does the government of the United States need to justify being primarily concerned with aiding the deprived citizens of America. It is impossible to follow the moral ideals with regard to all men equally; thus each man is allowed to choose toward whom he will concentrate his efforts, though, of course, it is best to help those most in need.

Even were it possible to follow the moral ideals with regard to all men equally, one would not be morally required to do so. One is not required to follow the moral ideals at all, much less to follow them with regard to all men equally. Of course one may choose to follow the moral ideals in this way, but such a choice will probably result in no action at all. What passes for such a choice is usually the choice to follow the moral ideals equally with regard to all those with whom one comes into personal contact. I do not see how this is in any way morally preferable to following the moral ideals with regard to some more traditionally specified group. What gives it an air of being morally preferable is that if one chooses to follow the moral ideals equally with regard to everyone with whom one comes into personal contact, one is less inclined to violate unjustifiably a moral rule in order to follow a moral ideal. But if one is clear about the distinction between moral rules and moral ideals, I see no advantage in excluding personal preferences, unless one decides to do that which will result in the greatest relief of evil regardless of any relationship to oneself.

I have up to now limited my discussion of ideals to moral and utilitarian ideals. One reason for this is that these are the only ideals that all rational men publicly advocate that one act on. All of the major religions of mankind urge their adherents to follow the moral and utilitarian ideals. But there are other ideals that are publicly advocated by some rational men. Various religions have put forward ideals which could be publicly advocated, e.g., that people develop certain personality traits. At its highest, religion has put forward the ideal of loving kindness, which goes beyond what is encouraged by the moral ideals. Although the emphasis naturally falls on the moral ideals, this is generally obscured because the language used is more appropriate to the utilitarian ideals. Most people prefer to talk about promoting good rather than preventing evil. The harm done by this kind of talk cannot be overestimated. Failure to distinguish between moral and utilitarian ideals has contributed to the mistaken view that promoting good justifies the violation of moral rules. It has also opened the way to the view that other ideals, even those that could not be publicly advocated, sometimes justify the violation of the moral rules.

Whenever the ideal that a religion supports rests essentially on a revelation, or scripture, viz., anything that is not known to all rational men, it cannot be publicly advocated. It is never morally justifiable to follow these ideals when this involves violating the moral rules. Failure to realize this has permitted the infliction of an extraordinary amount of evil. Nations, also, have put forward ideals that could not be publicly advocated. The evils caused by pursuing these ideals, even when this involves violating the moral rules, now outweigh the evils caused by the unjustified violations of the moral rules for religious ideals. Men of various races are putting forward ideals that cannot be publicly advocated and urging that they be followed even when it involves violation of the moral rules. It may be that the evil caused by racist ideals will outweigh the evils of both religious and nationalistic ideals. I am not maintaining that all of these ideals must lead to evil. If one recognizes that pursuit of these ideals does not justify violation of the moral rules, then many positive goods may come from following these ideals. Indeed, man needs some ideals beyond those provided by morality.

Although morality does not and should not provide a complete guide to life for all men, there is a sense in which it provides the supreme guide. The moral rules provide a guide to conduct for all men, that all rational men publicly advocate that they never violate for the sake of some nonmoral ideal. There are no nonmoral ideals or ends for which it is justifiable to violate a moral rule. In general, this view is largely accepted today. We would consider anyone who thought it justifiable to do what is morally wrong in order to promote some ideal or cause, a fanatic. In fact, this is an acceptable definition of a fanatic. A religious fanatic is one who thinks it permissible to do what is morally wrong in order to do what God commands, or his religion demands. A nationalistic fanatic is one who thinks it permissible to do what is morally wrong in order to advance the interests of his country. A racial fanatic is one who thinks preservation of his race permits his doing what is morally wrong. A humanistic fanatic is one who thinks that betterment of the human race makes it permissible to do what is morally wrong.

No end justifies immoral means. This is the proper understanding of the oft misused saying "The end does not justify the means." It should be clear from the above that morality is not humanistic in some of the more common senses of that term. It does not have as a goal the betterment of the human race. It does not have any positive goal at all. It seeks only to minimize evil. It sets the same limit on humanism as it does on the positive ideals presented by the different religions. As long as the positive ideal does not violate the demands of morality, it is compatible with the moral guide to conduct. Thus though morality does not provide a complete guide to life, it does provide a supreme one; nothing else is permitted to overrule it.

I have not yet discussed what I shall call the personal ideals. These are the ideals or goals that a rational man seeks for himself. Some of these can be publicly advocated, and some cannot. Philosophers and others have historically concentrated on those ideals that could be publicly advocated, and I also shall limit myself to these. Traditionally happiness has been considered that personal ideal which is sought by all rational men. However, happiness has been thought to consist of so many diverse elements that even were it accepted as the personal ideal sought by all rational men, this would not mean that all rational men had the same personal ideal except in a purely verbal sense. Happiness should not be confused with pleasure, though it has a close connection with it. A happy life is not the same as a life of pleasure. Although a life of pleasure may be a happy life, it also may not be, for one may not look back upon it with pleasure. A happy life is one that is remembered with pleasure, which a life of pleasure need not be, for one may come to regard it as a wasted life. Happiness is not remembered pleasure, but remembering with pleasure.

To say "This is the happiest moment of my life" is to make a prediction, but not in the literal sense that one is denying that she will ever have a happier moment. It is the prediction that one will remember that moment with great pleasure for the rest of one's life. Often the happiest times of one's life are those in which one is so absorbed in the activities of living and doing that at the time one often complained of having no time simply to enjoy life. This account of happiness, though obviously incomplete, still enables us to understand why happiness has been thought to consist of so many diverse elements; there are very many different things that rational men can remember with pleasure. The so-called Utilitarian paradox, that one best achieves pleasure by not aiming for it, seems not to be true for pleasure, but does seem to hold for happiness. Thus it seems pointless to list happiness as a personal ideal, for it is a goal that one is more likely to achieve by not seeking it directly.

In my discussion of the personal ideals, I shall discuss only those goals that a man is more likely to achieve when he sets out to attain them. Generally speaking, men think of the ideal life in two quite different ways. For some an ideal life consists primarily in the attaining of as many personal goods as possible. For others, an ideal life consists primarily in being a certain kind of person. In older and somewhat more colorful language, for some the ideal is a life of pleasure, for others a life of virtue. However, this colorful way of putting it is quite misleading. There are other personal goods in addition to pleasure, and virtue is not a homogeneous whole. Moreover, all rational men desire some goods, and all rational men wish to have some virtues. Indeed one might claim that the personal ideal shared by all rational men is to be a man of virtue and to have a high degree of all the personal goods, which is very close to Aristotle's definition of happiness. However, plausible as this seems, I think that it is false.

The lure of the *summum bonum* is almost irresistible. It is extraordinarily difficult to accept the view that there is no one thing, or some simple combination of things, that all rational men are seeking. Even those who realize the impossibility of formulating any intelligible account of a *summum bonum* continue to use the term. This is partly due to a failure to realize the diversity of personal goods. But the root difficulty is much more complex than this, and I shall not attempt to deal with it here. I have already shown that not all rational men seek all personal goods; that insofar as there is agreement on goals, it is an agreement to avoid suffering any evil. Thus we must allow different men to have different personal ideals, even if that ideal is describable as wanting to have a personal good. Some men may desire pleasure, in the ordinary sense of that term, others knowledge, and others certain kinds of physical and mental abilities. This latter ideal is often described as self-realization.

It would probably be less misleading to describe these different personal ideals as a difference in emphasis, but to do this would encourage the mistaken view that all men really want the same thing, only in somewhat different proportions. However, we must also guard against the similar error that each man has his own *summum bonum* or matter of ultimate concern, even though it may be different from some other man's. Most rational men have a number of personal goods that they wish to attain; and though one may be more important than any of the rest, it is rarely more important than all the rest put together. It is generally as misleading to talk about the *summum bonum* with regard to an individual man as it is to talk about it with regard to all men. Pursuit of these personal ideals clearly does not justify immoral means; but the failure to distinguish morality from other guides to conduct has obscured this, and so pursuit of quite worthy personal ideals has often led to immoral conduct.

But not all personal ideals involve attaining personal goods; some are concerned with becoming a certain type of person. Generally this involves certain traits of character or virtues. Virtues will be discussed in more detail in the following chapter, but something should be said here about their place in the personal ideals. Some virtues, which I shall call the "personal virtues"—e.g., prudence, temperance, and courage—are desired by all rational men. These virtues, however, generally form only a small part of one's personal ideals. The virtues that form the most significant part of some men's personal ideals are the moral virtues: honesty, trustworthiness, etc.—and other traits of character that are sometimes confused with them. For Plato and Aristotle all of the moral virtues went together under a name that we have come to call justice. Biblical thought added another virtue, sometimes called charity, or kindness. These two virtues—justice and charity, or kindness—were thought to comprise all of moral virtue by Hobbes and almost all thinkers after him. And as I shall show in the following chapter, they can be considered substantially correct. But as we have already seen from our discussion of morality, not all men wish to act morally.

Recently, as objective morality has fallen into disfavor, another trait of character has come to the fore as forming a significant part of the personal ideals of many people. The most popular name for this trait of character is authenticity. Authenticity is not to be understood merely as truthfulness, which would make it merely one of many specific moral virtues. Rather, authenticity seems as if it were designed to replace all of the moral virtues. In at least some accounts, authenticity requires only rationality and lack of hypocrisy. It is relatively easy to see how authenticity on this account seems to encompass all of the moral virtues. If we regard a rational man as necessarily making moral judgments, then he is involved in publicly advocating certain ways of acting. Since authenticity excludes hypocrisy, the authentic man must act in the way that he publicly advocates. Such a man will probably have all of the moral virtues. I do not know if such thoughts prompted those who advanced authenticity as a personal ideal for all, but it seems compatible with much that has been written on the matter. Even the emphasis on death fits in nicely here, as acknowledgment that one can die would lead one to publicly advocate following the guide to conduct provided by morality as we have described it. The same is true of acknowledging one's dependence on other people and on society in general. Interpreted in this way, authenticity is a worthy personal ideal; it is identical to the personal ideal of being a morally good man.

However, authenticity is not always understood in this way. The failure to distinguish morality from other guides to conduct, and the desire for one encompassing guide, affected the concept of authenticity, as it did more traditional ethical concepts. Authenticity most closely resembles the ancient Greek doctrine of living according to one's nature. The Greeks, of course, regarded man's essential nature as that of a rational being, and so living according to nature was interpreted very much like living rationally, but with no distinction made between living as reason requires and as reason publicly requires. However, today, man is no longer regarded as essentially a rational being. Thus authenticity requires man to follow his nature without telling him what that nature is. Perversion of the concept was inevitable. Authenticity was taken as requiring only that one act naturally, interpreted as acting as one feels, free from the artificial constraints imposed by society. No distinction was made between the constraints imposed by the moral rules and those imposed by nonmoral social conventions. Thus authenticity was felt to justify violating the moral rules. The "hero" of Gide's *The Immoralist* is someone who adopted the confused concept of authenticity as a personal ideal.

It should be noted that most of what I have said about the moral ideals does not apply to tolerance. Yet tolerance is regarded by some as one of the most important moral ideals. Tolerance is not a moral ideal. It is required by the moral rules. Tolerance, properly understood, does not involve doing anything; rather, it consists in not doing certain things. To be intolerant is to violate the moral rules with regard to someone because of some morally indifferent characteristic he possesses. A tolerant person will not seek to restrict the freedom or opportunity of any person because of the color of his skin, his place of birth, or his religious beliefs. An intolerant person is necessarily an immoral person, for he violates a moral rule unjustifiably. Legislation enforcing tolerance is completely justified, for it is simply legislation enforcing the moral rules. This is quite different from legislation that seeks to enforce the following of some moral ideal. Rational men can disagree about this kind of legislation. Those who say that you cannot make people moral by legislation usually fail to distinguish the moral rules from the moral ideals. Every civilized society enforces the moral rules. The criminal law is designed for precisely this purpose. You cannot make people follow a moral ideal by passing a law, for the passing of such legislation makes what would have been an action encouraged by a moral ideal into an action required by a moral rule. This seeming paradox is no argument against such legislation, but it may explain why some hold the silly view that moral action should not be enforced by legislation.

Neither morality nor tolerance requires one to give equal consideration to all views. Some views may not deserve serious consideration. But the expression of absurd views, even of immoral views, though not to be encouraged, should not be suppressed. Freedom of speech and related freedoms are not moral ideals; they are required by the moral rules. The only reason for violating a moral rule with regard to someone who expresses an immoral view is to prevent someone from suffering some evil. Thus the only justifiable limitation of freedom of speech is provided by the moral ideals. Dislike for, even disgust with, the views being expressed, does not justify violating a moral rule with regard to the person expressing the view. Similarly, dislike for or disgust with the personal preferences or habits of others does not provide a justification for violating a moral rule with regard to them. Cleanliness may be next to godliness, but it has little to do with morality.

It is important to distinguish the moral rules and ideals from those rules and ideals that are often confused with them. Failure to do so allows some to violate the moral rules with regard to those whom they dislike or with whom they disagree. Thus intolerance, which is immoral, masquerades as morality. This masquerade is no better when the intolerant are sincere than when they are not. In fact, when one sincerely believes that morality supports his intolerant actions, he is likely to cause more evil than when he is aware of the masquerade. Witness the evil inflicted on those who refuse to conform to the nonmoral social customs of a society. Witness the extraordinary evil caused by those who sincerely believed that it was morally right to persecute those who had different religious beliefs.

Religious tolerance is fairly well established now. Very few would hold it morally justified to violate the moral rules with regard to anyone because of his religious beliefs. I do not think that this is due primarily to an increase in moral understanding, but to a decrease in the importance of religious beliefs. The fundamentalist sects are notoriously less tolerant of people holding different religious beliefs than are the more liberal denominations. I do not believe this reflects a difference in moral character or moral understanding. It reflects what is admittedly the case, that religious belief is much more important to members of fundamentalist sects. Very few people are tolerant of different views on matters they consider important. Many people are quite prepared to violate the moral rules with regard to those who express sufficiently unpopular views on political matters. But tolerance only demands not violating the moral rules with regard to the person expressing the views; it does not demand politeness. The vigor of one's response to views one dislikes, particularly immoral views, is not restrained by tolerance. Tolerance simply demands that this vigor not express itself in the violation of a moral rule.

I do not want to be understood as maintaining that politeness is unimportant. Indeed politeness taken as a character trait involving acting so as to avoid giving offense to others may even be a moral virtue. But politeness is a moral virtue only when properly understood.

Politeness can never require either unjustified violation of a moral rule or conflict with justifiably following a moral ideal. Since one moral ideal is to teach people to follow the moral rules and ideals, it is a misunderstanding of politeness to think it requires one never to challenge someone who has put forward immoral views. Most people would probably prefer to continue this misunderstanding, for it takes some considerable courage to be rude in the service of morality.

The close connection between tolerance and morality makes it seem unlikely that anyone would seek to undermine the latter in order to promote the former. Yet this seems to be what those anthropologists who espouse ethical relativity are doing. These men wish to encourage tolerance of the customs and mores of the peoples they study. They hold, quite rightly, that it is morally unjustified for outsiders to come into a culture and try to force changes in the way these people live. Although they do not express it in this way, they hold that one should not violate a moral rule with regard to these people in order to get them to adopt a different way of life. However, they sometimes support this perfectly correct view by maintaining that there are no universal moral rules; that morality is completely a matter of one's own culture. But if my culture allows the violation of moral rules with regard to those who live differently, morality would provide no reason to be tolerant of the culture of different peoples.

The anthropologists' confusion is one that we have discussed repeatedly. They have failed to distinguish the moral rules from the nonmoral customs of a society. They wish to maintain that we should not impose our nonmoral customs on other cultures because doing so would be immoral. However, having failed to distinguish morality from those aspects of a culture which are peculiar to it, they do not have the concepts to express their views correctly. They advocate tolerance without realizing that in so doing they are advocating obedience to the moral rules. It is ironic that these people, who are so morally sensitive and sophisticated, should argue for the correct moral view by attacking morality.

Although this chapter is supposed to be devoted to the moral ideals, discussion of the moral rules continually seems to take over. I do not apologize for this. The moral rules are central to morality, not only from a philosophical point of view, but also from a practical one. Emphasis on the moral ideals results in a view of morality that is too idealistic. This is not only philosophically incorrect, it has bad practical consequences. An idealistic morality is too easy to dismiss as being all right in theory, but of no use in real life. To hold that morality requires everyone to follow the moral ideals is a misguided attempt to encourage such action. It is misguided because no philosophical theory will have much force in persuading people to follow the moral ideals. The result of this attempt may very well be to provide an excuse for those who wish to dismiss morality as impractical or too difficult for ordinary human beings like themselves. Distinguishing sharply between the moral rules and the moral ideals, and emphasizing the former, does away with this excuse. Morality requires that one obey the moral rules; it only encourages one to follow the moral ideals. The demands of morality are not too difficult for ordinary human beings.

Emphasis on the moral rules does not result in a purely negative morality. That the moral ideals are not required does not mean they are not encouraged. Those who wish to go beyond what is required by morality do have the moral ideals to provide them with a positive guide to life. I do not think that moral philosophy will persuade many people to follow the moral ideals. Those who are inclined to follow them generally will do so without the aid of moral philosophy. Those who are not so inclined generally will not do so, regardless of their agreement with a particular moral philosophy. Moral philosophy has as its primary practical function that of preventing people from doing what is morally wrong because of a misunderstanding of morality. Lack of the proper understanding of morality can lead to morally wrong actions. I believe that this book may result in some people avoiding an immoral action that they might otherwise have done. But I do not believe that this book will result in anyone doing a morally good action, i.e., following a moral ideal, which they would not have done without reading this book.

One may follow the moral ideals because he has compassion for his fellow man. Misguided compassion for one person may lead one to follow a moral ideal when this is the morally wrong thing to do. There is a possibility that an understanding of morality may prevent this. But a perfect understanding of morality, without compassion, generally will not lead one to follow the moral ideals. To have compassion for someone is to suffer because of his suffering. Thus compassion may lead one both to avoid causing anyone to suffer and to relieve the suffering of others. There are degrees of compassion, and most people have more compassion for those they love than they do for others. But it is not unusual for one to have some compassion for all mankind, even if it is only a very small amount. To see anyone seriously hurt, even though we do not know him, is distressing to very many people. The suffering of children usually arouses compassion in most people.

I do not use the term "compassion" as a term of praise. It is understandable how it comes to be used so, for we expect a compassionate man to be a kind man. But one need not act kindly because one is compassionate. Much depends on the degree of one's compassion. Even more depends upon the breadth of one's compassion. One who has compassion only for a limited group, such as his family, may be ruthless in dealing with other people. But even more depends on the actions that result from one's compassion. Even one who has a high degree of compassion for all mankind will not necessarily be a kind man. He may seek to relieve his suffering by trying to forget about others. This can be done in many ways: drink, drugs, searching for excitement and adventure, even complete dedication to some intellectual pursuit. He may even be overcome by his compassion and may hate those whose suffering causes him to suffer. Following the moral ideals is probably the least satisfactory way of relieving oneself of the suffering of compassion. One always has the sufferings of others clearly in mind. Nonetheless, there is some personal benefit to the compassionate person in following the moral ideals. He does get some pleasure in seeing some suffering being prevented.

But being morally good is not primarily a matter of feelings. It is a matter of action. The feelings are morally important only insofar as they lead to morally good actions. It is a confusion to hold that the morally good man is really no better than one who always acts selfishly, as each is simply trying to minimize his own pain and to increase his own pleasure. Apart from the fact that this is not even true (a compassionate man has other pains and pleasures besides those related to the suffering of others), it is beside the point. As long as your motive for following the moral ideals is not one that depends on people being aware of what you are doing, then it is morally insignificant what your motive is. Further, as we have already pointed out, a compassionate man has much more efficient ways of relieving his compassion than by following the moral ideals. We do not praise a man morally because he is compassionate, but because his compassion leads him to follow the moral ideals.

Compassion should be distinguished from love. One may have compassion for someone without loving him. To love someone is to take pleasure in his pleasure. This is what is common to all forms of love —of parents for their children, of a man for his wife, or of a saint for all mankind. Each kind of love includes something more than love, and one job for the psychologist is to determine statistically meaningful relations between love and various other feelings, desires, and actions. I am trying to provide some clear concepts so that he can begin to do this job. It is easy to see that love is intimately related to compassion. Generally we do not even talk of someone as genuinely loving another unless he also feels compassion for him. However, it is common to feel compassion for someone without loving him. Love without compassion is shallow, superficial, etc., but I do not think that we should deny it is love. But since it is so rare to love someone without feeling compassion for him, I shall consider love as always being accompanied by compassion. Again it should be clear that I am not using the term "love" as a term of praise. However, unlike compassion, the feeling of love is personally desirable.

The expressions of love, I call the acts of love. In the acts of love, I include sexual acts, for the acts of sex are among those in which one can express his love most directly. But there are many other ways in which one can express his love. Parents express their love for their children when they bring them toys in order to watch the look of delight on their faces. The spontaneous effort to give someone pleasure is the surest sign of love. People often treasure this far beyond the particular pleasure they have received. To be loved is to have someone take pleasure in your pleasure. To love someone who loves you is one of the most glorious things that can happen, for pleasure builds on pleasure as is possible in no other way. This is not merely true of love between a man and a woman, but also of love between parents and children or indeed between any two people. This is one reason why it is truly a loss to be unable to love. To be unable to love is to be unable to enjoy the pleasures of others. This means the loss of a significant amount of pleasure.

The proposed definition of love explains much of what we normally say about love. It explains why a behavioristic analysis of love is unsatisfactory. Love is not behavior; it is a feeling—a feeling of pleasure at the pleasure of another. But we can also see why behavior is so important in determining if one truly loves another. For if one loves another, one generally will act certain ways toward her. (Mistakenly, I always think of a loved one as a woman.) If I get pleasure from pleasing another, one would expect acts on my part in order to please her. It is now also clear how one can suddenly discover that one is in love with someone. What one discovers is the feeling of pleasure one gets in seeing her pleased. One often finds oneself going to considerable efforts to please her, and not considering them a sacrifice at all. Falling out of love is discovered in the same way. One discovers that one no longer gets pleasure in pleasing someone, that efforts to please her really are efforts.

Unselfish love, i.e., delight in the pleasure of another regardless of who caused it, is the most satisfactory kind. Unlike selfish love, which delights only in the pleasure that one causes oneself, it cannot give rise to jealousy. Jealousy is displeasure caused by the pleasure of one you love when that pleasure is not caused by yourself. One who loves another selfishly may actually seek to deprive her of pleasure that was caused by someone else. But it is not only love between men and women that can be selfish. A parent may have a selfish love for his children. It is even possible for a man to love God selfishly, though this would probably manifest itself in annoyance at others who seek to please God, rather than toward God himself.

If I love a woman selfishly and some other man pleases her, I am said to be jealous of him. But the phrase "jealous of him" is misleading. It should be "jealous because of him." He causes my jealousy by pleasing the woman I selfishly love. Exactly the same is true when brothers and sisters are jealous of each other. All love their mother selfishly, and each is displeased when she is pleased by another. Because one often envies the person who causes him to be jealous, jealousy and envy are often confused. But I can only be jealous of one who pleases someone I selfishly love, and I am jealous of him only for pleasing her. He is important only because of his relationship to the woman I love. It is the fact that she is pleased by another that causes my jealousy.

Envy is different. To envy someone is to be displeased because of his obtaining some good which you also desire. I can envy a man because he pleases some beautiful woman, but unless I love her, I cannot be jealous of him for that. Similarly, a child of one family can envy a child in another because that child's mother is pleased by her son, but he cannot be jealous of that child. He can only be jealous if his own mother is pleased by that child. Jealousy does not seem as bad as envy because in order to be jealous, one must at least love someone. Both jealousy and envy can lead to hate. To hate someone is to be displeased because of his obtaining some good, whether or not one desires that good oneself. Even worse, hate may come to include pleasure because of that person suffering some evil. Hate may thus not only be opposed to love, but also to compassion.

Although love is fundamentally a matter of taking pleasure in the pleasure of another, it so naturally becomes a matter of taking pleasure in any good obtained by another that often no distinction is made. We are said to love someone whenever we are pleased by his obtaining some good. Love in the basic sense is always love for individuals, for only an individual can feel pleasure. But in the natural extension, we can be said to love a country, and perhaps any other group or organization, when we are pleased by their achieving some good. When the country we love is our own, then love of country becomes pride in country. This pride, if it is felt only when the successes of the country are not obtained by immoral actions, is most properly called a feeling of patriotism. When pride is felt for successes even when obtained by immoral actions, then it is properly called a feeling of nationalism. Love of country, like all other love, needs to be restrained by morality. Without such restraint it leads to serious immoral actions.

That loving someone involves getting pleasure from him accounts for another extension of the term "love," viz., as when someone says "I love fishing" or "I love New Hampshire in the fall." But when we are talking about a person from whom we get pleasure, but one whom we do not love in the strict sense, then we should use the word "like." It is important to distinguish between liking someone and loving him, for it is possible to do the one but not the other. Too many young men and women have been told they were liked but not loved for there to be any doubt about this being possible. It may not be so clear that it is also possible to love someone and not like him. This rather sad state of affairs is often exemplified in movies by the innocent girl who falls hopelessly in love with the dashing criminal who treats her badly; the most well-known case is probably that of the professor in the movie *The Blue Angel.* A more common but less often remarked upon kind of example is that of parents with grown-up children who hold opposing religious or political views. That the parents and children do not like each other is clear to anyone who sees them together; that they, nevertheless, still love each other is clear to anyone who knows them.

Self-love, as spoken of by previous philosophers, can also be understood as a natural extension of love. A person who enjoys his successes, who is pleased when he achieves his goals, would be one who could be described as having self-love. Such a man need not be selfish; indeed, he may be among the morally best men. For to love oneself is not incompatible with loving others. On the contrary, it is very doubtful that someone who does not love himself will love others. One of the most delightful features of love is that the pleasure we get from loving one person may increase rather than decrease when we love someone else besides. A man's love for his wife often increases after he has a child whom he has come to love.

This short digression on love and related emotions is not entirely beside the point. I admit that it is primarily due to my dissatisfaction with other accounts of love. But it is important in discussing morality to distinguish clearly between love and compassion. It is also important to distinguish both of them from being concerned or caring for a person. When I talk of being concerned or caring for a person, I do not mean that one either loves him or has compassion for him. I mean only that the belief that doing something will help him to avoid suffering some evil is a motive for doing that thing. Compassion for people naturally leads one to care for them. But the degree of compassion is not necessarily linked to the degree of concern. The strength of one's concern is the strength of the motive, and that strength can be affected by many things besides one's compassion. It will certainly be affected by the way one has been brought up. It may be affected by one's religious beliefs. But there can be no doubt of the close relation between compassion and concern. A similar relationship is present between love and what I call taking an interest in a person. To take an interest in a person means that the belief that doing something will help him to obtain some goods is a motive for one's doing it. I shall regard taking an interest in a person as involving being concerned for him in the same way that I regard love as involving compassion.

It is often said that morality requires one to "Love thy neighbor as thyself." It should be clear that this is not correct. There are several different mistakes involved. First, morality does not require you to have any feelings toward anyone; it only requires you to act in certain ways. Second, morality does not even require that you act as if you loved your neighbor as yourself. Morality does not require that you regard the good and evil of another as of equal weight with your own. The moral rules require only that you avoid causing evil to your neighbor. Even the moral ideals do not encourage you to take as much interest in the good of your neighbor as you take in your own good. They do encourage being as concerned with the evil suffered by your neighbor as much as with evil suffered by yourself. It is because of this that the question "Who is my neighbor?" need not indicate any lack of the proper moral attitude, but only a realistic sense of one's power to act according to moral ideals. If "Love thy neighbor as thyself" is to be what morality requires, "love" must be changed to "compassion." Then "compassion" must be taken as "concern." Further, even understood in this way, it is not a statement of what morality requires, but only a way of encouraging action according to the moral ideals. This "only" does not mean that encouraging people to follow the moral ideals is unimportant; it is extremely important. But I refuse to confuse the demands of morality with what is encouraged by it. This confusion only encourages some people to dismiss the demands of morality as utopian.

People generally seem to prefer the loftiest kinds of statements when talking about morality. They can repeat these to each other, feel some sort of warm glow, and then forget all about it when they go about their daily lives. If someone presents some statement which does not demand very much, they often dismiss it as cynical. They dismiss it because it presents demands that can actually be followed by all men. "Love thy neighbor as thyself" is one of the favorite sayings. No one feels compelled to live by it; obviously only the very saintly can even approach it. "Live and let live," on the other hand, is often regarded as merely advocating the easy way out. But "Live and let live" is probably the best statement of what the moral rules demand. Do not interfere with others; do not cause them any evil. If one wishes to go beyond the moral rules to the moral ideals, one can change it to "Live and help live." These maxims do not have the emotional appeal of the more lofty statements, but they are maxims that all men can actually live by.

Morality should not be regarded as providing a guide by which all men should try to live, though with no hope of ever actually doing so. Morality should be regarded primarily as providing the rules which every man must obey no matter what his aim in life is. Only after this is clearly understood should morality be regarded as something which provides a positive guide to life. Morality has as its task the lessening of evil. Any action that seeks to lessen the amount of evil in the world is encouraged by the moral ideals. But morality has no final goal. The elimination of evil can never be reached as long as human beings continue to live. The task of morality is never-ending. The guide provided by morality can be followed by any man.

CHAPTER 8

VIRTUE AND VICE

Although the guide provided by morality can be followed by all rational men, it is more likely to be followed by those who have a good moral character. Indeed, this is little more than a tautology, as the criterion for determining the moral character of a person is the degree to which he follows the guide provided by morality. To raise up children so that they will act morally and to raise them up to have a good moral character are, generally speaking, simply two ways of saying the same thing. In a discussion of moral character, even more than in the discussion of other aspects of morality, the moral philosopher must keep in mind the raising of children. All rational men will publicly advocate that children be brought up to have a good moral character. This needs no argument, as it follows directly from the view that all rational men publicly advocate that all men act morally.

However, though there can be no disagreement that children be trained to act morally, there can be disagreement about how they should be trained to act in the desired manner. All will want this training to involve as little infliction of evil as possible and to be as effective as possible. The rational man's public attitude toward the training of children will parallel exactly his attitude toward punishment. He wants the most effective training because this offers the most protection for himself and those for whom he cares from violations of the moral rules. But he wants the training to inflict as little evil as possible because the child being trained may be someone for whom he is concerned. As with punishment, some rational men will place more emphasis on the one goal; others, on the other.

But even with this disagreement in emphasis, some points will be publicly agreed to by all. If a lesser punishment seems as effective in training as a greater, all rational men will publicly advocate using the lesser. (It seems, oddly enough, that lesser punishments may be even more effective than greater ones in training children. If this is the case, then there is no doubt that all rational men would publicly advocate using lesser punishments.) If it is as effective to train a child by rewarding him for making the morally right decision in a tempting or difficult situation as it is to punish him for making the morally wrong choice, then all rational men would publicly advocate training by reward. But it is extremely unlikely that children can be trained to act morally if they are never punished for unjustifiable violations of the moral rules. Although the rational man does not want any evil inflicted when it is not necessary for training, he is not against punishment when it is necessary. He and those for whom he is concerned must live with children when they grow up.

No rational man wants children to be trained to follow the moral rules blindly. He wants them to obey them in the manner specified by the moral attitude, for he knows that there are occasions in which reason publicly requires violating a moral rule. He would also like to encourage children to follow the moral ideals. Further, he wants children to be trained so that they act in these ways even when they believe that no one knows of their actions. He wants this because he knows that in life there are many occasions where one has opportunities both to act immorally and to do something morally good when there is little chance that anyone will discover it. As long as the motives the children come to use in explaining their moral action work even on those occasions when they believe no one knows of their actions, the rational man need not care what these motives are. The rational man's primary concern with motives is with their effectiveness in leading to the desired actions. However, he has one other concern: he does not want the motives to be such that they are more likely to result in more evil or less good to the person having them, or to others, than some other motives that are equally effective.

All rational men publicly advocate only that a man act morally, not that he act this way from certain motives. Some may reply to this that sometimes it is the motive which determines if he is acting morally or not. They grant that some actions are immoral no matter what the motive, viz., those in which we know that our violation of the moral rule will cause more evil than it prevents. But they hold that there are some cases where the motive determines the morality of the action. If I deceive in order to ingratiate myself or those I represent, then my action is immoral even if no harm is done. But if I deceive in order to save someone from suffering some evil, when the truth would hurt and have no future benefit, then my action may not be immoral. Similarly, killing an incurable cancer patient who had requested to be killed would be immoral if I did it in order to benefit myself or someone I cared for, but not if I did it in order to prevent the victim's suffering.

Persuasive as this reasoning sounds, it is false. It is not the motive which determines the morality of the action; it is whether one could publicly advocate that sort of violation. If one could publicly advocate the violation, then the violation is not immoral no matter what the motive. If one could not publicly advocate the violation, then it is immoral, regardless of the motive. Two factors serve to obscure this point: (1) We do not distinguish carefully enough between our moral judgment of the act and the moral judgment we make of a person who acts from certain kinds of motives. (2) We believe that certain kinds of motives lead people to violate moral rules even when they could not publicly advocate such violations, while other kinds of motives naturally lead only to violations that one could publicly advocate. It is primarily this second belief, which is probably true, that accounts for the false view that the motive determines the morality of an act. What determines the morality of a violation of the moral rules is whether one could publicly advocate such a violation. The motive, at most, determines the moral worth of the action, i.e., how much it indicates about the moral character of the agent.

A man's character is continually being shaped by the actions he performs. Violating a moral rule when one could not publicly advocate such a violation is usually acting hypocritically, and has a bad effect on one's character. A misunderstanding of psychoanalysis has led philosophers and others to the view that character is relatively unchangeable after the age of five. This misunderstanding is due to a failure to distinguish between character and personality. It may be true that personality is hard to change after an early age; it is not true of character. A child of five does not yet even have a character. It is primarily character, not personality, that we are concerned with in this chapter.

Personality traits primarily concern a person's likes and dislikes, not his actions. However, a person's likes and dislikes have an important effect on the way he acts, and we often judge what a person likes and dislikes by the way he acts. Indeed, the normal pattern is for a man to act according to his likes and dislikes. He is even acting irrationally if he acts contrary to his likes and dislikes without a reason. Thus words which refer to personality traits may be thought to apply primarily to actions. When we say that someone is shy, we may think that this means that he avoids meeting people. But shyness, as a personality trait, is primarily a matter of likes and dislikes rather than of actions. This can be seen from the fact that we can say of someone who acts like a politician at election time that he is really shy. Not all likes and dislikes become personality traits, but only those that any rational man could have.

Character traits are primarily concerned with actions. Indeed they are habits of acting. But not all habits of acting are character traits; only those are that can be judged by reason, i.e., those that all rational men would judge in the same way. Character traits are also habits of acting which have been formed, to some important degree, by free, intentional, voluntary acts. It is a tautology that each man is to some degree responsible for his character. If he were not at all responsible for it, it would not be his character. Personality is quite different. Although a man may change his personality by free, intentional, voluntary acts, most men do not. A man's personality is not something he need be responsible for. This can be seen from the fact that we talk of the personality of children before they reach an age at which they are held responsible for anything.

Personality traits and character traits are often closely related. Personality traits are sometimes used to explain character traits. Character traits are not generally used in explanations. We can, of course, explain a particular action by citing a character trait, but this is simply to fit it into a general pattern of behavior. Although personality traits and character traits are quite distinct, they are often confused with one another. This is especially true when the personality trait is one that could be used to explain the character trait. For example, to say that a person is sadistic is to cite a personality trait, viz., that he enjoys seeing pain inflicted on others. This personality trait may explain why a person is cruel, viz., he acts so as to inflict pain on others unjustifiably. People often fail to distinguish between being sadistic, which is a personality trait, and being cruel, which is a character trait. But it is important to make such a distinction, for a sadistic person need not be a cruel one, nor need a cruel person be sadistic. The failure to distinguish clearly between personality and character, and to recognize that only the latter is the concern of morality, has had serious consequences not only for philosophy but also in everyday life.

I am not denying the extraordinary impact of personality on character. Thus I do not wish to deny the importance of developing in children a personality that is most conducive to their achieving a moral character. Indeed, one would hope that children develop a personality such that they come to enjoy acting morally—and this is not an insignificant matter. But this should not lead us to neglect the important distinction between personality and character. Character traits are not only those habits of action that can be judged by reason, they are also those traits which reason can influence. Man does not act merely on the basis of his likes and dislikes; he is also capable of guiding his actions by reason. Reason can lead a man to act in a way opposed to his inclinations. A sadist may not be cruel or malicious even though he would enjoy being so. There are many factors that are important in forming a person's character: personality, though important, is only one; another is the actual actions of the person. For habits are usually strengthened by acting on them. Unfortunately, this is as true for bad habits as for good ones.

However, my primary concern in this chapter is not with character formation, but with the nature of specific character traits. Associated with each of the second five moral rules are specific character traits. Some of these are moral vices. Associated with the rule concerning deception is deceitfulness; with promises, untrustworthiness; with cheating, unfairness; with the law, dishonesty; and with duty, undependability. I realize that this is a somewhat arbitrary pairing of moral vices with moral rules; e.g., dishonesty might also be linked with the rule against deception. But these pairings are primarily for ease of exposition, and nothing is lost if one demands a more complex relationship. To have a moral vice is to have a habit of unjustifiably violating a moral rule. It is therefore not accidental that all rational men publicly advocate the prevention of those character traits that can be described as moral vices.

All the moral vices connected with the second five rules have corresponding virtues. In fact, except for deceitfulness, to which the corresponding virtue is truthfulness, the names of all of these other vices can be changed into those of the corresponding virtues simply by removing the prefix. These moral virtues are habits of obeying the moral rules as the moral attitude requires. Hence it follows that rational men publicly advocate the formation of these moral virtues. The moral virtues connected with the second five rules—truthfulness, trustworthiness, fairness, honesty, and dependability—are not very exciting. They are not those traits of character that we necessarily seek for ourselves, but rather those that we want others to have. It is obvious why this is so. We advocate obedience to the moral rules to avoid having evil done to us. Advocating obedience to the second five moral rules is no more than advocating that others acquire the associated moral virtues and avoid the associated moral vices. Of course, we must, at least, pretend to cultivate the virtues in ourselves, and thus we have the truth of the saying "Hypocrisy is the homage that vice pays to virtue."

The moral virtues and vices that we have been discussing, those connected with the second five moral rules, seem to lie on a single scale. As one becomes less truthful, he becomes more deceitful, less trustworthy, more untrustworthy, etc. We can rank people on this scale, and it makes little difference when we switch from the virtue to the vice. A person may be completely dependable, generally dependable, fairly dependable, somewhat undependable, usually undependable, or completely undependable. The virtue and the vice are such that as one moves away from the one end, he necessarily moves toward the other. The degree to which one has a particular moral virtue or vice is determined by the degree to which one unjustifiably breaks the corresponding moral rule. We can, in fact, state the second five moral rules in terms of either the virtues or the vices. Thus the rules might be either "Be truthful, trustworthy, fair, honest, and dependable" or "Don't be deceitful, untrustworthy, unfair, dishonest, or undependable." We shall see in Chapter 10 that this close association between the second five rules and the moral virtues and vices is of some importance.

Although most of what are normally regarded as the moral virtues and vices are connected with the second five moral rules, some moral virtues and vices are not. Cruelty, or maliciousness, is a moral vice which is not connected to any of the second five moral rules. In fact, it does not seem peculiarly connected to any of the first five moral rules. Rather a cruel, or malicious, person frequently unjustifiably violates any of the first five rules, i.e., unjustifiably inflicts evil on someone. Of course some people are more cruel than others; whereas some people are willing to kill and torture, others may only be willing to deprive of pleasure. But there are no distinct vices for each of the first five moral rules; only, perhaps, degrees of cruelty.

Unlike the moral vices connected to the second five moral rules, as cruelty decreases, we do not necessarily get an increase in what might be taken as the corresponding moral virtue, kindness. Between kindness and cruelty sits indifference. Unlike the moral virtues connected to the second five rules, honesty, fairness, etc., kindness does not consist in obeying the moral rules. Rather, kindness is the character trait that primarily involves justified relieving of evils. This explains the presence of indifference. Kindness is not simply lack of cruelty as honesty is lack of dishonesty. Nor is cruelty simply lack of kindness as dishonesty is lack of honesty. Lack of kindness is indifference; when regarded as a moral vice, it is known as callousness, and is closely related to cruelty.

I have listed only six moral virtues and seven moral vices, but I do not think that these are the only ones. On the contrary, any character trait that necessarily involves failing to follow the moral ideals or unjustifiably violating the moral rules is a moral vice; any character trait that involves justifiably obeying the moral rules or following the moral ideals is a moral virtue. If we wish, we can characterize moral virtues and vices without mentioning the moral rules or ideals. We can define them in terms of the attitudes of all rational men. A moral virtue is any trait of character that all rational men would publicly advocate that all men possess. A moral vice is any trait of character that all rational men would publicly advocate that no man possess. It is not my task here to list all of the moral virtues and vices. They will all be involved in a very intimate way with the moral rules and ideals. But it is worthwhile to point out that a number of character traits that have been considered by some to be moral virtues and vices actually are not.

Of the so-called cardinal virtues—justice, prudence, temperance, and courage—only justice seems a plausible candidate for being classified as a moral virtue. I have not discussed justice, because it does not seem to me to be a character trait that we normally assign to a person. I would suggest that if justice is to be considered a moral virtue, it should be understood in an extremely wide sense, characterizing a man who does not unjustifiably violate any of the moral rules. In this sense, of course, justice is not merely one moral virtue among many; it is the combination of all the moral virtues connected with the moral rules. I prefer not to talk of justice or of the just man, but rather to talk about the individual moral virtues. I should note, however, that though justice is necessary to moral goodness, and that lack of justice makes one immoral, being just only makes one not immoral and is not sufficient for moral goodness.

Prudence, temperance, and courage are not moral virtues at all, nor are their opposites moral vices. On the account of moral virtues as habits of obeying moral rules or following moral ideals, these three virtues do not even seem to be moral. Nor on the account of moral vices as habits of unjustifiably violating moral rules do imprudence, intemperance, and cowardice seem to be moral vices. However, if we characterize moral virtues and vices in terms of the attitudes of all rational men, it may seem that prudence, temperance, and courage fit the definition. It may seem that all rational men would publicly advocate that all men possess the character traits of prudence, temperance, and courage, and publicly advocate that no one possess the character traits of imprudence, intemperance, and cowardice.

Certainly every rational man would personally like to have the three cardinal virtues. But this is a somewhat different proposition. It is one thing for all rational men to want to have these cardinal virtues personally, and another for them to publicly advocate that all other men have them. If one were a rational egoist, he might very well prefer that all other men have the cardinal vices rather than the virtues, though of course he could not publicly advocate this. Further, no rational man would publicly advocate that those who were cruel or malicious acquire the personal virtues. This would increase the chances of his suffering the evil consequences of the moral rules being violated with regard to himself and those he cares about. Moreover, unlike the moral virtues, all rational men would personally like to have the three cardinal virtues, and to avoid the vices. Thus, I shall call prudence, temperance, and courage personal rather than moral virtues, and their opposites—imprudence, intemperance, and cowardice—personal vices. We could, in fact, define the category of personal virtues as those character traits that all rational men personally desire, and personal vices as those that no rational man personally desires.

Just as a proper understanding of the moral rules involves understanding the rational man's attitude toward them, so also does the proper understanding of the virtues, both moral and personal. We have seen that a rational man does not publicly advocate blind obedience to the moral rules, but in some cases may publicly advocate violating a rule. Dependability as a moral virtue is not blind obedience to duty; devotion to duty if not informed by reason may be a vice rather than a virtue. Similarly, if prudence, temperance, and courage are to be personal virtues, i.e., character traits that all rational men personally desire, then they must be understood in the proper way. Prudence cannot simply be timidity or a dislike of risks; a rational man may enjoy some risk-taking. Temperance cannot simply mean abstaining from smoking and drinking, for a rational man may desire to smoke and drink. Courage cannot simply be adventuresomeness or the enjoyment of risks, for a rational man need not enjoy all risks. Indeed on these accounts courage and prudence would seem to be incompatible. But if they are personal virtues, this cannot be, for a personal virtue is one that all rational men wish to have personally. Knowing they are incompatible, all rational men cannot want both of them. I shall try to provide a brief account of prudence, temperance, and courage, such that they are all compatible, and all rational men would like to possess all of them.

In saying that prudence, temperance, and courage are personal rather than moral virtues, I do not mean to imply that all rational men want these virtues only for their own self-interest. Although a rational egoist may desire these traits simply in order to benefit himself, a rational man who desires to act morally may want them in order to enable him to act morally. Prudence, temperance, and courage are not only an aid to the man pursuing his own self-interest, they are an equal aid to the man who seeks to act morally. Thus there is no suggestion that because prudence, temperance, and courage are personal rather than moral virtues they are somehow opposed to moral action.

The point of distinguishing between the personal virtues and the moral ones is to stress that the former have no necessary connection with being moral. It is possible for a man to be prudent, temperate, and courageous and yet to be thoroughly immoral. We might not call such a man prudent, temperate, and courageous, because to assign a personal virtue to a man is to praise him, and we hesitate to praise immoral men. Yet there is no doubt that a man can have the personal virtues without having any moral ones. But I think it extremely unlikely that a man could have the moral virtues without having the personal ones. This latter fact accounts, perhaps, for the inclination one has to consider these virtues as moral ones. I think this inclination should be resisted.

If prudence is to be a personal virtue, it must be a trait of character that all rational men, regardless of the personality they have, would like to have. Thus prudence cannot be a trait of character that appeals only to men who primarily enjoy the quiet pleasures, e.g., stamp collecting, but it must also appeal to those men who enjoy more rugged activities, e.g., mountain climbing. Prudence should not be confused with timidity, which is a personality trait, not a trait of character. A prudent man is one who carefully considers the consequences of his actions when these are likely to be serious, and who does not take unnecessary risks in seeking to reach his goal or satisfy his desires. This does not mean that the prudent man takes no risks, but he does not take them unless they seem to be the best way to obtain what he is seeking. A man who enjoys action and adventure is not excluded from being a prudent man. For him, risks are enjoyable. As long as he takes care to prepare himself, and has considered the evil risked in the light of the good to be gained, he may be a prudent man even if he is a lion tamer.

The prudent man is generally opposed to the rash or impulsive man, the man who undertakes a course of action that is likely to have important consequences without considering these consequences. This does not mean that the prudent man never acts on impulse, but he does not do so in cases where the consequences are likely to be momentous. The prudent man is one who has a concern for the future, who does not sacrifice a greater future good to a lesser present one through lack of concern for the former. We can define a prudent man as one who habitually acts rationally after considering the consequences of his action for himself and those for whom he is concerned, especially in those cases where his action may result in significant evil or loss of significant goods. Defined in this way, it is quite clear that prudence is a personal virtue. All rational men certainly want to avoid evil or the loss of any significant good for themselves and those they care for.

Temperance seems to be a part of prudence. But there is a difference in emphasis. Whereas prudence primarily involves concern for the satisfaction of future desires, temperance primarily involves the control of present desires. A temperate man is one who habitually acts rationally when in the grip of some strong present emotion or desire. This does not mean that temperance always demands the overcoming of this emotion or the refusal to satisfy the desire. Taken in this way, temperance does not seem to be a trait of character that would be desired by all rational men. Rather, considered as a virtue, temperance simply demands that one not allow a strong emotion or desire to make him behave irrationally. This permits circumstances in which it is not intemperate to satisfy one's desire or express one's emotion. Intemperance is a vice only if the indulgence of one's present desires or emotions leads one to act irrationally.

I am not attempting to describe temperance as it is ordinarily thought of; I am attempting to describe what temperance must be like if it is to be a personal virtue. Temperance is frequently regarded as merely abstention from, or great moderation in, the use of alcohol and tobacco. This is unfortunate. There is some need for the concept of temperance as a genuine personal virtue—one desired by all rational men, not merely by a genteel middle class. This is the concept of temperance with which philosophers have traditionally been concerned. A temperate man need not have weak desires or emotions, as the degraded concept suggests. If one does not have any strong desires or emotions, one has little need of temperance. For temperance consists in having that strength of character that allows one to resist a strong desire when to satisfy it would be irrational.

It is the "cool moment" aspect of rationality (Chapter 2) that provides the best background for understanding the concept of temperance. On the "cool moment" account of rationality, it is irrational for a man to act on a desire which in a cool moment he decided was significantly less important than the desire or set of desires he would frustrate by so acting. A man who is quick to anger may decide in a cool moment that giving vent to his anger results in the sacrifice of that which he considers significantly more important. Nonetheless, when he is angry, he may not be able to control his anger. He is unable to act rationally when in the grip of his anger. I call such a man intemperate. Generally the more important desires a man sacrifices by failing to control his present emotions or desires concern his own self-interest. But often the sacrificed desires concern not himself, but those he cares about. It can also happen that the more significant desire that is sacrificed is the desire to act morally. When this is the case, philosophers have often talked of "weakness of will." Thus lack of temperance is sometimes the cause of immoral action. This explains why some have regarded temperance as a moral rather than a personal virtue. However, defining a temperate man, as we have done, as one who does not let his present desires or emotions make him act irrationally makes clear that temperance is indeed a personal virtue. For all rational men desire it for themselves and those they care about.

A courageous man is one who habitually acts rationally in the face of danger or when he is suffering from fear. Since fear is an emotion, this may produce an overlap between temperance and courage. And indeed there are circumstances in which we would call some reactions to fear intemperate, though generally we call them cowardly. It should be no surprise that there is an overlap between the various personal virtues and vices. What distinguishes one personal virtue from another is the circumstance in which one acts rationally. This explains Plato's attempt to equate virtue and wisdom, for Plato treated all virtue as personal virtue. What distinguishes one vice from another is what causes one to act irrationally. Circumstances cannot always be clearly distinguished, nor causes always precisely picked out. So it should not be surprising that there are occasions in which it is equally appropriate to praise a man as either temperate or prudent, and others where we may condemn him for either intemperance or cowardice.

But there are standard situations in which it is clear that courage, not temperance or prudence, is called for. These circumstances are those in which one is faced with some clear and present danger. Being courageous does not require always facing the danger, and attempting to overcome it. Some dangers are severe enough to make a rational man modify his plans, or even to give them up entirely. If being courageous required always trying to overcome every danger, it would not be a personal virtue. Most, if not all, rational men would prefer not to have such a character trait. If courage is to be a personal virtue, it must consist in not allowing fear or danger to make one act irrationally. Courage should not be confused with adventuresomeness, which is a personality trait, not one of character. A courageous man must be one who after consideration of the danger involved acts in a rational fashion. He attempts to overcome it, if this seems most likely to benefit himself or those he cares about, and abandons his plans if this seems most beneficial. Only when understood in this way can courage be considered a personal virtue.

It is interesting, though I am not sure how important, that the three personal virtues seem to fit Aristotle's account of a virtue as the mean between two extremes. Prudence is the mean between rashness—i.e., too little concern for the future—and overcaution—i.e., too much concern for the future. The prudent man does not allow concern for the consequences of his action to paralyze him, but neither does he ignore these consequences. It is quite appropriate to advise someone to care not too much, yet not too little for the future. As a bit of practical advice, it might even be worthwhile to tell him to aim at erring in the direction of that extreme toward which he is not naturally inclined. All of this suggests what Aristotle says.

Temperance also is plausibly described as a mean between two extremes. On the one side, we have the extreme of intemperance or overindulgence, in general, a failure to control one's present desires and emotions. On the other side, we have asceticism or puritanism in which one refuses to satisfy any strong desire or display any strong emotion. This kind of generalized masochism is probably more common than one thinks. However, since it generally does not result in overt harm to others, it is not so commonly remarked upon. Thus intemperance is sometimes taken as the opposite of temperance, as if it were impossible to err by controlling one's present desires and emotions too much. But a rational man would advise one for whom he was concerned to steer the middle course between indulging all of his present emotions and desires and indulging none of them. And, again, it would be practical to tell him to err in the direction of that extreme toward which he is not naturally inclined.

The extremes between which courage lies are cowardice on the one side, and foolhardiness or rashness on the other. The former consists in letting fear or danger dissuade one from carrying out one's plans even though, all things considered, it would be rational to attempt to overcome the danger and proceed as planned. Foolhardiness or rashness consists in trying to overcome some danger when, all things considered, it is irrational to try to do so. However, when a man refuses to do something rash, we usually say he acted prudently rather than courageously. Conversely, even when it is prudent to try to overcome some danger, we generally praise a man for courage when he acts rationally. This, together with the fact that prudence is confused with timidity, and courage with adventuresomeness, explains why prudence and courage are sometimes thought to be incompatible.

Although courage is sometimes shown by the overcoming of fear, it is not necessary to fear in order to be courageous. Someone who recognizes the danger that he faces, but does not fear it, is no less courageous when he rationally decides to face it than the man who does so even though he fears it. We might praise more highly the action of the man who fears, as it was a more difficult act, but we would praise more the man who did not fear, as he is the kind of man we would prefer to be.

The courageous man is one who has the proper respect for the danger he faces; he does not let it overawe him, nor does he ignore it. To do the former would be to give up some goods unnecessarily; to do the latter would be to increase unnecessarily one's chances of suffering evil. The rational man does not desire either of these, but always seeks to minimize the chances of either himself or those he cares about losing some good or suffering some evil. As in the case of prudence and temperance, the rational man would advise the timid man to err on the side of foolhardiness, the adventuresome man not to fear erring on the side of cowardice. For this is more likely to result in their achieving the mean of courage.

Courage seems to have a more intimate connection with the moral ideals than either temperance or prudence. It is more natural to associate temperance with the moral rules, for, as noted previously, lack of temperance often results in violation of a moral rule. Although prudence is required if one is to act according to the moral ideals most effectively, it does not seem intimately connected with either the moral rules or the moral ideals. Courage, though sometimes required to obey the moral rules, is most often required in order to follow the moral ideals. It takes courage to prevent a mob from killing or torturing an individual. It takes courage to try to stop people from depriving others of their freedom and opportunity, especially when they have been doing it for a long time. It is no wonder that courage has often been considered a moral virtue, for it is so often required by those who would like to follow moral ideals. It is no wonder that it is often valued so highly, for it seems a rare commodity, and that which is rare is generally highly prized. But courage is not isolated from the values we have. The courage generally shown by parents when their children are in danger shows quite clearly that courage can be had when we value something enough. It is not, I think, a lack of courage that is primarily responsible for the few people who show it in the pursuit of moral ideals. Rather it is that so few people care enough about following moral ideals.

Just as there are many more moral virtues than the ones mentioned earlier, so there are many more personal virtues than the three cardinal ones. Fortitude, which is often confused with courage, is a personal virtue and consists in acting rationally when one is faced with continued hardship. Whether it can be considered a mean between two extremes, and in general whether all personal virtues can be so considered, is a question that I shall not attempt to answer. My primary concern has been to provide an account of the virtues such that their connection with the attitudes of rational men is clear. I have tried to provide an account of the moral virtues so that there could be no doubt about their intimate connection with acting morally. I have tried to show how they differ in this respect from the personal virtues from which they have not always been distinguished.

I should now like to show that the attitude that the rational man takes toward the moral virtues, and hence toward the moral rules and ideals, as well as the attitude he takes toward the personal virtues, depend upon man being the kind of being that he is. If man were not a being who could suffer the evils which are prohibited by the first five rules, then not only would these rules be pointless, but also the second five rules would lose their point. There would also be no point in advocating the acquiring of the moral virtues. Nor, as we shall see, would there be any point in acquiring the personal virtues. There is, then, a sense in which the first five moral rules are really fundamental in any account of morality, and even in a more general discussion of virtue and vice. This can be seen most clearly if we imagine a world in which rational beings would not publicly advocate obedience to any of the first five moral rules.

These beings must be such that they cannot be killed. If they die, and we can imagine it either way, they die from internal causes which cannot be affected by others. These beings would certainly have no need for a rule against killing, if they could even understand such a rule. Let us further suppose that these beings can suffer no pain. This is relatively easy to imagine, there now being some human beings who, due to a defect in their nervous system, feel no pain. Thus these beings would have no use for the second rule, "Don't cause pain," even if they could understand it. The third and fourth rules, "Don't disable" and "Don't deprive of freedom or opportunity," obviously belong together. Why the rational man does not want to be disabled or deprived of freedom or opportunity is that he thereby lessens his chances of escaping death and pain and of obtaining those things that he might desire or get pleasure from. But we shall imagine that our beings desire nothing but to contemplate the mysteries of the universe. Further, their ability, freedom, and opportunity to do so cannot be affected by anyone. Thus the third and fourth rules also become pointless, and perhaps unintelligible. To complete the picture, let us say that they get pleasure from nothing but this contemplation, and that no one can deprive them of it. Thus the fifth rule, "Don't deprive of pleasure," goes the way of the first four. And here we ensure that the second rule becomes pointless because there is no possibility of mental suffering.

It is not clear that beings such as we have described are rational. According to our description, they do nothing; except, perhaps, for contemplating aloud. There is nothing that allows us to distinguish this verbal behavior from a recording. These beings have no desires, goals, or aversions that can be affected by anyone. They show no purposive activity; in fact, they show no activity at all, except, perhaps, verbal activity. Even this is limited. They cannot interfere with one another at all. They cannot deprive one another of pleasure by talking too loudly and destroying the pleasures of contemplation. We are imagining beings who are completely independent of anyone else. They can neither be helped nor harmed in any way by anyone. Even if they are aware of others, they are completely indifferent to them. Such beings, which seem to be regarded as ideals by some religions and even some philosophers, are certainly quite different from human beings. We can, I think, regard them as rational beings only if we provide them with a history. So that we must first picture a group of beings like those which Shaw presents in *Back to Methusala*, and then allow for changes until the beings have the characteristics I have described above.

I am not sure that even with such a history we would regard such beings as rational. But even if we do, it is quite clear that the first five moral rules would have no application in a world populated solely by such beings. These rules have application only to people who can suffer the evils which the first five moral rules prohibit causing. It is pointless to have a rule "Don't kill" when no one can be killed. Similarly it is pointless to say "Don't cause pain" when no one can suffer pain, or "Don't deprive of pleasure" when it is impossible to do so. And if, in addition, no one has desires that can be thwarted by anyone else, then there is no point in having the rules "Don't disable" and "Don't deprive of freedom or opportunity." The beings we have described are such that none of the first five rules have any point with regard to them. The questions that now arise are "Do any of the second five rules have any point?" and "Is there any point in acquiring the virtues, moral or personal?"

The second five moral rules are justified; i.e., all rational men publicly advocate the moral attitude toward them, because violation of them generally results in someone suffering one of the evils prohibited by the first five rules. In the world we are now imagining no one can suffer any of the evils prohibited by the first five moral rules. Hence this justification of the second five moral rules no longer holds. Is there any other justification for these rules? Not only can I see no justification for the second five moral rules, but given this world of completely independent beings, I can see no justification for having any rules at all. There is no point in having rules if no one benefits from these rules. In the world we are now imagining no one would benefit from anyone following either moral rules or moral ideals. It follows immediately that there is no justification for the moral virtues, for all of the moral virtues are connected with the moral rules or ideals, and these are pointless in a world without evil.

The pointlessness of the second five rules, and consequently of the moral virtues associated with them, can be seen most clearly if we slightly modify our world without evil. Imagine the beings we have described at some earlier stage. Here they remember what it was like when they could be seriously harmed by others. Now in their joy at being free from the necessity to follow any rules, moral or otherwise, they take pleasure in deceiving, breaking promises, cheating, disobeying the law, and neglecting their duties. These beings therefore differ from the beings described in the previous example. They take pleasure in something other than mere contemplation of the world. But apart from this change, and any further changes that are required by this change, they are the same as the beings described in the previous example. No one ever suffers any evil as a consequence of deception, a broken promise, being cheated, a law being broken, or a neglected duty.

In this situation would a rational being publicly advocate the moral attitude toward the second five rules, or the acquiring of the associated virtues? I do not see why he would. He has nothing to gain from publicly advocating these things. Of course, having read Kant, he knows that it is impossible for everyone to deceive all of the time, never to keep a promise, etc. He is aware that complete universalizability of deception, breaking promises, etc., is impossible, self-frustrating, or unintelligible. Thus he publicly advocates sufficient obedience to the rules so that it is possible to break them. But since the whole point of establishing the rules is simply to provide the opportunity to violate them, he does not publicly advocate that everyone always obey them.

Consideration of this imaginary world shows the inadequacy of using the lack of formal universalizability as conceived by many philosophers, especially Kant, as the criterion of an immoral action. In this imaginary world, it is as impossible to completely universalize deception, promise-breaking, etc., as in our actual world. But whereas in our actual world it is immoral ever to do these things simply because one feels like doing so, in our imaginary world, it is not. No rational being in this world would publicly advocate that an evil be inflicted on someone because he violated one of the second five moral rules simply because he felt like doing so. However, all rational beings might publicly advocate punishment for a course of action reminiscent of an ordinary violation of the moral rules. These beings would publicly advocate that one not violate the moral rules all of the time; they might even publicly advocate punishing those who did. Punishment would consist in depriving the violator of the pleasure of violating any of the rules. For the only evil that can be inflicted on these beings is to deprive them of the pleasure of breaking the moral rules. But this punishment makes it clear that there would be another kind of activity for which these beings might advocate punishment. This would be any unauthorized activity designed to keep others from violating the moral rules. Any being who prevented others from violating the moral rules would, in this strange world, himself be acting immorally. He would be unjustifiably violating the one moral rule that retained its point in this world—the rule "Don't deprive of pleasure."

I do not deny that in the course of a moral argument one sometimes says "What would happen if everyone acted like that?" But I think that this question has more rhetorical than logical force. For one thing, it is not even clear what the question means. In the world we have been imagining, it is possible to ask someone who lies, "What would happen if everyone acted like that?" Part of the ambiguity in the question becomes clear if he should reply, "Do you mean 'What would happen if I and everyone else lied every time we spoke?' or 'What would happen if everyone lied whenever he felt like it?' It is only if you mean the first that lying becomes impossible, self-frustrating, etc. If you mean the second, then nothing much may happen at all." Violations of the second five moral rules are immoral, not because they are not universalizable, but because unjustifiable violation generally results in evil consequences. When considering violations of the first five rules, universalizability is even less important. For every violation of these rules has evil consequences. It is because of the evil consequences that result from violation of the moral rules that all rational men take the attitude toward them that they do.

Why should a rational man care if a given action can be universalized or not? In most cases it almost certainly will not be, especially if universalization is taken in the strong sense required by the theory. According to Kant, it is always immoral to violate the categorical imperative: "Act only on that maxim whereby thou canst at the same time will that it should become a universal law." There are extraordinary difficulties in applying the categorical imperative because almost any action can be claimed to be based on a maxim that one would universalize. If I steal from a man richer than I, even though I am not poor, I can claim that the maxim for my action was "Increase your income." It may be objected that I have left out the important aspect of my action, viz., that it involved stealing. But that is just the difficulty with the categorical imperative; it provides no guide in deciding which aspect of the action is important. Thus it provides no guide for determining how to formulate the maxim that one must be willing to universalize. By universalizing a maxim, I understand Kant to mean publicly advocating that everyone act on it.

But the difficulties in applying the categorical imperative are not the main thing wrong with it. It is simply false that one is acting immorally whenever he acts on a maxim which he would not publicly advocate that everyone act on. Even when one acts in a way that he would publicly advocate that no one act, he need not be acting immorally. He may only be acting imprudently or cowardly. Only if all rational men would publicly advocate that no one act in this way is acting in this way immoral. Usually this will involve violating a moral rule. Only when your action can be correctly described as a violation of a moral rule must you be willing to publicly advocate that everyone act in this way. But there is usually no need for one to justify his action morally, i.e., to publicly advocate it, unless he has violated a moral rule. It is absurd to demand that a moral man always will that the maxim he acts on be adopted by everyone else.

I do not want all men to become professional philosophers. I do not even want all qualified men to do so. There are quite enough professional philosophers. Those who are qualified to become professional philosophers are usually also qualified to enter some other profession. I think it preferable for many of them to do so. Yet, I do not think that anyone would consider me immoral for becoming a professional philosopher. Thus we can see the confusion that arises if we talk of willingness to universalize one's maxims of action as a necessary condition for acting morally. Lack of universalizability does not make an action immoral. However, if an action is a violation of the moral rules, unwillingness to universalize does make it immoral. This kind of action makes it more likely that someone will suffer an unwanted evil, and it is for this reason that all rational men publicly advocate liability to punishment for those who commit such actions.

Evil, or the possibility of avoiding it, is also what makes prudence, temperance, and courage worthwhile. The personal virtues become pointless in a world without the possibility of evil. If one does not need to be concerned with the future, nor to control one's desires, nor to face any danger, then one does not need prudence, temperance, or courage. It is the possibility of suffering evil that gives a point to the acquiring of the moral and personal virtues. Thus there is something to be said for those religious thinkers who "solve" the problem of evil by claiming that evil is necessary for the cultivation of those character traits, including both the moral and personal virtues, that we now value so highly. Of course, we now value these character traits so highly precisely because there is so much evil in the world, so that I am not clear how much force this "solution" has.

Let us now change the original imaginary world so as to allow the beings to deprive each other of the pleasure of contemplation by talking very loudly. Most if not all of the virtues become possible. For example, these beings might carelessly talk too loudly when particularly excited by something they were contemplating. This might invite reprisals by others. Thus the virtue of temperance would be desirable. Since reprisals might provoke counterreprisals, prudence would also be called for. It may be inappropriate to talk of courage, but fortitude would be possible. We could even imagine the point of some organization in which certain beings were designated as officials whose duty was to warn those who began talking too loudly and to punish those who did not heed their warnings. I do not know if we could generate the possibility of all the moral virtues with this simple world, but it is clear that some of them could be. The point of this example is to show that very little evil is required before some of the moral and personal virtues become possible again.

Let us now add the possibility of pain to this world; e.g., certain kinds of talk not only deprive of pleasure, but actually inflict pain. It may now be that all of the moral and personal virtues become justified again. Perhaps this accounts, in part, for the view of the classical utilitarians, that morality was concerned only with pleasure and pain. In the imaginary world we are considering, the utilitarians would not be so far wrong, but in the real world, their view is vastly oversimple. Not only is there the matter of life and death, but the ways in which one man depends on and can interfere with another are vastly more complex. Morality must be understood with reference to this world, not with reference to some more simple world.

CHAPTER 9

MORAL JUDGMENTS

H AVING PRESENTED AN ACCOUNT of moral rules, ideals, virtues, and vices, I shall now give an account of moral judgments. In the first chapter we saw that all previous accounts of moral judgments were inadequate because they provided no clear distinction between moral and nonmoral judgments. But though all previous accounts are inadequate, they all have something of value to say. The imperative theory, which regards moral judgments as a special kind of command, points to the fact that moral judgments are primarily used to tell people what to do or, more frequently, what not to do. This theory is most persuasive for moral judgments concerning actions that have not yet been performed. These judgments—e.g., "You ought to do it" or "You shouldn't do that"—do resemble commands in many ways. The commending theory is most persuasive for moral judgments about people. These judgments—e.g., "He is a good man"—do resemble the kinds of evaluations we make on plays, paintings, tools, etc. The emotive theory regards moral judgments as expressions of our emotions or feelings. This theory is most persuasive when we consider those moral judgments—e.g., "But cheating is wrong"—which are made when we wish to register our agreement or disagreement with what is being done. Suppose we see a good friend of ours cheating or about to cheat. Telling him that cheating is wrong would serve more as an expression of our feelings than it would inform him of something he did not know. The view that moral judgments are statements of fact seems plausible primarily when moral judgments are made in the context of a philosophical discussion. Given an account of the morally relevant features of a situation, to say that a proposed course of action is morally right is very like stating a fact.

The examples of moral judgments given in the preceding paragraph contain the words "ought," "shouldn't," "good," or "wrong." However, it is not because they contain these words that they are moral judgments. In fact, most moral judgments do not even contain these words. Rather than simply tell someone that he ought to do something, we usually say something more specific; e.g., "You promised to do it," or "It is your duty to do it." Similarly, in making moral judgments about people we do not generally say that they are good or bad, but something more specific, e.g., that they are kind and trustworthy, or cruel and deceitful. Moral judgments about actions also generally contain more specific terms than "right" or "wrong," such as "honest" and "fair," or "dishonest" and "unfair." Insofar as general terms are used in moral judgments, they are more likely to be the kinds of terms that do not usually appear in books on moral philosophy.

To make a moral judgment of an action, person, etc., is to judge the action by relating it to either a moral rule or a moral ideal. Further, the judgment must be one that we believe we would publicly advocate. How one describes what is involved in moral judgments will depend, in part, upon which definition of "publicly advocate" one uses. If one means by "publicly advocates" advocates when using only those beliefs that are required by reason, then actual moral judgments—e.g., "It was morally wrong to deceive him"—will involve some hypothetical judgment, such as the following: "If his action was a violation of the rule against deceiving, and he could not have publicly advocated such a violation because he knew that it was not for the benefit of the deceived or to prevent any evil, then his action was prohibited by public reason." It will also involve a factual judgment, e.g., His action was of the kind described above. If one means by "publicly advocates" advocates in order to reach agreement among all rational men, the description will be as follows: "Since his action was a violation of the rule against deceiving, and he could not publicly advocate such a violation because he knew that it was not for the benefit of the deceived or to prevent any evil, his action was prohibited by public reason." The first description emphasizes the dependence of the judgment on the facts slightly more; the second description seems to me to present a slightly more accurate account of what we usually mean. These descriptions are not meant to be analyses of "morally wrong"; I shall give an analysis of this phrase later in the chapter. Now I am simply emphasizing that moral judgments are judgments that involve both a certain content and a certain form.

I am not saying that a moral judgment must contain certain words. Whether a judgment is a moral judgment does not depend upon the words contained in it. A moral judgment can be made without actually saying anything at all; in some situations one can simply shrug one's shoulders. In fact, "good," "bad," "right," "wrong," "ought," and "should" are generally not used in making moral judgments, but in making nonmoral judgments. Nonetheless examination of these words will be of some value in getting clear about moral judgments. For each of them does occur in moral judgments that can be used to represent a wide range of similar moral judgments. By comparing their use in moral judgments to their use in nonmoral judgments, we may be able to clear up some problems that have arisen about the nature of moral judgments.

We say of an action that it is morally good, generally, when it is not in violation of any moral rule and is in accordance with some moral ideal. In most cases, giving to various charitable organizations, e.g., UNICEF, is morally good. Giving to museums, however, is generally following a utilitarian rather than a moral ideal. Working for organizations like the American Civil Liberties Union is also morally good. For these organizations seek to prevent evil without themselves violating moral rules. When the prevention of evil involves the violation of a moral rule, we have a more complex situation. We shall investigate it when we discuss what it is to say that an action is morally right or wrong. Refusing to act according to a moral ideal when this does not involve breaking a moral rule or some significant personal sacrifice and one has some special opportunity to do so is often called morally bad. An unjustified violation of the moral rules also is often called morally bad.

A morally good man is one who seldom or never does morally bad actions, and often or generally does morally good ones. But in judging a person we do not simply consider his actions, but also his intentions and motives. A morally good man must intend to do morally good actions and intend to avoid morally bad ones. We do not call a man morally good who accidentally acts in accordance with the moral ideals, and does not do morally bad actions simply because things don't turn out as he intends. This is a situation that generally occurs only in slapstick movies. It is worth mentioning to avoid the impression that it is only the consequences of a man's action that count toward his being judged morally good or bad. But consequences are important. The man who always tries to prevent evil but never does is not generally thought of as morally good. Of such a man, we may say that he means well; but some results are necessary before we call him morally good.

However, good results, even if intentional, are not sufficient to make a man morally good; motives are also important. A man who follows the moral ideals and obeys the moral rules, but does so simply or primarily from fear of punishment or desire of praise, is not usually considered a morally good man. A morally good man must do morally good actions and avoid doing morally bad ones for certain kinds of reasons. Generally we call a man morally good if he intentionally does morally good actions and avoids morally bad ones, and his motive for doing this is one that can be depended on to operate even when he believes that no one will know about his action.

From Chapter 3 we have an analysis of "good," "bad," "better," and "worse," when used in judgments describing particular kinds of things. A good x is an x that all qualified rational men would choose when they wanted an x for its normal function unless they had a reason not to. A bad x is an x that no rational man would choose. We can now see how the use of these terms in moral judgments fits the general analysis. A morally good man is one that all rational men would choose when they were selecting men to live with, unless they had a reason. A morally bad man is one no rational man would choose to live with, unless he had a reason. Unless they had a reason, all rational men would pick the morally better men when choosing men to live with. Thus all rational men would select the morally good man over the morally bad one. We can now see that moral judgments of men using the words "good" and "bad" are very similar to judgments made of tools, and even more similar to judgments made of athletes. This does not require that men be regarded as tools, or even as athletes, performing a function of any sort. It simply makes explicit the fact that a rational man is interested in the moral character of others because of the consequences for himself and those for whom he is concerned.

Before we can show that the use of the words "right" and "wrong" in moral judgments is very similar to their use in nonmoral judgments, we must provide some account of their use in nonmoral judgments. It is important that "correct" and "incorrect" can often be substituted for "right" and "wrong." In theoretical problems, an answer is right (correct) if all the people qualified to deal with this problem would agree on the answer. An answer is wrong (incorrect) if all qualified people agree that it is not the answer. If there is a disagreement among qualified people, then there may be no right or wrong answer to the problem. However, there may be a right answer, but we do not now know enough to determine what it is. We may either lack knowledge of all the relevant factors or appropriate techniques. The latter, in pure form, is primarily found in mathematics and logic. Here all that one needs to determine if a theorem is correct is to provide a proof accept-able to all qualified mathematicians.

In many cases lack of knowledge is due to lack of appropriate techniques. But in some cases, lack of knowledge of facts is simply due to failure on the part of people to look for them. If, in the absence of the agreement of all qualified people, we continue to maintain that a certain answer is right or wrong, we must be holding that some new technique or information can be found which will result in the agree-ment of all qualified people. If we do not believe this, then we must abandon calling our answer right or wrong. Otherwise we are doing no more than expressing our feelings. This is what those who adopted the verifiability principle were, in a misleading fashion, trying to say.

But it is not only answers to theoretical problems that are called "right" and "wrong." In practical matters, we talk of decisions or courses of action as being right or wrong. In these cases, what is right or wrong is often decided after the fact. We often call a decision right or wrong only after seeing whether or not it leads to the desired result. Where equally informed rational men would make different decisions, the one that leads to the desired result is usually called the right one. But that a man made the right decision does not mean that he is to be praised for it. He may have been simply lucky to do so. However, if a man generally makes the right decision, we tend to give him credit for it, even if we cannot see why his decisions generally turn out right.

Talk of intuition or insight is common here, and a man who gets such a reputation often acquires a number of followers, e.g., stock market analysts.

But sometimes all equally informed rational men would make the same decision. In these cases, we can talk about the right decision independent of its outcome. It is because of this kind of case that "right decision" does not mean simply "decision that leads to the desired result." We can imagine a case in which all rational men would agree that a man who decides to stay in a burning building rather than to climb down the fire escape has made the wrong decision, the man himself included. Yet it may be that the desired result, saving his life, was in fact achieved by his staying put, and would not have been achieved had he climbed down the fire escape. For it may be that an airplane brushed the side of the building, tearing down the fire escape while he would have been on it, and the wind from the plane was strong enough to blow the fire out. Thus he achieved the desired result by staying put, and would not have achieved it by climbing down the fire escape. But this does not alter the fact that the decision to do the latter was the right decision, and the decision to do the former, the wrong one. Thus decisions or courses of action, like answers to theoretical problems, are right when all properly qualified men would advocate them; they are wrong when no properly qualified man would advocate them. When there is disagreement, then the right decision may be the one that leads to the desired result.

A morally wrong action is usually an unjustified violation of the moral rules. Any action that can be called "morally wrong" can also be called "morally bad." However, this does not mean that "morally wrong" and "morally bad" mean the same thing. This should be clear from the fact that we often use "morally bad" to describe people, motives, and intentions, as well as actions, whereas "morally wrong" is usually restricted to actions. However, in talking of actions, the word "immoral" can generally be substituted for either. Nonetheless, there does seem to be a difference in emphasis between the two phrases. Since "morally wrong" is related to the nonmoral use of "wrong," it is generally used when we wish to emphasize the objective character of our judgment. A morally wrong action is one that *all* rational men would publicly advocate not doing. Since "morally bad" is related to the nonmoral use of "bad," it is generally used when we wish to emphasize that the action is to be avoided or not to be done. A morally bad action is one that all rational men publicly advocate *not* doing. Thus an unjustified violation of a moral rule can be called either "morally bad" or "morally wrong." Which phrase we use will depend on the point we want to emphasize.

The moral rules generally prohibit certain kinds of action rather than demand the performance of certain kinds. Thus the notion of violating a moral rule is usually much clearer than the notion of acting in accordance with one. Except for keeping a promise, doing your duty, and obeying the law, every action that does not violate a moral rule is in accordance with it. If an action in accordance with the moral rules is taken to mean one that is not a violation of the moral rules, then it would be incorrect to define a morally right action as one that is in accordance with the moral rules. For this would mean that an action like putting on my right shoe before the left was a morally right action. But in the first chapter, I noted that this kind of action was not subject to moral judgment. We generally talk of a morally right action only in those circumstances where we think the action reflects on the moral character of the person. These circumstances are primarily those in which a morally wrong action seems a genuine alternative. There are two classes: (1) those circumstances in which a person has or might be expected to have a strong desire or motive to violate a moral rule unjustifiably, and (2) those circumstances in which a person has or might be expected to have difficulty in discovering whether or not all rational men would publicly advocate violating a moral rule. We can, therefore, talk of two kinds of morally right actions. The first is where one ignores or overcomes some significant temptation. It is this kind of action that seems most straightforwardly related to one's character. The second kind of morally right action is done in circumstances where we think it difficult to determine what all rational men would publicly advocate. Here we often talk of moral insight. The former may involve only the moral rules; the latter almost always involves both the moral rules and the moral ideals.

The clearest case of a morally right action of the first kind is when we credit a man's personal virtues for his doing the morally right action. These are those cases where if he had done the morally wrong action, we would have said that it resulted from a lack of the appropriate personal virtue. It is this kind of immoral action that is appropriately described as proceeding from weakness of will. But not all morally right actions of the first kind are due to strength of will. Sometimes self-interest provides a strong motive for unjustifiably violating the moral rules, and it is not the personal virtues but the moral virtues that are put to the test. Philosophers have generally stressed the overcoming of self-interest as most important for this kind of morally right action. But often one must overcome the motives provided by love of one's family, one's religion, or one's country.

When family, religion, or country provide the motives for immoral action, then the overcoming of temptation is complicated by the difficulty in coming to see what all rational men would publicly advocate. It is no easy matter to see what would be publicly advocated by all rational men in the same situation. Morally irrelevant considerations are extraordinarily difficult to eliminate. That *my* family or country will benefit, and those I do not care for will suffer, are considerations that almost invariably affect my judgment. Distortion of the facts is almost inevitable. It is the recognition of the difficulty of making the right moral judgment in a case in which one is involved that accounts for the rule that judges disqualify themselves in such cases. Nonmoral considerations—e.g., that it is *my* family that is involved—usually lead to following a moral ideal when this involves unjustifiably breaking a moral rule. But sometimes uncritical obedience to the moral rules leads to the morally wrong action. Doing the morally right action when it involves overcoming one's habit of automatically obeying the moral rule is among the most difficult of all morally right actions.

When, given all the facts known by the agent (or which he should have known), all rational men would publicly advocate violating the rule in order to follow the ideal, then doing so is morally right. When no rational man would publicly advocate violating the rule in order to follow the moral ideal, then breaking the rule is morally wrong. When rational men disagree about whether to break the rule or not, then we cannot say that breaking the rule is either morally right or wrong. If we believe that some further information is now available which would lead all rational men to agree, then we can continue to maintain that the action is either morally right or morally wrong. But if we believe no information is available which would result in the agreement of all rational men, then to maintain that the action is either morally wrong or morally right is primarily to express one's attitude, which is better expressed by saying that the action either ought or ought not be done. But most moral disputes are disputes over the facts of the case, as is acknowledged even by those who hold that moral judgments are simply expressions of feelings.

The class of actions that I call justified exceptions to the moral rules is not the same as what is sometimes called a morally indifferent action. Those justified exceptions which all rational men publicly advocate are obviously not actions which are morally indifferent; they are morally right. Those justified exceptions which some rational men publicly advocate, while others publicly advocate the keeping of the rule, are not properly described as morally indifferent either. For this suggests that all rational men are publicly indifferent about such actions. Whereas it is most likely that though some rational men are publicly indifferent about these actions, some rational men would publicly advocate that they be prohibited and other rational men would publicly advocate doing them. The notion of a morally indifferent action suggests that all rational men agree that, morally speaking, it makes no difference whether the action is done or not. Insofar as there is a class of actions that can be described as morally indifferent, they would seem to coincide with the class of actions that I consider as falling outside the scope of morality. "Morally indifferent" resembles "morally right" in that one normally uses the phrase in describing an action only when one believes there is a real possibility that the action might be considered morally wrong.

The account of justified exceptions given above allows a more precise account of morally wrong than that given earlier. On that earlier account we said that a morally wrong action was usually an unjustified violation of the moral rules. We can now include as a morally wrong action one that is in accordance with a moral rule when all rational men would publicly advocate violating the rule in order to follow a moral ideal. This class of morally wrong actions differs from the unjustified violations of the moral rules in that only for the latter do all rational men publicly advocate punishment. To complicate the matter still further, it will sometimes be one's duty to violate a moral rule in order to follow a moral ideal. A doctor may have a duty to inflict pain on a person or to restrict his freedom in order to prevent much greater evil, and so may a judge or a policeman. Where we have not only a conflict of moral rules with moral ideals but of moral rules with one another, rational men may publicly advocate punishment for doing the morally wrong action. But in all of these cases we have not only the failure to follow a moral ideal, we also have a violation of a moral rule.

A man who never or almost never does what is morally wrong or bad and always or almost always does what is morally right, I call a morally righteous man. Note that such a man must sometimes follow the moral ideals. Of course, such a man must also have the appropriate intentions and motives, as we noted in the discussion of the morally good man. It is not necessary that a morally righteous man be continually tempted to do what is morally wrong. In fact, it is doubtful if a man who was continually tempted would be a morally righteous man. Although he may be tempted to do what is morally wrong from time to time, one would expect that situations that would tempt most men will most often not tempt him. Of two men facing the same temptation, we may praise the morally right action of the man who is tempted more than we praise the morally right action of the man who is not, but we admire the character of the latter more. This is similar to two men facing the same danger, where we praise the courageous action of the man suffering from fear more than we praise courageous action of the man who is not, but admire the character of the latter more. What I call a morally righteous man is sometimes called a conscientious man, a man of integrity, a just man, or sometimes simply a moral man. When justice is tempered with mercy, or the just man is also kind, he is what I call a morally good man. He is also called a kind man, a charitable man, a humane man, or sometimes simply a good man.

To call someone a morally good man or even to call him a moral man is to praise him. We normally reserve these praises for men we consider to be much better than we believe men usually are. I use the phrase "moral standards" to mean the standards used in determining how much moral praise or condemnation a man deserves. The higher the moral standard, the more morally right and good actions we require for a man to be praised as moral or morally good. The lower the moral standard, the more morally bad or wrong actions we require for a man to be condemned as immoral or morally bad. Some rational men have a higher opinion of how men usually act; they will demand more of a moral man than someone who has a lower opinion.

It is the opinion of how men usually act that determines how high or low one's moral standards are. If there is any way of narrowing the range of acceptable moral standards, it must be by narrowing the range of acceptable opinions about how men usually act. This latter narrowing can only be done by examining the way that men actually do behave. If no man has ever lived a full life without committing some immoral actions, it is pointless to demand no immoral actions before we call a man moral. If the morally best man we have ever heard of spent only one fourth of his time in following the moral ideals, it is absurd to demand that a morally good man devote half or all of his time to following the moral ideals. It is in discovering how men actually behave that psychology, sociology, and anthropology have relevance to morality. Thus it is not to be thought that the discoveries of the sciences have no relevance to morality. Our moral standards should be determined, in part, by the findings of the sciences I have mentioned. And a change in our moral standards will result in a change in our moral judgments.

Moral standards not only determine our moral judgments of people, but also those of particular actions. A judgment of the moral worth of an action is a judgment concerning how much the action indicates about the moral character of the person. Telling the truth when this has serious consequences for oneself is an action that has significant moral worth. Rescuing a child at great risk to oneself also has significant moral worth. Both of these actions are a strong indication of good moral character. A donation to charity involving no sacrifice has little moral worth, for it does not indicate much about the moral character of the person. Normally we talk of the moral worth of an action only when it is an indication of a good moral character. But we do sometimes talk of an action that is not morally wrong as being morally bad when we mean that it is a strong indication of bad moral character. Thus a morally bad action need not involve either an unjustified violation of a moral rule or the unjustified keeping of it.

I do not suggest that language is used with such precision, nor do I advocate, or even believe it possible, that it be used in this way in the future. However, I think the following may be of some value for being clear about the use of the phrases "morally good," "morally bad," "morally right," and "morally wrong." *Morally good* actions are those that all rational men publicly advocate doing, but do not publicly advocate punishment for not doing. *Morally bad* actions are those that all rational men publicly advocate not doing, without considering the question of punishment. *Morally right* actions are those that all rational men not only publicly advocate doing, but also generally advocate punishment for not doing. *Morally wrong* actions are those that all rational men not only publicly advocate not doing, but also generally publicly advocate punishment for doing. Thus the notions of morally right and morally wrong are closely connected with the notion of punishment, while the notions of morally good and morally bad are not usually connected with it. However, even on this account, it can be seen that "morally bad" and "morally wrong" are much more closely related to each other than are "morally good" and "morally right."

Judgments about the degree to which a person is responsible for some action which falls under the scope of the moral rules or ideals are judgments of blame and credit. In contrast with judgments of moral worth, which are usually made of morally good actions, judgments of responsibility are usually made of morally wrong actions. These judgments are intimately connected with excuses. If one is totally excused from responsibility for an action, then he gets no moral blame or credit for it. But, as we noted in the first chapter, one sometimes has a partial excuse. Thus one has to take some responsibility for the action, though not as much as someone who has no excuse. It is where we assign only partial responsibility that it is most appropriate to talk of credit and blame.

I call the standards one uses to determine how much credit or blame a person should get for a particular action "responsibility standards." These standards determine if one should get full credit or blame, partial credit or blame, or no credit or blame. Thus these standards do not usually result in what I call moral judgments, but in those judgments which determine to what degree, if at all, a person should be subject to moral judgment. The punishment for a certain kind of violation of a moral rule, e.g., disabling a person, is designed for the person who is fully responsible. To judge that he is not completely to blame is to decide that his punishment should be somewhat less than the normal punishment. This is why it is important what responsibility standards are adopted. For judging how much one is to be blamed affects how much he is to be punished.

The usual ways of talking about praise and blame have obscured the distinction between moral standards and responsibility standards. Praise is not the opposite of blame, but of condemnation, and is related to our moral standards. Blame and its opposite, credit, are related to responsibility standards. It is easy to see how the confusion arose. To call a man morally good is to praise him. We only praise a man as morally good if he does morally good actions. But the amount of positive moral worth that his actions have depends upon his being responsible for them. If an action that normally has a certain amount of positive moral worth is one for which we do not give complete credit, this will lessen the amount of moral worth. It will do so because by taking away some credit the action is no longer as strong an indication of the moral character of the person. Since the assignment of credit affects the assignment of moral worth, the two have usually not been clearly distinguished. In similar fashion, how much we condemn a man for an immoral action will depend upon how much we hold him responsible for it. Thus blame and condemnation are often not distinguished.

Another reason why praise and blame have been regarded as opposites may be that each is the dominant member of its pair. Judgments about moral worth are primarily made of morally right and morally good actions. There is no scale of rewards for ranking moral and morally good actions. Moral worth provides a plausible way of ranking moral and morally good actions on a single scale. Punishment does provide a scale for ranking immoral actions; hence there is little need for negative moral worth. Further, we are interested in discouraging all immoral actions; thus there is little point in ranking them. We are interested in encouraging moral and morally good actions, and ranking provides some extra incentive. Judgments of responsibility are primarily concerned with morally wrong or morally bad actions. There is little need to soften responsibility for morally good actions; no one suffers if more credit is given than is deserved. Sometimes it is important to soften responsibility for morally bad actions. Someone suffers more when he is blamed more than he deserves.

How much credit or blame a man deserves will depend upon the responsibility standards that are adopted. The stricter the standards, the greater the excuse needed to reduce the amount of blame. Stricter responsibility standards will probably result in people taking more care not to act immorally. But they will probably also result in more punishment being inflicted on people. Whether or not these statements are true cannot be determined *a priori*, but only by a study of how people actually behave. Just as the proper amount of punishment is determined by seeing what comes closest to maximum deterrence with minimum infliction of evil, so the proper responsibility standards are those that most closely approach this ideal. Psychology, sociology, and anthropology, all are relevant in determining the proper responsibility standards. But no science can decide between two different standards that result in the same amount of evil being suffered.

Some prefer stricter standards with fewer violations, though it is offset by an increase in the amount of punishment. Others prefer the more lenient standards, though the decrease in punishment is offset by an increase in violations. But of two standards both equally effective in discouraging violations, the more lenient is the better. This is exactly parallel to determining the amount of punishment. It is most unlikely that there is a unique determination of both how much a given violation should be punished and how much a given man should be held responsible. This is why the question of what a man deserves has never been answered to everyone's satisfaction.

In applying the responsibility and moral standards, considerations of person, group, place or time are as irrelevant as when applying the moral rules. What may make it seem as if these things are relevant is that we know that people in certain societies or in earlier times lacked some characteristics that are relevant in applying these standards. We do not blame some man in a primitive society for an immoral action as much as we would some person in our society. But this is not simply because he lives in a different society, but because we feel that people in that society lack some relevant characteristic, usually knowledge. We would assign the same amount of blame to someone in our own society who lacked these same characteristics. The standards used both in determining the moral worth of an action and in determining how responsible a man is for his actions are universal standards. They can be applied to all men in all societies.

"Ought" and "should" have often been considered peculiarly moral words. In fact, many have considered them to be the most important words to understand if one wanted to understand moral judgments. Although the two words cannot always be substituted for each other (in fact, it seems as if only "ought to" rather than simply "ought" can be substituted for "should"), it makes no difference to my points which word is used. Thus I shall use the one that sounds to me most natural in the context, and shall not be concerned about establishing conclusions about "ought" from premises about "should." Before I try to give an account of these words as they occur in moral judgments, I shall, as I did with the words "good," "bad," "right," and "wrong," try to provide an account of their use in nonmoral judgments. For, as the slightest consideration of these words shows, "ought" and "should" are most often used in nonmoral judgments, not in moral ones.

The following examples not only show some of the many nonmoral judgments in which "should" and "ought" occur, they also show that "ought to" and "should" are often interchangeable. "You should (ought to) see that movie." "You should (ought to) get some sleep." "I ought to (should) leave now." "You should (ought to) use a lighter shade of lipstick." "You should (ought to) have thought of that sooner." "He ought to (should) have an operation immediately." "He ought to (should) be up by now." "He should (ought to) have three teeth by now." "This bridge should (ought to) have four lanes each way." "All of us ought to (should) quit smoking." "I should (ought to) be studying for the exam now." "I know I should (ought to) have tried harder, but I didn't feel like doing it." "I know I should (ought to) be studying, but I don't feel like it." "There ought to (should) be more blue in that corner." "The lighting should (ought to) suggest a foggy night." "What should (ought) I (to) do now, wash the dishes, or make the bed?" "I don't know what I should (ought to) do."

It is, or should be, clear after looking at the sentences in the preceding paragraph that no simple account of "should" or "ought" will be adequate. To regard statements containing "should" or "ought" as commands is plausible for some of the examples given above but obviously implausible for others. It is, in general, most plausible for those sentences starting with "you" and in the present tense. It has less plausibility for sentences starting with "I," and has almost no plausibility for those sentences starting with "he" or in the past tense. In addition, some of the sentences do not seem to be imperatives in even the widest sense of that term—e.g., "He ought to be up by now," and "He should have three teeth by now."

Our discussion of "right" and "wrong" showed that they were used to describe answers either to theoretical questions or to practical questions. Thus it should not be surprising if "ought" and "should" are also used in two somewhat different contexts—although, as with "right" and "wrong," we should expect that the description of their use in one context will be very similar to the description of their use in the other. However, "right" and "wrong" seem to be more commonly used in theoretical judgments, whereas "ought" and "should" are most often used in practical judgments.

I shall start by attempting to describe their use in nonmoral practical judgments. As used in these judgments, the terms "ought" and "should" are used to advocate a course of conduct. When they are addressed to a particular person, they must advocate a course of conduct that a rational man concerned for that person would advocate. To say to a person that he ought to do something is to imply that the course of action being advocated is one which we, as rational men concerned for him, advocate, and usually suggests that we take an interest in him. To say to a person that he ought to do something, when we do not think that any rational man concerned for him would advocate that course of action to him, is close enough to lying to be a violation of the rule "Don't deceive." In fact, if you said "I think you ought to do it" and thought that the action was one that you as a rational man would not advocate to anyone for whom you were concerned, then you could properly be accused of lying. For to tell a person that he ought to do something is to imply that you are concerned for him.

Nothing said above should be taken as implying that in every situation there is only one course of action that ought to be followed. As we pointed out in Chapter 2, two rational men can act in incompatible ways and both be acting rationally. One person may say to me that x ought to be done, and another maintain that y ought to be done, where x and y are incompatible courses of action. Yet both may be using "ought" correctly. Disagreements about what ought to be done can have several different causes. Even though two people take an interest in me, they may disagree about what is really in my best interest. Even if they agree about what is in my best interest, they may disagree about the best way in which to obtain the desired goal. These disagreements can sometimes be settled, and sometimes they cannot. It may be that one person knows me or my situation better than the other, and upon acquainting the other with this additional information, both agree upon the course of action they would advocate.

There is also the possibility that even though all the relevant facts are known, two people will still disagree upon the course of action they maintain that I ought to follow. In these situations, where there is no right course of action, the course of action that we say ought to be followed will generally reflect our own individual attitudes and desires. Thus an economist and a banker, advising a young man with the ability to be either, may very well advise him to follow different careers, even though they do not disagree on any facts, and both are interested solely in the welfare of the person they are advising. In these cases, it might be better to say "If I were you, I would" rather than "You ought," but one cannot say the latter phrase is being misused in this sort of situation.

There are, however, situations in which every rational person acquainted with the relevant facts and concerned for the individual or individuals involved would advocate the same course of action. All qualified doctors might agree that I ought to have an operation immediately. One is mistaken when he says that I ought to do x, if, given all the facts, no rational man concerned for me would advocate my doing x. Thus, unlike commands, statements containing "ought" or "should" can be mistaken. Of course, someone can make a mistake in *giving* a certain command. One may not mean to say what he did. Also obeying the order may produce results other than those intended. However, a person giving a command need not have any concern for the individual to whom he gives the command. But if you tell a person that he ought to do something, what you tell him to do must be something that a rational person concerned for him might advocate his doing. If it is not, you were either mistaken in telling him he ought to do it, or you were deceiving him.

It should not be thought, however, that every practical judgment containing "should" advocates a course of action for the welfare of the person to whom it is addressed. To say that it must be such that a rational man concerned for me might advocate my doing it, does not rule out the possibility that doing it might not benefit me personally. Thus it is not incorrect to tell me that I ought to do something that will benefit someone else, especially, but not solely, if I am interested in that other person. We often tell people what they ought to do in order to benefit someone in whom they are interested. This is a perfectly acceptable use of "ought." If we take an interest in a person, it is rational to advocate his doing something to benefit someone in whom he takes an interest, even if his doing it will not benefit him personally.

Thus we have the possibility of even greater disagreement among rational men about what I ought to do. For one course of action might benefit me personally; another might benefit someone for whom I am concerned. Given all the facts, it may therefore be that rational men will disagree about the course of action they advocate for me to take. One may advocate a course of action designed to benefit me personally; another may advocate a course of action designed to benefit someone in whom I take an interest. But in either case, it is correct to tell me that I ought to do x, only if x is a course of action that a rational man concerned for me might advocate, and if it is one which you, in fact, being concerned for me, do advocate.

This analysis of "ought" is easily adapted to statements in the first, second, or third person, and in either present or past tense. When I say that I (you, he) ought to do x, I mean that I, as a rational person concerned for myself (you, him), advocate that I (you, he) do x. When I say that he ought to have done x, I mean that I, as a rational person, concerned for him, would have advocated that he do x. In some cases, we may be making an even stronger claim, namely that all rational men would advocate his doing x, or would have advocated his doing it.

I realize that it may sound somewhat strange to talk of my advocating a course of action to myself, but on reflection I hope that this strangeness will disappear. It is not at all unusual for someone to tell himself that such and such is the rational thing to do. Nor is it always the case that one does what he considers the rational thing to do. Thus the proposed analysis accounts as well for statements such as "I know I should have done it, but I didn't feel like it" as it does for the more straightforward statements like "You ought to have an operation."

There is also no difficulty in adapting the analysis to statements such as "This bridge ought to have four lanes each way," and "The lighting ought to suggest a foggy night." Insofar as these statements are addressed to someone who is going to build the bridge or to control the lighting, they are to be understood in the same way as second person, present tense statements containing "should." If we do not wish to rewrite the statements, they can be understood in the following way: "I, as a rational man concerned for the people affected by the bridge (lighting), advocate that the bridge have four lanes each way (that the lighting suggest a foggy night)." Here, again, one may or may not be claiming that all rational men would agree. Whether one is claiming that or not will become clear from what one does if someone disagrees with what one says.

So far I have been concerned solely with the use of "ought" in nonmoral practical judgments. I shall now turn to the use of "ought" in nonmoral theoretical judgments—judgments such as "He ought to be up by now" and "He ought to have three teeth by now." "Ought" is used much less often in judgments of this sort, and most accounts of "ought" have completely ignored its use in this kind of judgment. In these judgments, nothing is being advocated, much less commanded; rather something is claimed or asserted. Depending on the context, "He ought to have three teeth by now" can be taken as a prediction that he now has three teeth or as a claim that he deviates from the normal, generally, though not always, with the suggestion that this is a bad thing. If we do not know how many teeth he has, then our statement is most likely a prediction. If we know that he only has one tooth, it is a claim that he has fewer teeth than is normally expected of a boy his age.

The prediction and the claim are much more closely connected than they seem at first glance. For the prediction is generally made on the basis of one's belief about how many teeth boys of his age generally have. Of course, both the prediction and the claim can be made on somewhat narrower grounds than what is normal for boys of his age. If, for example, everyone in his family has been an early teether, then "He ought to have three teeth by now" can be based on one's beliefs about the age that his brothers and sisters got their teeth. What must be the case, however, is that one have some basis for his remark. If one says "He ought to have three teeth by now," and upon being asked why, he cannot provide any reason, then he has misused the language. We should use "ought" in nonmoral theoretical judgments only when we have beliefs that would lead some rational man to accept the judgment. Of course, sometimes, a belief that leads one rational man to accept a judgment will not lead another one to accept it; but this is a consequence that we should now expect.

Disagreements about whether to accept this kind of "ought" judgment sometimes turn on whether to accept the beliefs that are used to support it. Thus disagreements over these judgments can sometimes be settled by finding out the facts; but not always. Rational men may differ in the weight they give to the support provided by certain facts. There are times, however, when the facts are such that any rational man acquainted with them would accept certain "ought" judgments. Suppose we know that a child has always napped for one hour and then played quietly in his bed for another hour. Then his mother's remark made one hour and forty-five minutes after he went to sleep that he ought to be up by now would be acceptable to all rational men.

So that just like nonmoral practical judgments, nonmoral theoretical judgments containing "ought" sometimes make a stronger claim, sometimes a weaker one. If we say "He ought to be up," then we must at least be claiming that we have some beliefs, which would lead some rational men to accept our judgment. The presence of new information can drastically change our assessment of a judgment. For example, in the case of the mother's remark about her child being up from a nap, information that the child had been given a sleeping pill just before he went to bed today would make us less likely to accept the mother's judgment. Since "ought" judgments are generally made on the basis of many beliefs, a change in one or more need not affect our assessment of an "ought" judgment, but sometimes, as in the example sketched above, it will.

Nonmoral theoretical judgments can be analyzed into a kind of nonmoral practical judgment, viz., I as a rational man advocate believing this prediction or claim. A rational man would advocate believing a prediction or claim only if it was supported by some belief which he accepted and which he thought provided adequate support for the prediction or claim. Thus nothing is lost by analyzing these nonmoral theoretical judgments into practical ones. However, a nonmoral theoretical judgment containing "ought" should always be distinguished from a nonmoral practical judgment containing the same words. But it is a testimony to the power of language that there are occasions on which a theoretical judgment is made with the tone of a practical one, and vice versa. There are even cases in which it is not clear which of the two is meant. Thus "He ought to be up by now," said of a husband rather than a baby, could be either a practical or theoretical judgment. There may be times when even the person who made it is not clear which she meant. So that if you asked her, "Do you mean that you think he's up, or that you think he ought to get up?" she may be unable to answer, or will reply "Both. I think he is up, but if he isn't I think he ought to be."

This may be the time to emphasize again that I am not primarily concerned with providing an account of ordinary language. I am, at most, providing an account of an "idealized" ordinary language. By "idealized," I do not mean a better one, i.e., one that all rational men would prefer, but only one that has less flexibility and more precision than ordinary language. As will be most apparent in the account of "ought" and "should" as they occur in moral judgments, there is no absolutely clear distinction between making a moral judgment and making a nonmoral one. But I believe that these distinctions are helpful. Understanding the analysis that I have given should provide a clearer understanding of the actual use of moral judgments and of nonmoral ones.

Moral judgments containing "ought" or "should" are practical judgments in which a man advocates acting according to the moral rules or moral ideals, e.g., doing morally right and morally good actions. They are practical judgments that a rational man will publicly advocate. I am not maintaining that all practical judgments that a rational man publicly advocates are moral judgments. What I call a "utilitarian judgment," telling someone that he ought to follow the utilitarian ideals, is a judgment that a rational man would publicly advocate. I am maintaining that a moral judgment must be one that would be publicly advocated. If I claim to be making a moral judgment when I say "You ought to do x," then I must be willing to make that judgment to any rational man in similar circumstances. Similar circumstances are those in which the same moral rules or ideals apply, in which the rational desires of the persons involved are the same, and in which the amount of evil to be avoided, prevented, or caused is similar.

This is what gives moral judgments their universal quality, a characteristic that all moral philosophers agree that they have. For in making the moral judgment "You ought to do x," I am implying that I, as a rational man, publicly advocate doing x—i.e. advocate that all rational men in similar circumstances do x. This universal quality distinguishes a moral judgment containing "ought" from most nonmoral judgments containing the same words. When I tell a friend that he ought to do x, I am not committed to telling everyone in similar circumstances, if it can even be determined what similar circumstances are, that he ought to do the same thing. But if I make a moral judgment, then I am committed to making that same judgment to any man in similar circumstances.

As I pointed out previously, there is sometimes disagreement among rational men about what ought to be done. It follows from this that sometimes two rational men will make incompatible moral judgments about what ought to be done. If these disagreements cannot be settled, two or more rational men will publicly advocate different courses of action. In this situation, a rational man who makes a moral judgment is expressing his personal public attitude. But of course he is not doing just this. For even if there are several different courses of action that might be publicly advocated by rational men, there are many more that no rational man would publicly advocate.

Thus even where there is disagreement among rational men about what action ought to be done, if they are making moral judgments, there is a very distinct limit to what they can say. The course of action that the rational man advocates in making a moral judgment must be one that he would advocate in all similar cases. Thus agreement about the moral judgment to be made can sometimes be achieved, not by producing new information, but by getting the person to see that he would not make this same judgment if some other person was involved. But even in those cases where rational men cannot agree about what morally ought to be done, there is agreement about what the relevant considerations are, and about what considerations are not relevant. Thus, though they may disagree about this case, they can agree that if the facts were somewhat different, they would agree. There are some cases in which all rational men must agree on what morally ought to be done.

All rational men must publicly agree that one ought to do what is morally right, and that one ought not to do what is morally wrong. This is a mere tautology. But, given the analysis of morally right and morally wrong, it shows that moral judgments about what one ought to do are capable of being mistaken. Someone making the moral judgment that *x* ought to be done can be shown that he was mistaken by showing that doing *x* is morally wrong. Further, moral judgments about what one ought to do, even if they cannot be lies, can be deceitful. For we can know that an action is morally wrong and claim to be making the moral judgment that one ought to do it. Thus moral judgments containing "ought" or "should" cannot be made simply according to the whim of the person making them. In some cases, only one moral judgment is correct. In others, there may be a number of permissible moral judgments, though this number will generally be quite small in proportion to the moral judgments that are not permitted.

There are two distinct kinds of moral judgments in which "ought" occurs. One is that moral judgment in which one publicly advocates obeying a moral rule. The other is that in which one publicly advocates following a moral ideal. In either of these cases, one may find complete agreement, or partial disagreement. We have already pointed out that there are occasions in which not all rational men agree that one ought to obey a moral rule. It is equally clear that rational men can disagree about whether one ought to follow a moral ideal. In fact, in the latter case there is room for much more disagreement. For though all rational men publicly advocate following the moral ideals, they do not, as with the moral rules, publicly advocate that everyone always follow them.

When "ought" is used in those moral judgments advocating obedience to a moral rule, and no rational man would publicly advocate violating the rule, then "ought" has a stronger sense than when advocating following the moral ideals. For in these cases all rational men not only agree in publicly advocating obedience to the rule, they also publicly advocate liability to punishment for disobedience. We can describe this sense of "ought" by saying that it is used when all rational men publicly demand that a certain course of action be followed. This may be that sense of "ought" which Kant had in mind when he talked of a categorical imperative.

It is this sense of "ought" that philosophers seem to have in mind when they use the words "oblige" and "obligation." I prefer not to use these words. It seems to me that these words have their normal use only in connection with the three positively stated moral rules: "Keep your promise"; "Obey the law"; "Do your duty." To stretch the use is to invite misunderstanding. I have not been concerned with these words because there is no philosophically important reason to distinguish the positively stated rules from the negatively stated ones. It is not that there are no philosophically interesting things to say about obligation; it is only that these things do not have any important bearing on moral philosophy.

One need not be concerned for a person in order to make a moral judgment that he ought to do x. However, when actually making a moral judgment to some person about what he ought to do, one is generally expected to have some concern for him. If I tell a person for whom I obviously have no concern "You ought to do x," even if I intend this to be a moral judgment, he may legitimately reply, "You can't tell me what I ought to do; you don't care about me." The legitimacy of this reply stems in part from the fact that moral and nonmoral judgments are not totally distinct. Although we can tell anyone that a certain action is morally right or morally wrong, when we say to someone that he ought to do something, even when making a moral judgment, we suggest that we are concerned for him. Thus most moral judgments telling someone what he ought to do also must have a characteristic of a nonmoral judgment, namely that one be concerned for the person to whom one is making the judgment. This brings us to the question we shall discuss in the next chapter, "Why should one be moral?"

CHAPTER 10

WHY SHOULD ONE BE
MORAL?

M<small>ANY PHILOSOPHERS HAVE HELD</small> that the question "Why should one be moral?" is a senseless or pointless question. I believe that this is due to their misunderstanding of the question. They interpret the question as "Why would a rational man publicly advocate that one be moral?" Taken in this way, the question is pointless, for the answer is obvious. All rational men must publicly advocate that everyone act morally. But the question is not a request for a moral judgment. Rather, it is a request for a nonmoral practical judgment. Understood in this way the question becomes "Why would a rational man concerned for me advocate that I be moral?" This is not a senseless question. It may very well be that some rational men concerned for me will advocate that I not be moral. However, some rational men concerned with me will advocate that I be moral. Why they would advocate this provides the answer to the question "Why should one be moral?"

This question must be asked by someone who thinks you are concerned for him. To really appreciate its force, consider that you have been asked it by one of your children or a younger sister or brother. What would you answer? There are many things you could say. You could point out that it was generally in one's self-interest to be moral, that people who were moral were generally happier than those who were not. When talking to those whose character is not yet formed, this point takes on even more significance. If you were religious, you could add that God wants one to be moral, and that he will reward those who are. But you could say more than this. You could talk of your ideal of a man—one with all the virtues, moral and personal—and say that you wanted him to be such a man. To want him to become your ideal of a man certainly shows your interest in him. You could talk of integrity and dignity, pointing out that since he must publicly advocate obedience to the moral rules, it would be hypocritical not to be moral himself.

Finally you could point out to him that though you were concerned for him, you were also concerned for others, and that in large measure, you advocate his being moral, not so much out of your concern for him as out of your concern for everyone. There is nothing wrong, morally or otherwise, with advocating a course of action to someone for whom you are concerned, which is not advocated out of concern for him. As long as you would advocate this course of action to anyone for whom you are concerned, you need not advocate it out of your concern for him. If you have instilled in him a concern for others, then this final answer will have the most force. If you have not, then there is a good chance that none of your answers will seem persuasive.

Many attempts to answer the question seem to take it as asking for reasons of self-interest for being moral. But though it is usually in one's self-interest to be moral, it will sometimes not be so. It is not even always in one's self-interest to seem moral, though in any well-run society it almost always will be. But no answer in terms of self-interest is completely satisfactory. What is desired by those who ask the question "Why should one be moral?" is an answer that will apply always, and not just generally. What is desired is an answer in terms of the intrinsic nature of morality.

This was partially realized by Plato, who tried to offer reasons of self-interest for being moral, but at the same time to make these reasons intrinsic to morality. The result of this was to make morality intrinsically self-interested, though with a strange kind of self-interest, viz., harmony of the soul. But as we have seen, acting morally is not necessarily in one's self-interest. There is a connection between self-interest and morality, but any attempt to make this direct results in a distortion of the concept of morality or of the concept of self-interest, or both.

However, not all reasons are reasons of self-interest. As we have seen, reason is a wider concept than self-interest, and allows a concern for the welfare of others. Thus in asking "Why should I be moral?" one need not be asking, and, I think, generally is not asking "What's in it for me?" but rather "What is the point of my being moral?" Since being moral is usually regarded as simply obeying a certain set of rules, it is not self-evident that there is anything to be gained by anyone by his acting morally. This is especially true if there is no distinction made between those moral rules which can be justified, either with or without reference to the customs or institutions of one's society, and those which do not have a justification at all. In many societies the genuine or justifiable moral rules are not distinguished from those rules or traditions which the society, by some accident or design, has grouped together with them.

Thus I should imagine that the question "Why should I be moral?" or its practical equivalent in many circumstances, "Why shouldn't I do it if I want to?" is most often asked in connection with rules concerning sexual relations. "Why should I refrain from having sexual intercourse before marriage?" Simply to say it is immoral to have sexual relations outside of marriage is not a sufficient answer. If no one is hurt, what is wrong with my breaking what my society considers a moral rule? The question "Why should I be moral?" can only be answered if restricted to justified moral rules. To the general question "Why should I be moral?" we must agree with others who have said this question is unanswerable as it stands. But this agreement masks a larger disagreement. Others have not made the distinction between justified moral rules and unjustified ones. They have simply used morality to mean justified morality. They would say that there was no answer to the question "Why should I obey the justified moral rules?" This is not what I am saying at all. I am simply pointing out the obvious truism, that there is no intrinsic reason to obey unjustified moral rules.

It could, of course, be claimed that there is an intrinsic reason to obey even unjustified moral rules: namely, you will be punished if you are caught violating the rules. Though this answer is correct, its very correctness shows us that it is not the answer we were looking for. For this answer gives us no better reason for obeying the justified moral rules than for obeying the unjustified ones. But our analysis of morality makes clear why punishment is not just accidentally connected to violation of the moral rules, and thus explains why this answer has some force. However, "You will be punished" does not really answer the question "Why should I be moral?" but only the question "Why should I seem moral?" One might, of course, claim that it is impossible to seem moral without being moral. But this claim, though it may hold generally, certainly does not hold universally. We are interested in finding a reason that holds universally.

One way of making this answer hold universally is to bring in God. God always knows if you are really moral or only seem to be, and he will punish you if you are not really moral. Thus some claim that belief in God is a necessary support of morality. But this claim is a version of the view that only self-interest, in this case avoidance of the wrath of God, can provide the reason for acting morally. The answer in terms of religious self-interest avoids one of the difficulties that all answers in terms of natural self-interest have. It is simply false that it is always in our natural self-interest to act morally. However, the religious self-interest answer is not primarily an answer to the question "Why should I be moral?" but rather to the question "Why should I do as God commands?" Of course, if God commands us to be moral, then we do have an answer to our original question also.

The religious self-interest answer to the question "Why should I be moral?" is not the only religious answer. There is also what I prefer to call the genuine religious answer, viz., the love of God. The genuine religious answer to the question "Why should I be moral?" is that God will be pleased if you are. And since God knows when one only seems to be moral, it provides a reason for actually being moral. But this reason, like that of religious self-interest, does not distinguish moral from nonmoral rules. In both cases we obey the moral rules because God happens to command us to. However, it does make sense for God not to command us to obey the moral rules; and in fact, to command us to break one of the rules unjustifiably. God commanded Abraham to sacrifice his son Isaac.

On a practical level, the most serious defect with both religious answers is that they depend upon the belief in a God, and a God of a very special sort, viz., one who commands obedience to the moral rules. A rational man need not believe in such a God. So these answers provide no reason at all for him to be moral. What we want is an answer that all rational men must acknowledge as a reason. I say only that it would be acknowledged as a reason by any rational man, not that it would provide a motive for all rational men. I am not claiming to be able to provide an answer to the question "Why should I be moral?" such that every rational man, if aware of this answer, would act morally. On the contrary, I emphatically deny the possibility of such an answer, as it would have as a result that all immoral action was due to ignorance or irrationality.

Some would not find this consequence, that all immoral action is due to ignorance or irrationality, unacceptable. On the contrary, Plato tried to show, at least on some interpretations, that no one ever knowingly did evil. However, Plato did not clearly distinguish between immoral action and irrational action. It is generally true that anyone who acts so as to bring evil on himself or those he cares about is acting either unknowingly or irrationally. It is not true that all immoral action is either unknowing or irrational. Immoral action usually involves doing evil to those we do not care about (or care about enough) in order to please or benefit ourselves or those we do care about. There is nothing irrational in this, unless we accept the very dubious Platonic account of the harmony of the soul.

There is a great temptation to accept such an account. Freud has often been twisted in such a way as to yield the conclusion that the immoral man is always sick. But though most murders may be due to mental illness, it is completely implausible to account for all immoral action in this way. The wicked suffer torments of the soul only if they have a certain kind of superego, which all of them do not have. Even if all of the wicked do suffer some pangs of conscience (a very doubtful view), it is very likely that their ill-gotten gains very often more than compensate for such pangs. To hold that the wicked never profit from their wickedness is a view that I, as much as anyone, would prefer to be true. Unfortunately, all of the evidence appears to show that it is false. But there is another view, which I think my account of morality supports, namely, that a moral man stands a better chance of being happy than an immoral one. I think the evidence appears to show that this view is true. I am only denying that there is any plausible account of human nature such that it is never in one's self-interest to unjustifiably violate a moral rule.

The question "Why should I be moral?" is most likely to be asked by those concerned with morality, such as Glaucon and Adimantus; thus we should be wary of dismissing the question as a request for proving the self-interest of morality. Providing an answer to this question is one good way of distinguishing bogus from genuine or justifiable morality. If we cannot give an answer to it, then we should begin to question the justification of that morality. But we do have a justification of some moral rules. With regard to these rules we should be able to give a satisfactory answer; though, of course, not one in terms of self-interest.

The moral rules prohibit causing evil. This provides us with a ready-made answer to our question. One should be moral because he will cause someone else to suffer evil if he is not. Note that this is a moral reason or answer to the question "Why should one be moral?" As such it should apply in all cases rather than merely generally. We can now distinguish between being moral and the reasons for being moral. Included among these reasons is what I shall call the moral reason, to avoid causing evil. Note that this is a perfectly acceptable answer to the question. It is one that might serve to convince someone who had actually asked the question. Pointing out to him that others will suffer because of his immoral action may be sufficient to make him give up that course of action. For he may not have thought of this, or have given it sufficient weight.

It is because one usually knows the moral rules before one knows their justification that it is possible to fail to distinguish justifiable moral rules from unjustifiable ones. And it is primarily the presence of unjustifiable moral rules that leads some to ask "Why should I be moral?" It is important and interesting that "Because you will cause someone to suffer evil if you are not" is an appropriate answer only when asked about the justifiable moral rules. It also keeps open the possibility of distinguishing between actually being moral and only seeming to be so. It thus differs from all religious answers. It is also an answer that derives from the point of morality itself, not one that has only an accidental relation to morality.

However, though this answer can always be given to anyone contemplating a violation of the first five rules, it is not always an appropriate reply to someone contemplating the violation of one of the second five rules. And it is with regard to the second five rules that the question is more likely to be asked. Although violation of any of the second five rules generally results in someone suffering evil, some unjustifiable violations of each of the second five rules do not result in anyone suffering evil. Thus, when no one will suffer evil, one may wonder if one should tell the truth when doing so would be contrary to one's interest. Why should one be moral in this case? The straightforward answer "Because you will cause someone to suffer evil" is not adequate here. Although this would be an appropriate answer for not lying most of the time, it does not seem appropriate in the particular case we are considering.

I am not concerned now with the question "Why in general shouldn't I deceive, break my word, cheat, disobey the law, or neglect my duty?" The answer to these questions is the same as for the first five rules: "You will cause someone to suffer evil consequences." Thus it might seem as if the answer to the question "Why in this particular case shouldn't I deceive, cheat, etc." is "It is likely or probable that your act will cause someone to suffer evil consequences." But in some cases this is not true. It is not likely or probable that your act will cause someone to suffer evil consequences. From the fact that disobeying these rules generally results in someone suffering evil consequences, it follows that many individual acts of this sort are likely to have these consequences. But it does not follow that some particular act is likely to have them. It is the offering of this reason in the cases where it does not fit that renders it suspect. It is a good reason not to violate a moral rule on a particular occasion that it is likely or probable that your act will cause someone to suffer evil consequences. But it is not a good reason when this is not likely or probable.

I now wish to provide an answer to the question "Why should I be moral?" when this is asked of a justifiable moral rule, and cannot be answered by "Your act will cause or is likely to cause evil consequences to someone." Otherwise I must admit that there is an unbridgeable gap between the justification of the moral rules and the possibility of always answering the question "Why should I be moral?" But even admitting this gap in some cases should not make us overlook that there is no gap in the most important and most clear-cut cases. Thus the justification of the moral rules provides an answer to the question "Why should I be moral?" in very many cases. The answer is not a religious one or one of self-interest, but a moral one —one which is intrinsic to morality.

We are now dealing with a very limited class of actions, those actions which are an unjustifiable violation of some moral rule, and yet one cannot say that someone will suffer (or is likely to suffer) evil consequences because of that act. These are those violations of the second five rules, particularly the last three, when a single violation causes no harm; but one cannot publicly advocate such violation because general violation would have serious evil consequences. Here the moral virtues come into play very importantly. We noted that no moral virtues are specifically connected to each of the first five moral rules. We do not need them, for our moral reason is sufficient to offer an answer to the question "Why should I be moral?" But each of the second five moral rules is connected quite tightly to a moral virtue: to the rule concerning deceit we have truthfulness; to promises, trustworthiness; to cheating, fairness; to obeying the law, honesty; and to duty, dependability.

The answer to the question "Why should I be moral?" when it is not likely that my action will have evil consequences for anyone is connected to the moral answer by means of the virtues. As noted in Chapter 8, virtues and vices are built on habit and by precedent. Following the moral rule generally builds the virtue, and contrary action generally builds the vice. The reason for following the moral rule in the peculiar situation when no one would be harmed by an unjustified violation sounds like a prudential one; i.e., it builds your character. This may sound more like a Platonic reason of self-interest than a moral reason. But it is not, for a virtuous man is much less likely to cause evil consequences to others. Building one's virtue makes one less likely to unjustifiably break moral rules when it is likely that this will cause someone to suffer evil consequences.

It should not be surprising that the moral answer to the question "Why should I be moral?" is direct and universally connected with the first five moral rules, and only generally and indirectly connected to the second five. For we saw in the justification of the moral rules that the first five rules provided the basis for the second five. Hence it is not surprising that the moral answer to the question "Why should I be moral?" is indirect when applied to these second five rules. But, though indirect and involving the moral virtues, the second five rules are by no means loosely connected with the moral reason. The moral virtues, when properly understood, necessarily lead to causing less evil than the vices. However, blind following of the moral rules, especially the second five, could be disastrous.

I have admitted that the moral answer to the question "Why should I be moral?" sometimes requires one to make use of the virtues. But the virtues need not figure solely as an aid to the moral answer to the question. There is what could be called the virtuous answer to the question "Why should I be moral?" This answer makes use of the fact that some men aspire to a good character. The most plausible view of a good character is that it contains all of the virtues, both moral and personal. If one aspires to a character of this sort, then he must act morally. For clearly one cannot have the moral virtues unless he acts morally. One who acts morally because he aspires to a good character need not even be concerned with others. Rather he need only be concerned with attaining a goal that he has set himself. It is certainly a worthy goal, one that all rational men would publicly advocate that all men aim toward. I do not think, however, that the virtuous answer will have much appeal to anyone for whom the moral answer has no force. Although one needs no reason for aspiring to a character which includes the moral virtues, it is very unlikely that one will aspire to it unless he does have a reason. The most persuasive reason for wanting such a character is the moral reason. But the virtuous answer, like the moral answer, is one that has an intrinsic connection to morality. Further, it always provides a direct answer for being moral.

There is a third answer that has an intrinsic connection to morality. This answer makes use of the fact that, as a rational man trying to reach agreement with all other rational men, one must publicly advocate the moral attitude toward the moral rules. One may be persuaded to act morally because reason, including his own, publicly requires acting in this way. I call this answer the rational answer to the question "Why should I be moral?" If one aspires to act in the way that reason publicly requires, then he must act morally. The rational answer is quite similar to the virtuous one; neither one requires concern for anyone else. Yet both can always provide a direct answer for being moral. However, neither of them by itself seems to me to be very persuasive. Of course, one needs no reason for wanting to act as reason publicly requires. But unless one accepts the moral reason as persuasive, I do not see why he would want to act in this way.

There is one illegitimate motive for wanting to act this way. It is illegitimate because it is based on a confusion. The confusion involves the relationship between what reason publicly requires and what reason requires. "Reason publicly requires acting morally" simply means that all rational men publicly advocate acting morally. "Reason requires acting morally" means that it is irrational to act immorally. As I have continually pointed out, and shall discuss again later in this chapter, reason does not require acting morally; it only allows acting in this way. Reason does not require acting in the way reason publicly requires. If one does not clearly distinguish between what reason requires and what reason publicly requires, then he may conclude that it is irrational to act immorally. It seems likely that Kant was involved in this confusion.

But though I believe that neither the rational answer nor the virtuous answer is as important as the moral answer, I believe that they are important. It may be that some men have been brought up so as to desire to have a character including all the moral virtues, and that other men have been brought up to desire to act in the way that reason publicly requires. If they have, I have no desire to discourage them. More important, these answers strengthen the moral answer. It may be that the moral answer, making no reference to oneself, is, by itself, not enough to persuade most people to act morally. Thus these latter two answers, though grounded in the moral answer, go beyond it and carry some significant force of their own. Indeed, this is evidenced by the fact that some common emotions, with obvious power to move men, seem related to these answers as well as to the moral one.

Compassion is intimately connected with the moral answer. Combined with a proper understanding of morality, compassion may lead one to genuinely accept the moral answer. I believe that those who ask "Why should I be moral?" do not lack the necessary compassion. They do have compassion for others, but they do not see how morality, which they regard as simply a traditional set of rules, has any relationship to it. The moral answer is the answer they want, if only they can be made to see it. That they have compassion is shown by the fact that they often suffer remorse when they actually do harm someone, even if unintentionally. To suffer remorse is to suffer because of some harm you have caused. Thus remorse is simply compassion felt in some special circumstances. The special circumstances are those in which you consider yourself responsible for someone suffering some evil. Thus a compassionate man will often feel remorse when acting immorally. Violations of the first five rules are most likely to cause remorse.

The emotion most closely connected with the virtuous answer is pride. Of course, pride is appropriate to more than one's virtues. One can take pride in one's abilities, work, family, or country. One can take pride in anything that one believes makes him superior to other men. To feel pride in something is to feel pleasure because one believes that thing makes him superior to other men. Since all rational men consider, at least publicly, a character containing the moral virtues to be superior to one not containing them, it is obviously appropriate to take pride in one's moral virtues. He who does take pride in his moral character will suffer shame when he acts immorally. To feel shame is to feel sad due to loss of pride or because of something that one believes makes one inferior to other men. The desire to maintain one's pride and to avoid feeling shame provide strong motives to some for being moral. Pride and shame are also closely related to the moral ideals. One often feels pride when acting on the moral ideals, and shame is commonly caused by failure to act.

The feeling of guilt seems most closely connected with the rational answer. One is found guilty of having unjustifiably broken some rule. Although guilt is often most closely associated with legal rules or laws, one can also be guilty of having unjustifiably broken some moral rule. Feeling guilty is anxiety due to one's belief that one is guilty. Children often feel guilt when they violate the rules laid down by their parents or teachers. But adults may not feel guilt unless the rules they violate are ones that they consider justified. The rational answer emphasizes that the moral rules are rules toward which all rational men, including oneself, publicly advocate obedience. Thus for one who accepts the rational answer, feeling guilt is unavoidable when he acts immorally. The desire to avoid feeling guilt may provide a strong motive for acting morally. Unjustified violation of the second five moral rules seems to be the most common cause of feeling guilt.

The rational answer can also be used to explain and justify some of our talk about conscience. This should not be surprising, as pangs of conscience are often considered identical to guilt feelings. By regarding conscience as one's public attitude, we can come to understand how this identification was made. Letting your conscience be your guide is equivalent to acting as you publicly advocate. Going against your conscience is doing what you know you would publicly advocate not doing. Regarding conscience as one's public attitude rather than as the superego takes conscience out of psychology and brings it back to morality where it belongs. However, it is easy to understand how conscience came to be identified with the superego. Most of what our public attitude tells us to do, we learned from our parents. Concerned primarily with the explanation of behavior and not its justification, Freud and his followers made no attempt to distinguish between the internalized parental teaching which was justifiable and that which was not. Thus conscience was swallowed up by the superego, and lost its moral significance. By identifying conscience with one's public attitude, we give conscience back its traditional moral authority.

The rational answer is also connected with the concept of authenticity. Authenticity excludes hypocrisy. Hypocrisy is not exactly deceit, but is closely related to it. It consists in advocating that others act in a way that one does not intend to act oneself. Some people have maintained that authenticity is all that is required for acting morally. That is correct only if one is trying to reach agreement among all rational men. Since such a person must publicly advocate acting morally it is plausible to maintain that an authentic man is a moral man. Being authentic such a man will act in the way that he publicly advocates that all other men act. In somewhat older terminology, which I prefer, such a man would be called a man of integrity.

If one takes cheating as the model of immoral action, he may look upon the moral rules as the rules which govern the game of life. Looking at them in this way, he may regard it as beneath his dignity to be immoral. He may think that if he cannot win the game of life without violating the moral rules, he does not deserve to win. One who views morality in this way may also find the rational answer most persuasive. The difference between dignity and integrity is very small. I think, however, that dignity has a closer relationship to pride. To act beneath one's dignity is to suffer shame; to violate one's integrity is to suffer guilt. A man of dignity is one who truly believes "It matters not whether you win or lose, but how you play the game." But unless one accepts the moral answer, I do not see why one should accept the moral rules as the rules for the game of life.

Although I believe that pride, and a desire for authenticity, integrity, or dignity may lead one to act morally, I doubt that they will do so unless one also has compassion. However, if one has pride and integrity, in addition to compassion, then he has additional reasons for being moral. Being moral is required to avoid not only remorse, but also shame and guilt. But all of these reasons have an air of self-interest about them. I do not think self-interest, no matter how far it is extended, provides the fundamental reason for being moral. The fundamental reason for being moral is to avoid causing evil for others. The fundamental reason for being morally good is to prevent others from suffering evil. All of the other reasons seem to me to have little force unless this reason has force—although I grant that the force of the moral reason is increased significantly by the addition of these other reasons.

I have provided a number of answers to the question "Why should one be moral?" Some, like the answers in terms of self-interest and those which involve religious belief, I have found wanting. For I think that these answers do not really address themselves directly to the question. I admit that acting morally is generally in one's self-interest; indeed I have tried to show why this is so, but I cannot admit that it is always so. Further, I think that those who ask the question are not really looking for an answer in terms of self-interest but one which explains the point of morality. The religious answer may satisfy some, but I, personally, do not find it self-evident that I should do what it is claimed that God commands. The answer that I find most satisfactory is the moral answer. This answer is truly an answer to the question. It stems from the very nature of morality. Once one accepts this reason, I think it can be supported by other reasons: those involving pride, integrity, and dignity. But the fundamental reason for being moral is to avoid causing evil for others.

I think that this is the best one can get in the way of reasons for being moral, unless one is prepared to make some highly dubious hypotheses about human nature, or the nature of the world. I am not prepared to make these hypotheses. First, any that would even be plausible would provide no better reasons than these reasons. Second, I think these reasons are good enough. They are good enough reasons to make it completely rational for any person to be moral at any time. However, I do not claim—in fact, I deny—that they are good enough reasons to make it irrational for one ever to be immoral. Although the moral reason, even with its supporting reasons, will not lead all rational men to act morally, it will lead some. Further, even those who do not accept the moral reason for acting morally would be rational if they did so.

Some might take the previous paragraph to be an admission of ultimate failure to answer the question "Why should I be moral?" I have stated, or at least implied, that it is perfectly sensible to ask "Why should I avoid causing evil for others?" Thus it might be concluded that giving the answer "You will avoid causing evil for others" does not really answer the question. But this conclusion is not warranted. Simply because it is sensible to ask "Why should I avoid causing evil for others?" it does not follow that avoiding causing evil for others does not provide an adequate reason for being moral. The objection claims that if I can sensibly ask "Why should I do X?" when X is the reason for doing Y, then X can't be an adequate reason for doing Y. But when stated in this general way, we can see the mistake involved. It is due to a concept of a reason which we have shown to be false, that an adequate reason for doing a particular action is one that all rational men will act on.

What some people desire when they ask the question "Why should I be moral?" is an answer that will show that reason requires acting morally, not merely that it is allowed by reason to act so. But as I have tried to show, reason rarely requires acting in one way rather than another. I think that the reluctance to accept this answer is due to the belief that reason does always require one kind of action—acting in one's own self-interest. The equation of rational action with action in one's self-interest is so strong that the question "Why should I do X?" is often taken to mean no more than "How will doing X be in my self-interest?" Thus the question "Why should I be moral?" is considered not really answered by "Because you will avoid causing evil for others." Although this gives me a reason of sorts for being moral, it is not really the right kind of reason. Not all rational men will act in accord with it. Supposedly, the only answer that all rational men will act on is "Because it is in your self-interest." I have admitted that this answer cannot always be truthfully given.

I should now like to show that the answer "Because it is in your self-interest" is not a reason that all rational men must act on. However, first I should like to discuss a slightly different question so as to provide as close a parallel to the moral case as possible. Let us consider the question "Why should I be prudent?" This is a question that is asked, though perhaps not in exactly these terms, by many people, especially by teen-agers. Just as "Why shouldn't I do it if I want to?" is sometimes equivalent to "Why should I be moral?" so it is also sometimes equivalent to "Why should I be prudent?" In the former case, my answer is "You will cause evil for someone"; in the latter, "You will suffer evil yourself." We are inclined to think it perfectly rational to go on and ask "Why shouldn't I cause evil for others?" but to be irrational to reply "Why shouldn't I cause myself to suffer evil?" This inclination is not merely due to a prejudice in favor of oneself over others. The two questions are not usually asked in the same circumstances. When we ask "Why shouldn't I cause evil for others?" a further clause is generally understood, viz., "if it benefits me." The question is really "Why should I be concerned for others rather than myself?" I have already stated that reason does not require being concerned for others, especially when it is at some cost to oneself.

The question "Why shouldn't I cause myself to suffer evil?" is not understood in the same way, i.e., with the unstated clause "if it benefits me." With the question "Why shouldn't I cause myself to suffer evil?" the unstated clause is generally something like "if I want to." When asking why we should not harm others, we implicitly contrast concern for others with self-interest. When asking why we should not harm ourselves, we contrast self-interest with passions. Someone who smokes, or drinks, or takes drugs when told that these activities will harm him may reply, "So what, I want to." Here if we think the harm is great enough, we consider the action irrational. Thus it seems as if asking "Why shouldn't I cause myself to suffer evil?" is, if it is a serious evil, an irrational question—one that no rational man would ask. Hence it seems that the answer "You will harm yourself if you do that" is one that all rational men would accept for not doing something, whereas "You will harm someone else if you do that" is not acceptable to all rational men.

But we are still not clear enough. When asking why I should not cause evil for others, I contrasted this with benefiting myself. However, when I asked why I should not cause evil for myself, I did not contrast it with the prevention of evil to others, but with a desire to do something irrational. It is not that, considered by themselves,

"Why shouldn't I harm others?" is a perfectly sensible question and "Why shouldn't I harm myself?" is a senseless one. The sense of the question depends upon the unstated clause that goes with the question. It is not senseless to ask "Why shouldn't I harm myself?" if the unstated clause is "if I can thereby prevent harm to others." This question with this unstated clause is one that is asked, though perhaps not in these words, by many people, particularly young men and women. It is not unusual to hear a father try to persuade his son not to join the Peace Corps or not to join the fight for civil rights, by pointing out that he will harm himself. And it is not unusual to hear the son reply that this is not a good enough reason, that avoidance of harm to himself does not take precedence over trying to help others. Thus it can be seen that "Why shouldn't I harm myself?" is not always a senseless question. Avoidance of harm to oneself does not always provide a reason that all rational men will act on.

It is, of course, possible to call irrational all those who are willing to sacrifice their own interests for the interests of others. But one who did this could only do it by arbitrarily defining rational action as action done for one's own self-interest. We do not ordinarily limit rational action in this way, as I showed in Chapter 2. Since it is rational to sacrifice your interests for the interests of others, the reply "You will harm yourself if you do that" is not a reason that all rational men must act on. It does provide a good reason for not doing something, but in doing this it does no more than the reply "You will harm someone if you do that." The two reasons are on a par. It is allowed by reason to guide one's action by either one. Of course, one who accepts the avoidance of harm to others as the more important reason will be a moral man, while one who considers his own self-interest most important will probably not be. But neither man will be irrational. Thus, while I have shown that reason allows acting morally, I have also shown that it allows acting immorally.

Thus it seems as if reason is of no use as a guide to action. This, of course, is not so; reason is incompatible with many kinds of action, as pointed out in Chapter 2. But it is true that in the important decisions about whether to act morally, reason does not provide the guide. When morality and self-interest conflict, even when morality and the interests of friends or family conflict, reason takes no sides. Disappointing as this conclusion seems at first, we should see that any other conclusion would be worse. Were reason ever to prohibit acting morally, we would be forced, in the case of conflict, to advocate either irrational or immoral behavior. If reason was always to require acting morally, we would be forced to regard all immoral action as irrational, including that which was clearly in the self-interest of the agent. Contrasted with either of these alternatives, the conclusion seems far less disappointing than before.

I have shown that reason does not always require acting morally, and I have also shown that reason does not always require acting in one's self-interest. However, I have shown that reason always allows one to act morally or to act in one's self-interest. But there is a danger that one will come to think that reason prohibits acting in any way that is both immoral and contrary to one's self-interest. This has not been shown. Indeed, it is false. Reason allows action that is both immoral and contrary to one's self-interest. This has generally been overlooked by philosophers who have considered all rational actions to be either moral actions or those of self-interest. Further, they have often held that these two kinds of actions not only exhaust the category of rational actions but that they are mutually exclusive. Thus some seem to hold that self-interest cannot provide additional motives for acting morally, and that morality always requires one to act contrary to one's self-interest.

It should be immediately clear that morality cannot always require one to act contrary to one's self-interest. So many actions that are in our self-interest fall outside the sphere of morality that this view is not even plausible. Further, even when our actions are covered by a moral rule or ideal, it may be in our self-interest to act morally. This becomes clear when we remember the various common emotions that are so intimately connected with the various answers that were given to the question "Why should one be moral?" It is in our self-interest to avoid shame, guilt, and remorse, and often we must act morally if we wish to avoid them. Further, the risk of punishment and the enmity of those affected by the immoral action may also lead one to act morally. Thus it should be clear that self-interest and morality are not mutually exclusive. In a country with a good government, self-interest and morality often provide reasons for doing the same action.

It is commonly thought that when self-interest and morality both require acting in a certain way, reason prohibits acting in any other way. We have seen that the desire for revenge may lead one to act irrationally. Hate may have the same result. Thus philosophers have often thought that were they to show that self-interest always requires acting morally, they would have shown that immoral action is irrational. We have already seen that self-interest does not always require acting morally, but even if it did, this would not have made reason prohibit acting immorally. There are other reasons for acting immorally besides reasons of self-interest. These reasons are beliefs that our action will benefit some person or group in whom we take an interest. Such a belief may lead us to act even though we know the action is both immoral and contrary to our own self-interest. Parents often act immorally for the sake of their children, when they would not do so for themselves. Their interest in their children is greater than their concern for themselves and for morality. Lovers not only sacrifice themselves, but others, for the sake of the loved one. Reason need not prohibit such actions.

It is important to realize that a rational action can be both immoral and contrary to one's self-interest. Failure to realize this, together with the view that all rational actions are either required by self-interest or by morality, leads to the view that whenever a rational person sacrifices himself for others he is acting morally. But violating the moral rules when one could not publicly advocate such a violation is immoral even if one is willing to sacrifice one's life in performing the violation. Unjustified violations of the moral rules which are contrary to one's self-interest are not just a logical possibility. On the contrary, without underestimating the amount of evil caused by immoral actions done from motives of self-interest, I think that considerably more evil has been caused by immoral actions that were contrary to the self-interest of the agent. Religions have provided motives for men to act in ways that were both immoral and contrary to their self-interest. Some of these actions may have been irrational—i.e., no one was believed to have benefited from them—but some were thought to benefit some people, either in this life or the next. The amount of evil caused by self-sacrificing immoral actions for religious reasons is incredible. So many men have not only slaughtered others but risked their own lives in advancing the interests of their religion that it is impossible to hold that self-interest is the sole cause of immoral action.

But religion is only one of many sources of reasons for being immoral. One is often immoral in order to advance the interests of one's social or economic class. And sometimes these immoral actions require some sacrifice of self-interest. Men often act both immorally and contrary to their self-interest, in order to advance the interests of their race or ethnic group. But today probably the greatest and most serious source of reasons for being immoral come from one's country. Many men are not only willing, but anxious, to sacrifice their lives for their country even when their country is engaged in an immoral war. The evil caused by immoral actions due to nationalism probably outweighs the evil caused by the immoral actions due to all other reasons put together. Taking an interest in one's country need not lead to immoral actions. To be willing to do whatever is in the best interests of one's country, except act immorally, is the mark of a patriot. A nationalist is one who is willing to advance the interests of his country even when this requires him to act immorally. To keep patriotism from degenerating into nationalism is impossible without a clear understanding of morality.

Pointing out that self-interest does not always provide the motive for immoral action is important for avoiding confusion. We have seen that self-interest often is not even an opponent of morality, but often sides with morality against the demands of country, race, or religion. But, in fairness, it should also be pointed out that religion, country, and race may provide reasons for morally good actions when self-interest would lead to immoral action. In other words, self-interest, religion, race, and country—all provide reasons which sometimes support morality and sometimes support immoral action. Why then has self-interest received so much attention as the opponent of morality? Mostly, I think, because of a misunderstanding of morality, and probably also because of an oversimple account of rational action. But there is another reason. Suppose one accepts morality as the supreme guide; that is, one limits his actions to those allowed by morality. Such a man, if he acts so as to benefit his race, religion, or country, will often be acting in a way indistinguishable from a man who follows the moral ideals. This is not true of the moral man who acts only in his own self-interest.

Morality requires concern for others. So also do patriotism, religion, and concern for one's race. Morality differs from these others in that it necessarily encourages equal concern for all. But, as mentioned above, if one does not violate the moral rules unjustifiably, the moral ideals encourage him to minimize the evil suffered by any group of persons for whom he is concerned. If self-interest provides the only motive for his actions, then he will never be a morally good man. But acting out of patriotism, racial pride, or religious motives may lead him to be morally good. However, though race, religion, and country, unlike self-interest, may provide motives for morally good actions, they also provide more powerful motives for immoral action. Indeed, except for those motives provided by the moral answer and related answers, the motives which have the most power for moral good also have the most power for moral evil. But when religious conviction, racial pride, and patriotism come together in a man who has great compassion for all mankind, as they did in Dr. Martin Luther King, Jr., moral goodness achieves such power that even death seems to be overcome.

I realize that the question "Why should one be moral?" will be answered differently by different rational men. I would expect most readers of this book to advocate that one be moral and to give some or all of the answers to the question that I have provided in this chapter. However, I am fully aware that some people, lacking that concern for all mankind that is essential for dependable moral action, may not advocate that someone for whom they are concerned be moral. A rational father, perhaps with bitter experience with men outside of his family, may advocate to his son not to be moral, but only to seem to be. Such a man might provide his son with reasons why he should not be moral. He may argue that he will generally get the best of others if he is immoral and that he will be able to satisfy his own desires and the desires of those whom he loves much more completely and easily. In some situations this may be extremely persuasive, but in others it will not.

Much more common will be the father who advocates to his son to put his country above all else. He can also provide some powerful reasons for his son to adopt this course of action. His life will have a largeness of purpose and ideals, which are lacking to the man who is concerned only with himself and some few loved ones. Indeed, such a man may have all the rewards that are normally associated with a moral life, including great honor and esteem. Putting one's race or religion above all else may be supported by similar reasons. It is not a service to morality to minimize the persuasiveness of these answers; they do not lose their persuasiveness if we ignore them. However, I think we may now have arrived at that stage in human history where the moral answer may prove to be more persuasive to many to whom it is clearly presented. Many men now do have a concern for all mankind, and many religions now support this concern. Many nations have come to realize how small the earth is. And the evils that result from dividing the races have become apparent to all.

Those who think it difficult to give an affirmative answer to the question "Should I be moral?" should realize that it is also difficult to give an affirmative answer to the question "Should I be immoral?" And the difficulty of providing persuasive answers to the question "Why should I be moral?" is no greater than the difficulties of providing persuasive answers to the question "Why should I be immoral?" Unfortunately, in some societies, and in some parts of all societies, the answers to "Why should I be immoral?" may be more persuasive than the answers to "Why should I be moral?" It is, I think, the most important measure of a society—which answers are most persuasive to most of its citizens.

CHAPTER 11

MORALITY
AND SOCIETY

In the preceding chapters I have tried to describe as completely as possible the sphere of morality. I presented a complete list of the basic moral rules and ideals and provided a justification for them. It was shown how these rules and ideals provide a guide to conduct and a basis for moral judgments. I have tried to show that given the same facts, all rational men will agree on the answer to most moral questions and that all of their disagreements will take place within a much larger area of general agreement. This is because the only relevant matters in deciding a moral question are knowledge of (1) the relevant moral rules and ideals, (2) the amount of evil to be avoided, prevented, or caused, (3) the rational desires of the people affected, and (4) the effect that the violation of the rules, if allowed, would have. Where the facts are not in dispute, moral disagreement arises from different weight being given to a moral rule or ideal or from differing views of what is to be considered a greater evil.

By limiting the moral sphere in this way, I sought to remove the vagueness and confusion that have come to be considered an integral part of moral philosophy. But the price to be paid for this precision and clarity is a sharp reduction in the area of life to which morality is relevant. It is not merely due to linguistic error that philosophers have not distinguished moral judgments from other value judgments.

Nor is the failure to distinguish the guide to conduct provided by morality from other guides to conduct simply an oversight. Philosophers, more than most men, desire completeness. They want a system that encompasses everything. One of the distinguishing features of a metaphysical system is that it includes everything.

Moral philosophers have also wanted a system that would tell all men how to act all of the time, not just some of the time. Although some philosophers might agree with much of what I have said about morality, almost all of them would claim that it was incomplete. Most previous moral philosophers have attempted to provide complete guides to conduct, or at least the outlines of such a guide. They would claim, quite correctly, that I have been primarily concerned with how men ought not to act, not with what they ought to do. My reply to this claim is to admit that even with the moral ideals, morality does not provide a complete positive guide to conduct. Even if one decided to live according to the moral ideals, each man would have to decide for himself the way in which he would do so. We do not want all men to be doctors, yet being a doctor is certainly one way in which to devote one's life to the moral ideals.

We do not even want all people to devote themselves primarily to promoting the moral ideals. Wouldn't it be an excessively dull world if no one was primarily concerned with promoting pleasure, a utilitarian ideal? Shouldn't we be extremely hesitant to disparage in any way those who are primarily concerned with discovering new knowledge, another utilitarian ideal? Thus rational men might not always agree about publicly advocating that a particular person devote more time to following the moral ideals even though this would not involve violating any moral rules. Not all rational men would agree that the Beatles ought to devote more time to following moral ideals. Some might prefer that they continue to concentrate on following a utilitarian ideal, i.e., providing enjoyment to people by their music. But no rational man would publicly advocate that they or anyone violate a moral rule in order to follow a utilitarian ideal.

It may seem to follow from my view that governments are generally immoral. For governments often violate one or more of the moral rules in order to act on utilitarian ideals. Not only this, but given that I list not only promoting pleasure, but also increasing opportunity as a utilitarian ideal, it seems that I am forced to condemn as immoral government taxation in order to promote the arts or better schools for all. This seems to follow because in these cases taxation deprives people of opportunity or pleasure, not in order to prevent the deprivation of opportunity or pleasure, but in order to increase opportunity and pleasure. But the conclusion that it is immoral to tax in order to support a superior school system seems to be contrary to our ordinary thinking about the matter. In fact, it is not uncommon for people to condemn as immoral a government, e.g., the state of New Hampshire, which does not tax people in order to support a better school system.

I do not wish to maintain the kind of paradox that philosophers used to glory in. Therefore I must either show why our intuitive judgments are mistaken or why the paradoxical conclusion does not follow from what I have said. I am not sure that it is positively immoral not to tax in order to support a better school system. I am certain that it is generally not immoral to do so. Thus I shall try to show why the conclusion that it is immoral to tax in order to support a better school system does not follow from what I have said.

In order to do this, I must do a little political philosophy. According to what I have already said, governments not only may tax, but also may deprive people of their freedom, opportunity, and pleasure in other ways in order to achieve certain moral ideals. Thus it not only is, but ought to be, allowed to governments to deprive people of these in order to prevent war. For war brings death, pain, and disability—the three greatest evils. Although phrases like "Give me liberty or give me death" have a powerful rhetorical force, they have little appeal to the reason of most men. The death penalty is almost universally considered more serious than life imprisonment. It is hard to conceive of someone outside of prison being deprived of freedom any more completely than he is by life imprisonment. Thus governments are generally allowed to deprive their citizens of a substantial amount of freedom in order to prevent the greater evils that generally accompany war.

For the same reason governments are allowed to restrict freedom in order to prevent serious internal disorder. Civil war usually brings with it even more evil to the citizens of a state than war with some foreign power. Riots and general lawlessness threaten many with the possibility of serious evil. Hence governments are allowed to limit the freedom of people in order to prevent civil disorder. As long as governments have a moral justification for limiting freedom, then they are not being immoral in doing so. Of course, people will sometimes disagree whether the prevention of evil is sufficient to justify the violation of a moral rule. Most of these disagreements are due to a disagreement about the facts. How serious is the risk of evil? How much freedom needs to be deprived in order to prevent it? No abstract general theory is of any help in settling these questions.

From what I have said, it also follows that governments may tax and otherwise limit freedom in order to support medical research. For medical research is an indispensable aid in following the three positive moral ideals of preserving life, relieving pain, and lessening disability. For the same reason governments may provide support for the training of doctors and nurses, the building of hospitals, and in general, do all those things which will help prevent people suffering the evils of death, pain, and disability.

But though the government may violate the moral rules in order to follow the moral ideals, this does not distinguish the government from an individual. For an individual may also sometimes violate a moral rule in order to follow a moral ideal. That one of the duties of government is to prevent the suffering of evil by its citizens also does not distinguish the government from some private citizens. For it may be the duty of some private citizens, e.g., doctors, to prevent others from suffering evil. Thus insofar as the government violates the moral rules only in order to follow a moral ideal, there is no problem in fitting governmental action into what has already been said. The problem arises when the government violates a moral rule in order to follow some utilitarian ideal. For I have claimed that it is not justifiable to violate a moral rule in order to follow a utilitarian ideal.

The social contract theorists provide one answer to this problem. According to one interpretation of the social contract theory, we agree to obey the laws if the government agrees not only to prevent evil, but also to promote the general welfare. On this account, it is the duty of the government to promote the general welfare. Thus in doing so, it is not merely following a utilitarian ideal, it is also obeying the moral rule "Do your duty" or "Keep your promise." Since it is generally acknowledged that a better school system promotes the general welfare, the government has a duty to support a better school system. In carrying out this duty, it is permitted to deprive people of some freedom, opportunity, or pleasure. For were it not permitted to do this, it would be unable to fulfill its duty. Although this argument can also be applied to support of the arts, it is not quite so persuasive here. There is not so close a connection between support of the arts and the general welfare, as there is between a better school system and the general welfare.

Although this argument seems to me very plausible, I prefer to see if I can provide one which is more closely related to my account of morality—I hope that it will be adequate for my purposes. Let us first distinguish between the moral rules. With regard to the second five moral rules all rational men would publicly advocate that they may sometimes be broken in order to follow the moral ideals. Of course, there will be disagreements on how much evil must be prevented before such a violation is justified, but this is a familiar problem. The difficult question is whether governments can violate the second five moral rules to promote utilitarian ideals. Though I hope that this would never be necessary, it seems to me that some rational men might publicly advocate allowing this, especially if no one is to be harmed and those who are the victims of the violation are the same ones who are to be benefited.

No rational man would publicly advocate the violation of one of the first three rules in order to follow some utilitarian ideal. Although there may be particular cases in which a rational man would be willing to suffer death, pain, or disability in order to achieve some good, he would not be willing to let someone else decide when he should suffer these evils and for what goods. No rational man would publicly advocate that the government have the authority to violate one of the first three moral rules in order to follow any utilitarian ideal.

The fourth and fifth rules, "Don't deprive of freedom and opportunity" and "Don't deprive of pleasure," remain. They are the only ones which can be plausibly described as being as much concerned with goods as with evils. The first three rules demand that one avoid causing evil, the next two that one avoid causing loss of goods. This being the case, it is quite plausible that rational men would publicly advocate that government be allowed to violate these rules in order to follow utilitarian ideals. To allow government to do this would simply be to allow the government to take away some goods in order to promote others. Of course, the good that is promoted must be significantly greater than the good that is taken away. But if this limitation is heeded, then it seems that all rational men would publicly advocate that government have the authority to violate the fourth and fifth moral rules in order to follow utilitarian ideals.

Although what I have said accounts for governments violating the fourth and fifth moral rules for utilitarian ideals without thereby being immoral, more must be said. If all rational men would publicly advocate the violation of these moral rules for utilitarian ideals by government, why would they not also publicly advocate the same kind of violation by individuals? One answer is that in every society there is only one government but many individuals. If individuals were allowed to violate these moral rules in order to promote utilitarian ideals, the resulting disorder would lead to the evils that all rational men wish to avoid. Allowing the government to violate these moral rules in order to follow utilitarian ideals does not lead to disorder.

Another answer is that we do allow individuals to violate the moral rules with regard to someone else if they have good specific reasons for thinking that the person has a rational desire to have the rule disobeyed with regard to himself. Similarly, governments are allowed to violate the moral rules with regard to their citizens if they have good specific reasons for thinking that the citizens have a rational desire to have the rule disobeyed with regard to themselves. Thus the justification of government violation of the fourth and fifth moral rules in order to follow utilitarian ideals is like the justified violation of a rule when the person or persons, toward whom one disobeys the rule have, or would have if they knew the facts, a rational desire to have the rule disobeyed.

What we have now said may make it seem as if there is absolutely no difference between governments and individuals. Although I intended to reduce the difference between what is morally justifiable for governments to do and what is morally justifiable for individuals to do, I do not wish to maintain that there is no important distinction to be made. Governments are not merely individuals; there is at least one morally significant difference between them. Whereas individuals need never violate the moral rules, governments must often do so. By simply enforcing those laws that are necessary in order to prevent violations of the moral rules, it deprives people of freedom and opportunity. Since the government must violate the moral rules, it is faced with a decision about the way in which it will do so. The government needs money and must get it from its citizens, but the manner in which it gets it, e.g., income tax or sales tax, is a matter for decision. Whatever decision it makes will result in different people being deprived of different amounts of money. Since the government violates, though justifiably, the moral rules with regard to all of its citizens, it is in a different relationship to them than any individuâl is with regard to his fellow citizens.

This differing relationship blurs the distinction between the utilitarian ideals and some moral ideals. The distinction between preventing the depriving of freedom, opportunity, and pleasure and increasing freedom, opportunity, and pleasure becomes somewhat arbitrary. Promoting what I call the utilitarian ideals can often be plausibly described as following the moral ideals, for the government may claim that it is simply trying to lessen the amount of freedom, opportunity, and pleasure that it takes away from its citizens.

Thus I wish to allow that governments differ from individuals in that for governments, the distinction between some moral ideals and utilitarian ideals becomes more blurred. However, this does not put governments outside of the moral sphere. For governments cannot justifiably violate any moral rule unless some rational men would publicly advocate the violation of that rule. The difference between governments and individuals lies in this, that in some cases it could be publicly advocated that the government violate some moral rules for utilitarian ideals when it could not be publicly advocated that this be done by individuals.

All rational men would publicly advocate that the government violate the moral rules in some situations, and no rational man would publicly advocate that it violate them in others. However, the bulk of the cases, at least of the important ones, will be those in which rational men disagree about whether the government should violate the moral rules or not. Of course not all disagreements will concern whether the government should violate the moral rules; some will concern how they should do it. In the making of political judgments, i.e., using moral rules and moral and utilitarian ideals in judging governments, more must be considered than is considered in moral judgments of individuals. The more that must be considered is the amount of good that will result. Political judgments thus differ from moral judgments in that good as well as evil is a relevant consideration. This is a direct consequence of the fact that for governments the distinction between the moral and utilitarian ideals becomes less significant. It was undoubtedly the classical utilitarians' preoccupation with governmental action that led them to ignore the important distinction between good and evil.

Although distinguishing between moral and utilitarian ideals is less important when talking of governments, this does not make political judgments about governments significantly different from moral judgments about individuals. A morally righteous or, when talking of governments, a just government is one that seldom or never does what is morally wrong, and always or usually does what is morally right. A just government almost never unjustifiably violates any of the moral rules with regard to any of its citizens, nor does it do so with regard to other governments or individuals. Almost all violations of a moral rule by a just government are those that at least some rational men would publicly advocate. Of course, since rational men sometimes disagree, there may be disagreement about whether a government is just or not. But as with other moral disagreements, one would expect that given all the facts, a particularly difficult task when talking about governmental action, there will be a large measure of agreement. Disagreements should continue only in a very limited sphere. Like individuals, governments are judged not only by their actions, but also by their intentions and motives. If the government in power does what, to the best of its knowledge, will cause the least amount of evil, then it does not become unjust because its action actually caused more evil. But, like individuals, good intentions are not enough to make a government just. The results must generally be the intended ones. Thus an inefficient government may not be an unjust one, but neither will it be a just one.

The necessity of government to constantly violate the moral rules makes the distinction between a just government and a good one more difficult to make than the parallel distinction between a morally righteous man and a morally good one. Nonetheless there is some point in the distinction. A just government is one that by positive action, as distinguished from not acting, neither intends to nor does unjustifiably violate any of the moral rules. A just government does not unjustifiably increase the evil suffered by anyone, but a just government may not be a good government. A morally good government, or simply a good government, is not only just, but intends to and does follow the moral and appropriate utilitarian ideals. A good government is one that by its positive action decreases the amount of evil suffered and increases the amount of good enjoyed. Thus a government can be just without being good, if it does not follow the moral or utilitarian ideals, but simply refrains from unjustifiably violating the moral rules. A good government must also be a just government. A government that is unjust is not a good one, no matter how much it attempts to decrease evil and increase good. For if it is unjust, this means that it unjustifiably violates the moral rules; and this would never be publicly advocated by any rational man.

Although it is generally difficult to judge individual laws, it is sometimes possible to do so. A just law neither intentionally nor unintentionally unjustifiably violates a moral rule. If a law intentionally violates a moral rule unjustifiably, it is an unjust law; if it does so unintentionally, it is simply a bad law. All just laws are good ones. This last statement needs to be defended, for it seems that there could be a just law that was not good. That is, the law neither decreases evil nor increases good, but neither does it intentionally or unintentionally unjustifiably violate a moral rule. But there cannot be a law meeting this description. For if a law is not a good one, i.e., neither lessens evil nor promotes good, then it is bad, for it limits freedom or opportunity unjustifiably. Thus an unnecessary law is a bad one. By an unnecessary law I mean a law not needed either to lessen evil or to promote good.

I have been talking about governments and laws in such a way as to leave the impression that I am overlooking the obvious fact that governments are composed of men and that laws are made by these men. Although I am aware of these obvious facts, I do not think there is any simple way, if there is any way at all, to replace talk about governments and laws with talk about the men who compose the former and make the latter. Although it is extremely unlikely, a good government may be composed primarily of bad men, and a good law may be passed by men whose motives were morally bad. It is far more likely that a bad government be composed primarily of good men, and that a bad law be passed by men whose motives were morally good. Of course, most often, good governments will be composed of good men, and bad governments, of bad men; good laws will be passed with good motives, and bad laws with bad motives. But the goodness and badness of laws and governments are not to be judged by the goodness or badness of the motives responsible for the former or the moral character of the men who compose the latter.

The men who compose the government and who make the laws are subject to the moral rules in exactly the same way that all other men are. This means that they are required to obey the moral rules except when they could publicly advocate violating them, and that they are encouraged to follow the moral ideals. It may be suggested that unlike others they are required to follow some of the moral ideals. For it is acknowledged by all that one duty of governments is to protect their citizens from the evils resulting from violations of the moral rules. Thus those in government are not merely encouraged to follow those moral ideals which urge one to prevent the violation of moral rules, they also have a duty to follow these ideals. I agree that in their role as members of the government, they do have such a duty, but since it is their duty, I do not think this changes their relationship to the moral rules and ideals. People outside of government often have duties which require them to do things that would otherwise only be encouraged by the moral ideals. One is following the moral ideals only when one is doing something beyond what is required by one's duty or by one of the other moral rules.

In these days, when everyone is aware of the vast number of deprived persons in almost every country, it may seem that more is required of men, especially men in government, than simply to obey the moral rules. To say that following the moral ideals is only encouraged, not required, seems to provide an easy way out for those who selfishly seek to preserve the status quo. Much as I would like to show that morality prohibits doing nothing to minimize the evils suffered by others, I cannot see how I can do so. Of course such men are not morally good, but not to be morally good is not necessarily to be morally bad. Further, no practical purpose would be served by distorting the concept of morality to make it require everyone to be morally good. If men do not wish to be morally good, even a correct account of morality will not persuade them to be.

Even though it will probably have little practical effect, I should like to point out that the account of morality presented so far does not provide the easy way out that it seems to. If no one were to be morally good, then it would. But one need not be naively optimistic to believe that in every country, and in every government, there are some morally good men. If these men introduce good laws, those that aid those citizens who are deprived, then the moral rules require that one not oppose such legislation unless one could publicly advocate such opposition. To do so is to unjustifiably violate either the fourth or fifth moral rule. So although the moral rules do not require legislators to introduce good laws, they do require them to do nothing to prevent such legislation being enacted. Thus holding that morality only encourages, but does not require, following the moral ideals does not allow for the preservation of a society with all of its social evils. If there is at least one morally good man, then morality requires that no one stand in his way as he seeks to eliminate the evils of his society. If there is not even one morally good man, no understanding of morality will be of any use.

Clearly much more needs to be said to clarify the relationship between morality and government. To be completely clear about this relationship one would have to develop a complete political theory, i.e., a theory about the rational man's public and private attitude toward government. I hope to do this some day, but in this chapter I am only concerned with showing that most of what I have said about morality applies to governments as well as to individuals. I have been concerned to show the universality of the moral rules and ideals; to show that they apply not only to the actions, intentions, etc., of private individuals, but also to those of governments.

I conceded that when talking about governments the distinction between moral and utilitarian ideals became blurred. I now want to give another reason for this blurring. Rational men may disagree about whether to say that we are lessening the deprivation of freedom and opportunity, or whether we are simply increasing freedom and opportunity. The disagreement will stem in part from disagreement about the minimal amount of freedom and opportunity that citizens in the society should have. This "should have" is difficult to interpret; primarily, I think, it means "a rational man knowing the resources and problems of the society would publicly advocate every citizen having." But I think that there is also something of "a rational man knowing the resources and problems of the society would expect every citizen to have." All rational men, knowing the resources and problems of a society, would regard members of that society with less than some minimal amount of freedom and opportunity as deprived. When one got above this amount, rational men might disagree, some claiming that those who did not have some higher amount were being deprived, others claiming that they were not.

Generally speaking, those who advocate governmental action seem to prefer talking of following the moral ideals rather than the utilitarian ones. They seem to claim that in a society with these resources and problems, no person should have less freedom and opportunity than will be provided by the governmental action they advocate. Indeed, they generally claim that even this governmental action will still leave too many people with less freedom and opportunity than the minimum they should have. Those who oppose governmental action seem to claim that everyone or almost everyone has at least the minimum amount of freedom and opportunity he should have. For them governmental action is designed not to lessen the deprivation of freedom and opportunity, but simply to increase the amount of these goods. They oppose this kind of action because they feel that governmental action invariably results in depriving people of freedom and opportunity, and they do not think that it is justifiable for government to violate a moral rule for utilitarian ideals.

Nowadays those who advocate more governmental action are called liberals; their opponents, conservatives. There are, of course, differences in belief about the practical effects of governmental action, but generally even when the effects are agreed upon, there is often disagreement among liberals and conservatives. Conservatives generally place more emphasis on the moral rules; liberals tend to emphasize the moral ideals. A related difference is the degree to which one views the government as an individual, i.e., the degree to which one thinks the distinction between utilitarian and moral ideals breaks down when dealing with governments. Extreme liberals would seem to hold that it breaks down completely; extreme conservatives, that it does not break down at all. Extreme conservatives would hold that the only duty of governments is to prevent evil, not to promote good. They count any governmental action that seeks to increase good as following a utilitarian rather than a moral ideal. Extreme liberals hold that with regard to government the status quo is of no importance, and thus there is no distinction between lessening evil and promoting good. In keeping with the present trend to deplore extremism of any sort, I do not accept either of these views.

Extreme liberals do not recognize the importance of the status quo in moral matters. For them, the appropriate governmental action is one which more evenly distributes the freedom and opportunity enjoyed by members of the society. They see nothing wrong in depriving certain people of opportunity in order to give the same amount of opportunity to others who now have less. Of course, taking a thousand dollars from a very rich man and giving it to a very poor one probably gives significantly more opportunity to the poor man than it takes away from the rich man. Thus I do not regard the negative income tax as an extreme liberal measure. Further, attempts to help those people who are deprived, even though this involves depriving others of some good, are usually justifiable. But if the people to be aided are not deprived, public reason will require a significant difference between what is given and what is taken away. Morality does not allow a government to deprive some people of goods unless a significantly greater amount of good will result. Here there will be disagreements among rational men.

I regard the dispute between liberals and conservatives as limited to violations of the fourth and fifth moral rules. So I do not regard the extreme liberal as a classical utilitarian, simply advocating the greatest happiness for the greatest number. I think utilitarianism not only an incorrect position, but an extremely dangerous one. It is never justifiable to violate the first three moral rules in order to follow the utilitarian ideals associated with the fourth and fifth rules. One who holds that it is justifiable to do so, as a classical utilitarian might, opens the door to the most extreme forms of totalitarianism. Communism, as practiced, is classical utilitarianism in action. It is devoted to the greatest happiness for the greatest number regardless of the consequences for some. Strange as it may seem, the path from John Stuart Mill, who defended liberty on utilitarian grounds, to communism, which denies it on the same grounds, is both short and easy to travel. Although the originators of the greatest happiness principle certainly did not intend it, their principle can be used to justify governmental actions which everyone would consider immoral. Thus I have more than an academic interest in distinguishing my position from utilitarianism.

I have already shown that governments cannot be considered exactly like individuals, for they are constantly forced to violate moral rules. Thus it is clear that I cannot accept extreme conservatism. It is simply a fact that governmental action has the effect of increasing the freedom, opportunity, and pleasure of some, and decreasing it for others. Thus, in the real world, the distinction between moral and utilitarian ideals does indeed become extremely blurred when applied to governments, especially governments of any size. However, insofar as both liberals and conservatives accept what I have said about the moral rules and ideals, and their application to government, they will not be extreme. For they will both acknowledge that a government is justified in breaking a moral rule only if those responsible for the violation could publicly advocate that the rule be broken in this case. If they agree on this, then their disagreement on whether the government should undertake a certain course of action is a rational one. Nothing in my theory can be expected to settle it. But I think that employing the concept of public advocacy in deciding political issues would have far more significant consequences than is initially apparent.

Not only does morality not solve the issues between conservatives and liberals, as long as they are not extreme, it does not solve any of the moral issues on which fully informed rational men would publicly advocate different positions. Thus morality often leaves an individual with that dreadful freedom of choice about which some existentialist thinkers have written so fully and brilliantly. Often there is no morally right course of action. Even if one is a moral man, one is forced to choose between alternative courses of action. The anxiety caused by these choices is easily understood. One knows that he must either violate a moral rule or fail to prevent some evil, but he knows that neither choice is required by public reason. This kind of situation cannot but be distressing to any moral man. Morality often fails to provide a clear answer to the genuine moral perplexities that confront us. This explains, in part, why such morally sensitive people as the existentialists generally are, have claimed that objective morality is a fraud or useless or both. But this reaction, though understandable, is not justifiable. Just because morality does not always provide a clear answer, it does not follow that it never or even generally does not. Of course those cases where morality provides a clear answer are not morally perplexing. So they have not attracted the attention of those concerned with moral perplexity. To desire morality always to present us with one clear answer may be a rational desire, but it is irrational to discard morality simply because it does not satisfy this desire.

It is not surprising that there has been a reaction to the existentialist rejection of morality. Nor is it surprising that those reacting have accepted the basic premise of the existentialists, that there are no justifiable moral rules. Thus we have those works, lately become so popular, by theologians which decide the most perplexing moral issues in the most simple fashion. These works claim to be presenting a new kind of ethic or morality, sometimes called situational or contextual ethics. They claim to do away with the need for moral rules. Of course, this claim is false. The situations that these men consider present moral dilemmas precisely because they seem to demand, or at least to allow, the violation of a moral rule. Like the existentialists, these theologians have become overly impressed with the obvious fact that there are occasions when it is justifiable to violate a moral rule—even occasions when it is the morally right thing to do. They have falsely concluded that there are no moral rules.

These men are not presenting a new morality; they are not even denying the old morality. At most they are attacking a kind of moral fanaticism, which holds that it is never justifiable to violate any moral rule. But having confused a fanatical view of moral rules with a rational one, they claim to have discarded moral rules entirely. If one is to find any positive value in these works, one must consider them as helping to solve a very limited, though important, problem that often arises in morality, viz., deciding what to do in those situations when rational men publicly advocate different courses of action. If we take them to be dealing with this limited problem, then their answer, "Consider what God would do," is seen to be a legitimate one. In fact, one of the tasks of religion seems to be to provide a positive guide to moral action in those cases where morality does not provide a clear answer.

Religion also has another task connected with morality, namely that of providing men with motives for being morally good men. On the lowest level, this is done by claiming that God rewards men who are morally good and punishes those who are morally bad. On the next level, there is an attempt to inculcate a love of God, so that one is morally good because it pleases God. Religion can also try to get men to care for their fellow men, and so promote what I call the moral reason for being morally good. It can promote human concern in several ways: first, by trying to get men to see other men as their brothers; second, by providing as a model some person who did have a concern for all mankind. So religion can provide some real support to morality.

However, there is always a risk that when morality is supported by religion, there will be a blurring of the boundaries of morality. Since religion may provide the motive to some people for being moral, they may fail to realize that it is not religion which determines what is moral. Thus these people may fail to distinguish between a religion's support for morality and a religion's support for its own particular religious rules or ideals. This is extraordinarily dangerous. It leads some people to brand others as immoral when they are not immoral at all but simply fail to conform to the rules or ideals of some particular religion.

This problem becomes especially acute in those cases discussed earlier, viz., those cases in which there is no morally right course of action. It is a proper function of religion to offer guidance in these cases. Since these cases are truly in the sphere of morality, it is very easy for one to conclude that the answer given by his religion is *the* morally right answer. But it is not. This is not to say that it is a morally wrong answer, but simply to repeat that in this kind of situation there is no morally right answer. The occurrence of this kind of situation makes possible talk of Christian Ethics, Jewish Ethics, Moslem Ethics, etc. Christian Ethics differs from Moslem Ethics where there is no morally right course of action. A rational Christian will publicly advocate that one thing be done, while a rational Moslem will publicly advocate that something else be done. But one must be very careful here, for it is very easy for the Christian to claim falsely that the Moslem is immoral, and vice versa. In truth, neither will be. But both must be extremely clear about the nature of morality, and distinguish it sharply from what their religion tells them to do. Otherwise it will be almost impossible for them to keep from falling into this dangerous error.

The words of the prophet Micah, "What doth the Lord require of thee, but to do justly, to love mercy, and to walk humbly with thy God," are a stirring testimony to the support that religion can give to morality—and to the dangers that attend such support. For Micah, the

Lord commands us to do what is morally right and what is morally good, and thus he provides a powerful support for morality. But the Lord also requires one to walk humbly with Him, and Micah does not distinguish this requirement from the requirements of morality. Thus one may be led to think that a man who does not fulfill this last requirement is to be condemned in the same way as one who does not fulfill the first two. Thus atheism has often been condemned as immoral. But as Hobbes clearly pointed out, there is no ground for calling the atheist unjust. Pride may be a sin, but it is not a moral vice. Humility is neither a moral nor a personal virtue, though it may be a trait that is conducive to moral virtue.

The problem posed by religious support of morality is part of a larger problem which often goes by the name of ethical relativity. I have claimed that morality is universal, that the justified moral rules and ideals are the same everywhere and for everyone. But there is a sense in which this is obviously not true. It is not true that everyone, everywhere, accepts all and only the moral rules and ideals as I have formulated them. The problem of ethical relativity is usually put forward as if it is a problem that arises because different societies accept different moral rules and ideals. But the problem arises as much within a given society as it does between different societies. As we have already noted, followers of a certain religion may not distinguish between the moral rules and other rules put forward by their religion. The Ten Commandments combine moral and purely religious rules. I do not wish to maintain that there is no difference of opinion about what rules are moral rules. There may even be a difference of opinion about what rules are justified moral rules. But I think this latter difference of opinion can be settled. If it is settled, then I think that the former difference of opinion should be settled also. There is no point in continuing to call something a moral rule if it is acknowledged that it is not a justified moral rule.

Thus it seems to me that differing ethical beliefs are no more a problem for morality than are differing beliefs about the correct explanation of a given phenomenon a problem for science. If people have not thought enough about a problem, or do not have the necessary information or techniques, then it is not surprising that they do not arrive at the correct solution. It is impossible to overestimate the amount of stupidity in the world. Most people have not thought enough about the nature and justification of the moral rules. Hence it is not surprising that they do not distinguish between genuine or justified moral rules and rules which only seem to be moral rules. In almost all, if not all, societies and religions, the moral rules are not distinguished from some nonmoral rules. What I have attempted to do in this book is to distinguish clearly the moral rules from all other rules. I have tried to show that the sphere of morality does not cover all of life. By limiting morality, I have sought to provide a guide to conduct that all rational men would publicly agree upon. I have also sought to limit the area in which rational men would seek to impose their own views on others. For it is a consequence of accepting this account of morality that it is morally unjustified to deprive anyone of freedom, opportunity, or pleasure, let alone to disable him, cause him pain, or kill him, because he will not conform to a way of life not demanded by the moral rules.

But, it may be objected, since I include among the moral rules, the rules "Obey the law" and "Do your duty," my supposed universality is a universality in name only. For what is according to the law in one society may be contrary to it in another. What one society considers a duty, another society may not. So when we come to specific cases, what is moral in one society may be immoral in another. This must be admitted, yet the consequences are not as damaging as they may seem. First, we have eight moral rules, which do not differ in content from society to society. Second, in any society, the specific act is considered to be moral or immoral by application of the same criterion. Would one publicly advocate violating the rule? It is not considered an argument against the universality of morality that people promise to do different things; therefore, in specific cases, failure to do quite different things can be immoral. Such an argument would rightly be considered absurd. It is not immoral of me not to meet someone at the airport if I have not promised to do so; it is if I have. What makes the latter act immoral is that the moral rule concerning promises applies to it.

What is different about the rules "Obey the law" and "Do your duty"? As far as I can see, nothing. In one society it is immoral to have more than one wife; in another society it is not. But there is no problem here: in one society there is a law against having more than one wife; in the other there is not. What makes the specific act immoral or not is that the moral rule about obeying the law applies to this case in one society and not in the other. In one society it is immoral for grandchildren not to take care of their grandparents; in another society it is not. But in one society grandchildren have a duty to provide for their grandparents, and in the other they do not. Again what makes the specific act moral or immoral is that a moral rule either applies or it does not.

But, it may be objected, some laws require the violation of a moral rule, and for no good reason. We may have a duty to violate a moral rule, and for no good reason. But we may also have made a promise which if fulfilled would require violation of a moral rule for no good reason. The case of promising need be no different from the two others. In these cases, we have a conflict of moral rules; and hence the moral ideals come into play, and also considerations about the amount of evil to be caused, prevented, or avoided. Thus I do not see how the inclusion of the rules "Obey the law" and "Do your duty" affects the universality of morality any more than the inclusion of the rule "Keep your promise." The moral attitude allows for the universality of the moral rules while at the same time leaving room for justified exceptions to the rules. The confusion between a rule being universal—i.e., applying to all rational men without consideration of person, time, place, or group—and its being absolute—i.e., admitting no exceptions —has been one of the main sources of ethical relativity.

Since a moral judgment is one that a rational man must be willing to publicly advocate, it is not possible to equate a moral judgment with a judgment made on a moral matter, i.e., that which is subject to moral judgment. Unfortunately this has not generally been recognized. Most of the so-called analyses of moral judgments have not in fact been analyses of moral judgments, but merely analyses of judgments made on moral matters. Considered in this way, they can be seen to be extremely plausible. Most people's judgments on moral matters are simply expressions of their feelings that are aroused by consideration of the act they are judging. Most people do not even consider whether their judgment is one that they would publicly advocate, or rather they do not consider this unless their judgments are challenged. If emotivism is considered as an analysis of the unreflective judgments on moral matters made by most men, I think it probably correct.

The feelings that are aroused by consideration of an act of which a moral judgment is appropriate usually reflect the views of one's society. Thus ethical relativism is also largely correct if taken as an analysis of the way in which most people make judgments on moral matters—especially if we consider unreflective judgments, those made simply on the basis of one's feelings. But not all judgments of moral matters are unreflective. After reflection some people make judgments of moral matters which conflict with the views which are dominant in their society. Indeed, some people, though undoubtedly a very small number, make judgments of moral matters which conflict with the way they presently feel toward the act in question. There is often a considerable time lag between coming to see what the correct moral judgment of an act is and coming to feel toward that act the way one thinks one ought to feel.

If one knows that he would not be willing to publicly advocate his judgment, then he is not making a moral judgment. But usually one does not know this. Usually one does not consider whether he would be willing to publicly advocate his judgment. Sometimes one may even believe that he would be willing to publicly advocate his judgment, but further reflection convinces him that he would not. It is this latter case that is most appropriately called making a mistaken moral judgment. It is not surprising that people often make mistaken moral judgments. It is no easy matter to see what one would publicly advocate. One must consider what one would advocate if one did not know who the parties involved were, but knew only the morally relevant facts. Sometimes considering the act with the two parties reversed is helpful. But not always. A judge should not consider what he would advocate if he were the criminal. What he must consider is what he would publicly advocate.

The distinction between moral judgments and judgments made of moral matters allows one to make a simple statement about moral progress. Moral progress occurs as judgments of moral matters become moral judgments. This assumes, of course, that these judgments are not hypocritical. It is generally not realized how many judgments of moral matters are not even intended to be moral judgments. Many people realize that their judgments cannot be publicly advocated, but do not care about this. They are not concerned with reaching agreement among all rational men, but only with a limited number. In primitive societies, this often includes only the other members of the society. In civilized societies, it may not even include this much. Some people make judgments that could only be agreed to by people with a similar social status. Some people make judgments that could be accepted only by people of the same race or religion. Indeed, in large societies a man is usually considered a highly moral man if his judgments of moral matters could be agreed to by all members of his society. Since most of the moral matters that one makes judgments of are matters concerning only those people in one's society, it is easy to overestimate the extent of moral progress. A man whose judgments of domestic matters make him seem a most moral man often is seen not to be so when he makes judgments of foreign policy.

One of the lesser, but nonetheless significant, evils of war is the reversing of moral progress. People whose judgments of moral matters had been genuine moral judgments no longer make the same judgments. Especially when the moral rules are violated by their country, they make judgments that they could not possibly publicly advocate. They no longer care about reaching agreement among all rational men; they care only about reaching agreement among their fellow countrymen. They even condemn as unpatriotic those who continue to make genuine moral judgments of such matters. Thus nationalism overwhelms morality, not only as the basis for action, but also as the basis for judgment. Confusion about morality often allows nationalistic judgments to pass for moral ones, a confusion often not only supported by the leaders of the country but often shared by them. Sometimes, however, nationalism is explicitly put forward as superior to morality. "My country, right or wrong" is a slogan that war makes respectable even in the most civilized societies. Thus war often causes people to lose that decent respect for the opinion of mankind that morality demands.

To act morally is to act in the way that one could publicly advocate when the action is covered by either a moral rule or a moral ideal. It is very easy to forget this final qualification and to equate moral action with any action that one could publicly advocate. There is no great harm in this; acting as one could publicly advocate does rule out immoral action. However, ignoring the qualification tends to blur the distinction between acting morally and acting according to the utilitarian ideals. This tends to obscure the important fact that morality is concerned with the minimization of evil, not with the maximization of good. The Golden Rule, though it provides a guide that closely resembles the moral guide, is not identical with it. Nor is there any simple way in which to modify it so that it does. "Do unto others as you would publicly advocate they do unto you," though it eliminates many objections to the Golden Rule, still encourages one to do more than the moral guide. Changing it to the negative, "Do not do unto others what you would publicly advocate they not do unto you," may be equivalent to the guide provided by the moral rules, but it leaves out those actions encouraged by the moral ideals. If one thinks of politics as involving more than morality, as requiring not only moral action, but also acting on the utilitarian ideals, then the Golden Rule, in its positive modification, can be regarded as the political guide to life.

The moral guide can perhaps be best summarized in that ancient command "Eschew evil; do good" where this is understood as meaning "Obey the moral rules; follow the moral ideals." It is unfortunate that the most familiar moral injunctions have to be modified or interpreted before they provide an adequate summary of the moral guide to life. I should have liked to be able to present an account of morality simple enough to be compressed into a saying as forceful as the more familiar moral injunctions. However, the best I can think of is "Always be just; be kind when you can." To which religion would add "And let the kindness be loving-kindness." Far more forceful is the patently deriva-tive "What doth morality require of thee but to do justly and love mercy?" It is not mere coincidence that the familiar moral injunctions come so close to expressing the view of morality described in this book. For I do not consider myself as having presented a new moral-ity, but simply as describing with more precision the nature of the morality which has been preached by all of the great moral and reli-gious teachers of mankind.

The importance of presenting a precise account of morality lies primarily in the effect it may have on people's behavior. For though I am unable to hold that if one knows what is morally right he will always do it, I do think that many men of good will do what is morally wrong because they are unclear about the nature of morality. Thus I fully agree with Hobbes's remark quoted at the beginning of this book, "the utility of moral and civil philosophy is to be estimated, not so much by the commodities we have by knowing these sciences, as by the calamities we receive from not knowing them."

But philosophical understanding, such as that provided by this book, is not enough. People must come to care for all other men. Yet it is extremely hard to come to care for all other men if it is clear that they do not care for you. To the deprived citizens of a country it is clear that other men do not care for them. To show them that other men do care, government must actively seek to eliminate all deprivation. It is also necessary for the natural compassion of mankind to be broadened and deepened. This is a task for art and religion. They, and not philosophy, have the power to increase man's compassion and to widen its scope. More important, this compassion must yield a concern for mankind which is active even apart from the compassion that generates it. Parents and teachers, indeed all those who are responsible for the teaching of children, have a crucial role. For if a child does not learn to care for others while he is young, it may be impossible to teach him when he is older. I have shown what morality is. Others are needed to teach men to follow it.

INDEX

Guides to life, 4, 10, 134–35, 214, 238
Guilt, 206

Habits, 153
Happiness, 135–36, 200
Hate, 146, 213
Health, 25, 48
Hedonism, 10
Heroism, 58
Hobbes, Thomas, xiv, 8, 21, 137, 233, 238
Honesty, 137, 155
Humanism, 135
Hume, David, 25–27
Humility, 233
Hypocrisy, x, xviii, 93, 138, 152, 155, 197, 207

Ideal observer, 100
Ideals, 133–34; see also Moral ideals, Personal ideals, Utilitarian ideals
Immoralist, The (Gide), 139
Impartiality, xviii–xix
Imprisonment, 57, 219
Impulsiveness, 159
"Incorrect," see "Correct and incorrect"
Indifference, 42, 156
Indulgence, see Overindulgence
Infanticide, xxi
Insight, 177
Integrity, 207–208
Intemperance, 160, 162; see also Temperance
Interest, taking an, 147
Intolerance, 140
Intuition, 177
Irrationality, see Reason
Isolation, man in, 38–39

Jealousy, 145–46
Johns Hopkins University, xiv
Judgments
 aesthetic, 53–54
 legal, 126
 moral, see Moral judgments
 of moral matters, xviii–xix, 236
 nonmoral, 186
 political, 223–24
 practical, 187
 theoretical, 187, 190
 utilitarian, 192
 see also "Good" and "bad," "Ought"

 and "should," "Right" and "wrong"
Justice, 137, 157, 181, 224, 238
Justification, x, 33, 166–67
 of exceptions, 180
 of first five moral rules, 76–101
 of second five moral rules, 102–27
 rational, 33

Kant, Immanuel, xiii, xiv, 5, 9, 167, 194, 205
Kennedy, John F., 22
Killing ("Don't kill"), 29–30, 40, 42, 78–80; see also Death
Kindness, 137, 156, 181, 238
King, Martin Luther, Jr., 215
Knowledge, 48, 50

Language, xiii, 12, 21, 182, 191
Law ("Obey the law"), 90, 114–18, 120–21, 126, 139, 225
Liberalism, 228
Love, 144–48
 self-, 147
Lying ("Don't lie"), 103–104, 168

Maliciousness, 154, 156
Man
 in isolation, 38–39
 in the company of others, 38–42
 in a world without evil, 164–67
Man and Citizen (Hobbes), xiv n.
Marriage, 111
 and sexual relations, 112–13, 198
Martin, Jim, xxii
Masochism, 31–32, 40, 43, 81–82, 85, 162
Medicine, 49, 130, 220
Mental illness, 200
Menza, Victor, xxii
Mercy, 181, 238
Micah, prophet, 232–33
Mill, John Stuart, xiv, xix, 7–9, 10, 50–51, 229
Money, 57
Moore, G. E., 10–11
Moral answer, 201, 208, 218
Moral attitude, 96–98, 101, 116–17, 125, 151
Moral ideals, xix, 19, 74, 128–49
 concerned with evil, 130–31
 paired with moral rules, 128
 and personal preferences, 132–33